THE KRUGER NATIONAL PARK

Hunting party in the Lowveld, *c.* 1900

THE
KRUGER NATIONAL PARK
A Social and Political History

Jane Carruthers

UNIVERSITY OF KwaZulu-Natal PRESS

Copyright © Jane Carruthers 1995

All rights reserved. No part of this book may be reproduced in any form or by electronic or mechanical means, including information storage and retrieval systems, without permission in writing from the publishers: University of KwaZulu-Natal Press, Private Bag X01, Scottsville 3209, South Africa • Email: books@ukzn.ac.za • www.ukznpress.co.za

ISBN 978 0 86980 915 0

Reprinted 2013

Cover photograph by Duncan Butchart.
All other photographs courtesy of James Stevenson-Hamilton and the National Parks Board.

 Printed in South Africa by Interpak Books

Contents

List of Maps and Illustrations   vii
Acknowledgements   ix

Prologue   1
A Wildlife Paradise: The Nineteenth-century Transvaal   7
Imperialists and Sportsmen, 1902–1910   29
Creating a National Park, 1910–1926   47
Politics and the Park after 1926   67
The 'Other Side of the Fence': Africans and the Kruger National Park   89
'Playing God': Wilderness and Science   103
Epilogue   119
Notes   123

Bibliography   141
Index   165

Maps and Illustrations

Maps

	Page
Location of the Pongola Game Reserve, 1889	20
Singwitsi and Sabi Game Reserves, 1903	34
Transvaal Game Reserves, 1910	50
Kruger National Park, 1926	76
Kruger National Park, 1995	102

Illustrations

Hunting party in the Lowveld, *c.*1900   *Frontispiece*

Following page

The Drakensberg near Mtimba Road, 1904   12
Trophies of Game Ranger Harry Wolhuter
Africans and whites collaborated in the nineteenth-century hunt.
View near Pretoriuskop, *c.*1902

Warden's annual trek, *c.*1910   38
James Stevenson-Hamilton, 1899
Ranger Leonard Ledeboer
Warden's quarters at Sabi Bridge, 1907

Advertising poster designed by Stratford Caldecott, *c.*1928   56
Stevenson-Hamilton and Mr and Mrs A.J. Crosby
Stevenson-Hamilton's office, 1914
Jan Smuts, Julius Jeppe and John Rissik
South African Railways publicised the Sabi Game Reserve
Paul Selby promotional literature, 1926
Minister of Lands, P. Grobler, 1926

	Following page
Travelling conditions for the first tourists	80
Tourists camping out in the Kruger National Park, c.1930	
Satara supply store, c.1930	
Skukuza rest camp, c.1929	
Balule rest camp for Africans, 1930	
Gustav Preller and guests at Skukuza, 1930	
Punda Maria rest camp under construction, 1933	
Unveiling the plaque to Paul Kruger, 1933.	
The newly established National Parks Board, 1927	
An African policeman apprehends a poacher.	94
Pretoriuskop entrance gate, 1928	
Ranger J.J. Coetser and African police, October 1922	
Kumane picket, 1906	
African police in the northern section, 1909	
African police quarters at Sabi Bridge, 1911	
Witwatersrand Labour Association bus to the gold mines	
Ranger Duke with African tenants using the railway trolley, 1908	
Stevenson-Hamilton at Tshokwane, 1913	110
Stevenson-Hamilton in his retirement	
Early wildlife photo taken in the Kruger National Park	
Vermin culling: lion skulls at Sabi Bridge, 1924	
Frederick Courteney Selous, the famous Victorian hunter	
Early wildlife photo taken in the Kruger National Park	
An elephant carcase being loaded after a culling operation	
Scientific research conducted by the National Parks Board	

Acknowledgements

Much of this book had its origins in a thesis entitled 'Game protection in the Transvaal, 1846 to 1926' for which I was awarded a doctoral degree by the University of Cape Town in 1988. I thank again those who assisted me in that earlier work as well as those who have been involved in this book.

For their critical appraisal I am deeply indebted to Professor Basil le Cordeur (University of Cape Town); my colleagues in the Department of History at the University of South Africa, especially Dr Gregor Cuthbertson; Professor Roderick Nash (University of California, Santa Barbara); Dr William Beinart (University of Bristol); and Mrs Cynthia Kemp. The National Parks Board has been most helpful throughout the project, in particular, Dr U. de V. Pienaar (former Warden of the Kruger National Park and former Chief Executive Director of the National Parks Board), Dr G.A. Robinson (Chief Executive Director of the National Parks Board) and Dr Salomen Joubert (former Warden of the Kruger National Park). Mr James Stevenson-Hamilton gave me access to his father's private papers and photograph collection and has always been enthusiastic and helpful.

The assistance of libraries and archives is invaluable to any historian and I thank the staff of the following institutions: The Brenthurst Library, Johannesburg; the University of Cambridge; the Johannesburg Public Library; the National Parks Board, Skukuza and Pretoria; the Public Record Office, London; the State Archives, Pretoria and Cape Town; the University of South Africa; the University of the Witwatersrand and the Wild Life Society of Southern Africa, Pietermaritzburg.

Mr Duncan Butchart's contribution of the cover picture, sketches and maps is greatly appreciated.

As far as the publication of this book is concerned, I could not have collaborated with a more capable and friendly team than Ms Margery

Moberly, Publisher, and Dr Jenny Edley, Editor, of the University of Natal Press, and I thank them for their hard work and close attention to detail.

Finally, I would like to thank my husband, Vincent, who has supported me in every possible way.

JANE CARRUTHERS

Prologue

National parks fulfil an important cultural function in that they are the tangible embodiment of those elements of the natural environment which citizens consider worthy of state protection. They therefore evoke a love of the country for its intrinsic, rather than for its political, worth. Thus a national park is not merely a physical entity, a geographical area, or a suite of ecosystems and species, but a mirror of society and a vigorous symbol.

The Kruger National Park is one of South Africa's most famous symbols, both nationally and internationally. Indeed, for many people, South Africa is epitomized by two concepts: its former political philosophy of apartheid; and the Kruger National Park. However, unlike the evils of apartheid, the symbolism of the Park is powerful because nature conservation is thought to be intrinsically 'good' and the Park has come to represent values which are generally considered to be morally sound. Within the Kruger Park – a large area of some 19 000 square kilometres – the rich fauna of the subcontinent is displayed in its natural habitat. In this wildlife wonderland, visitors are encouraged, educational material is generated, scientific research is undertaken, and revenue is collected.

However, certain important aspects of the history of the Kruger National Park, because of the appeal of its strong moral overtones for the white middle class, have been neglected in popular accounts. It is these lesser known – but nonetheless crucial – elements which form the subject of this book. First, the Kruger National Park is an ambiguous symbol: it does not have the same meaning for everyone. Rather, it conjures up different values and ideals for different groups of people. For foreign tourists, it is a showcase for the wildlife of southern Africa. For the local, mostly white, middle-class public, wildlife viewing is an important aspect of a trip to the Kruger Park, but the Park is also a place of recreation and a romanticized reminder of how the landscape might have looked before twentieth-century modernization. While driving around the Park in their motor vehicles, guidebooks at hand, or while enjoying the facilities of the many sophisticated camps, visitors can savour a feeling of recuperation and spiritual regeneration.

In the lives of impoverished Africans, however, what the Kruger National Park has to offer by way of aesthetic beauty has little relevance. Many people, particularly those in areas adjoining the Park, who live in extreme poverty, and who have in the past been deliberately excluded from enjoying or sharing in any of the recreational and educational benefits of the Kruger National Park, hold quite different views. For them the Park's name and ethos have come to symbolize strands in the web of racial discrimination and white political and economic domination. It is for this reason that from time to time there are strong cries for the abolition of the Kruger Park, and calls for its partition among neighbouring communities sorely in need of agricultural land.

It is important to appreciate that the Kruger Park is not a world apart, but that its history has closely reflected that of the larger South Africa. In most guidebooks and popular accounts, the Kruger National Park is removed from its historical context and is scrutinized as though it were an island, quite separate from the real world of conflicts within society, of national politics or economics. As will become clear, however, national parks cannot be divorced from the society which created them, and in the history of the Kruger National Park the changing interface between culture and nature in South Africa can be seen and evaluated.

The story of nature conservation in southern Africa has become embedded in a mythology which often bears little relation to fact, and it is therefore necessary to delve into the past anew to gain a fresh and more accurate interpretation. The myths surrounding nature conservation have arisen because the subject is so often construed in the light of an evangelical crusade in which 'good conservationists' are arrayed against 'evil exploiters and poachers'. This simplistic view leaves no room for understanding or appreciating either the socio-political nuances or the harsh realities of the politics of natural resource conservation. In general, accounts of the history of nature conservation in South Africa tend to be distorted and inaccurate. Real and complex matters have been transformed into spurious moral battles between 'selfish' and 'unselfish' interests, or between heroes and villains. Aiding the emergence of this strong mythology is the fact that academic historians in South Africa have generally avoided the field of environmental history, leaving it in the hands of journalists, scientists and administrators in the conservation field, who are untrained in the techniques of historical research, and who have a passion for their cause.

Histories of the Kruger National Park surface in many publications. There are the 'official' histories,[1] reminiscences of wildlife officials,[2] introductory chapters to field guides and other environmental literature,[3] general tourism tracts,[4] or entertaining articles in popular magazines. Most of these are proselytizing – even emotional – in nature. Personalities such as Paul Kruger, deemed to have advanced the 'struggle' for nature conservation, have been elevated to the status of heroes,[5] while opponents are denigrated, notwithstanding the role they may have played in shaping the policies which were eventually implemented. Negative aspects are brushed aside and no historical background has been provided. The absence of scholarly primary research has, moreover, resulted in many imaginative embellishments, and errors and inaccuracies have been repeated so frequently that they are now self-perpetuating. With the immense human pressures being put upon conserved areas in southern Africa, the time has come to re-evaluate how the Kruger National Park came to be.

Environmental history is a developing field in South Africa. In the United States it is a well-patronized academic endeavour and serious works have included analyses of wildlife protection strategies, the evolution and growth of national parks, the impact of forestry, fire, water supply and drought, environmental attitudes, and environmental and animal ethics. With its splendour of flora and fauna, the southern African region cries out for similar attention from historians. The sub-continent has not only the largest variety of mammals of any zoo-geographical region in the world, but also one-tenth of the world's avifauna and representatives from almost all the living orders of reptiles. Many species are spectacular, many are beautiful, and a number are endemic to the region. For centuries this wildlife has attracted international attention and the museums and botanical gardens of Europe have been assiduously filled with specimens from South Africa. While natural scientists have for centuries taken cognizance of our ecological wealth, it is only within recent years that historians have begun to turn their attention to it. There are signs, however, that environmental history is beginning to form a significant dimension in the South African historiographical tradition. Previously all historians, whether liberal, nationalist or Marxist, ignored the physical environment in their concentration on human interaction. There is now the realization that intra-human events are markedly influenced by environmental conditions, and that the nexus between culture and nature requires exploration. Important historical research has recently been accomplished on the relationship between nature and agricultural developments, the ecological effects of political dispossession, and how social engineering has affected environmental protection.[6]

The more accurate view of the history of the conservation and exploitation of nature, which is beginning to emerge, indicates that a medley of attitudes and motives need to be studied. This historical investigation of the origins and early development of the Kruger National Park, in the context of the Transvaal from the nineteenth century until about 1960, aims to unravel some of these strands. And, in doing so, to establish that what is generally regarded as being ecologically commendable came into existence for a variety of reasons – among them white self-interest, Afrikaner nationalism, ineffectual legislation, élitism, capitalism, and the exploitation of Africans – all unrelated to moral virtue.

The perspective of this work is thus wider than the repetition of anecdotes relating to the early period of the Kruger National Park, and some readers may be disappointed that stories of brave and exciting encounters, or narratives of the reminiscences of pioneering game rangers, are not included. The time has come, however, to look behind the collation of administrative and legislative facts, and even beyond the biographies of individuals, however interesting these may be, and to interpret the Kruger National Park within the broader history of the country. In the new South Africa all voters will be in a position to make demands on politicians, and changes to nature conservation philosophy will certainly ensue. An understanding of what has happened in the past may therefore be facilitative in planning the way ahead.

The aim of this work is therefore to analyse how and why the Kruger National Park has come to exist in its modern form. It sets out to explain the principles and philosophies behind the Kruger National Park, and for this reason it is not a book about *what* has happened so much as about *why* it happened. In a chronological but also thematic manner, it explores the ideas which have underlain nature conservation strategies and examines how these have found formal expression in governmental policy. In doing so, the place of nature in society is examined, demonstrating that attitudes to wildlife conservation reflect many of the characteristics of the society which initiated them. Nature conservation policies are highly political issues and they cannot be evaluated if they are treated separately from the milieu in which they first emerged. The Kruger National Park is not – and has never been – divorced from the socio-economic concerns of South Africa. Its origins and later history gain interest from being understood in this wider context.

Two technicalities need explanation at the outset. The first is that one of the principles of law imported into southern Africa from Europe with white settlement is that while domestic animals constitute private property, ownership cannot be vested in wild animals. Therefore wild animals have the status of *res nullius* and possession of them can only occur once the animal has been killed or captured. For this reason there is no private law protection of wild animals, and protection can only be accomplished by the state through special legislation. Wildlife conservation therefore largely reflects the attitudes of the dominant group responsible for law-making. On occasion, attempts have been made to constitute wildlife as private property, but these have not so far been successful.

The second technicality concerns the terminology used in connection with nature protection. In popular speech, generally no distinction is made between 'protection', 'conservation' and 'preservation' and they are used interchangeably and loosely. At present, conservation is the most commonly employed noun and, for this reason, it is used throughout this book. However, 'conservation' and 'preservation' can have specific and distinct meanings and these also find a place in this work. Conservation – often called wise usage – is the management and utilization of any resource in such as way as to ensure its perpetuation; it is the modern doctrine of sustainable yield. Preservation on the other hand, is posited on a principle of non-utilitarianism and demands the prevention of any active interference whatsoever. The practice is considered to be conservative and thought to be wasteful. However, despite these differences, the main principle involved in both 'conservation' and 'preservation' is the affording of some kind of safeguard, and so 'protection' is also appropriate in this regard.

Over the years there have been many legal provisions and administrative policies affecting wildlife, and prevailing ideas, attitudes and beliefs have mutated with them. The many arguments in favour of wildlife protection have, for example, included 'conservationist' arguments prompted by material considerations which have stressed the careful utilization of wildlife on account of its economic value. These have impacted upon notions of a more idealistic nature (often, but not always 'preservationist'), which have highlighted aesthetics, the sentimental attachment to a rural past, an escape from the pressures of urban living, and nationalism as expressed symbolically in terms of the landscape. In this way, nature protection had an emphasis and direction in the South African Republic before 1900 different from that in the Transvaal Colony during the period 1900 to 1910. This in turn differed from the ideology of the early Union of South Africa and a shift occurred again in the mid-1920s. Changing circumstances of the 1930s in South Africa affected the Kruger National Park directly. After the Second World War, the modern science of wildlife management was forged within the Park and has reigned supreme into the 1990s. With the change in government in South Africa in 1994 have come new legislative structures to govern nature conservation. Dominant attitudes to wildlife protection and national parks may well change with them, bringing a new dispensation into the conservation scene. Wildlife conservation policies have not been homogeneous and do not derive from a single cause. Rather, because at their core they relate to resource allocation, they are often contradictory and paradoxical and have been shaped more by extrinsic social, economic and political circumstances than by deliberate conservationist intentions. This is unlikely to change.

A Wildlife Paradise
The Nineteenth-Century Transvaal

A desire to protect nature can be traced far back into the southern African past, and many conservationist philosophies conjoined to produce the modern national park ideal. Thus, when the Kruger National Park was established in 1926 it was not a sudden event, but the culmination of many movements containing many strands of protectionist thought.

For centuries before European colonization, the inhabitants of the subcontinent utilized the natural environment for shelter, food and subsistence. The practicalities of life combined with cultural taboos to ensure that overexploitation of resources did not occur.[1] Because hunter-gathering communities were nomadic, their constant movement resulted in sustainable exploitation and in the consequent survival of sufficient plant and animal life to feed succeeding generations. In such a Stone Age society, there was no political hierarchy, wealth or trade; food could not be stored or transported for any distance. A strong sharing ethic meant that there was no impetus to consume more than was needed by a small band of people at any one time. San rock paintings attest also to the respect, even veneration, that hunter-gatherers had for wildlife, and to the significance of the hunt in their spiritual life.[2]

With the advent of the Iron Age, a cultivating and pastoral lifestyle brought different imperatives for wildlife exploitation. Trade and the protection of crops and livestock from predators necessitated conservation strategies somewhat akin to those of medieval Europe. The accumulation of wealth led to divisions along social and class lines and these, in turn, politicized hunting. Desirable wildlife species came to be controlled by the élite who alone could initiate a hunt, control trade in wildlife products, and enjoy the spoils of certain species. There were even royal hunting preserves, out of bounds to commoners, the best known of which was Shaka's game reserve in the Umfolozi district of Zululand, set aside in the 1820s. Strict protection proscription extended to clan totems, such as crocodile or lion, which could not be destroyed. In addition, the population of pre-colonial hunters was small relative to the abundance of wildlife.[3]

The relationship between man and beast changed with white settlement and wildlife became a point of contact between African people and European ideas. Whites introduced both a strong market economy and firearms, and these together tipped the scales towards over-exploitation. In 1654, a mere two years after the Dutch East India Company's colonization of the Cape, Governor Jan van Riebeeck was obliged to intervene in order to prevent the extermination of penguins on Robben Island, which were salted in the same manner as herrings. He issued the following decree: 'In order to prevent the islands from being rendered altogether devoid of these birds, we gave orders that henceforth instead of thrice daily, food should be served only twice . . .'[4]

Other conservation measures followed in the Cape, particularly after the British occupation at the beginning of the nineteenth century which brought with it the strict wildlife legislation which pertained in Britain. However, state legislation was always difficult to enforce because of the extended nature of the Cape Colony and the difficulty in apprehending offenders. Indeed, colonial expansion probably occurred largely because the abundant wildlife resource attracted people ever further into the interior. Wildlife products could be used for trade and for subsistence, and while they retained an economic value, it was impossible to curtail exploitation. Conservation legislation was simply ignored.

In addition, Christianity, the dominant settler religion, excluded pantheistic beliefs in the intrinsic power and value of nature such as those held by the hunter-gatherers. Rather, Christianity enjoined its adherents to tame and civilize nature in the service of mankind and material progress. The western legal system facilitated this process of wildlife decimation, because wild animals belonged to no one. Any injunctions against over-exploitation were therefore ignored, because there was a generally held conviction that killing wildlife was not a real crime, unlike the theft of domestic stock which was private property. The widespread use of improved firearms ensured that the number of wild animals declined steadily, two species even becoming extinct – the blue antelope, *Hippotragus laucophaeus*, and the quagga, *Equus quagga*.

Despite the futility of legislation, by the mid-nineteenth century, the Cape Colony could boast of sophisticated hunting restrictions (enacted in 1822) which provided for certain closed seasons, special protection for elephant, hippopotamus and bontebok, restrictions on killing pregnant and immature animals, stringent anti-trespassing provisions, and even embryonic state game reserves established at Groenekloof near Malmesbury in 1822, and at Knysna in 1856.[5]

Until well into the nineteenth century, although the Cape fauna had been almost exterminated, wildlife in the interior of the region survived. When the main thrust of white penetration from the south began, people were astounded at the variety and abundance of wildlife they encountered north of the Orange and Vaal rivers, and in the region now known as KwaZulu-Natal, and began to destroy it in earnest. In these interior districts wildlife utilization promoted wealth, enabling trekboer pastoralists to expand their cattle herds, and providing them with items of trade as well as domestic necessities. In the markets of Grahamstown and Fort Willshire, ivory and hides commanded high prices and these commodities were continuously augmented by hunting deeper and deeper into the interior where the Cape legislation did not pertain.

The first whites to explore north of the Vaal River, early in the nineteenth century, were small numbers of trekboers, traders, naturalists, explorers and missionaries, and their respective professions determined what their attitudes to the indigenous wildlife would be. The majority hunted commercially, often with the assistance of African communities. Robert Scoon and David Hume were two of the best known early hunter-traders in ivory. Both Scoon and Hume had immigrated from Scotland in 1817 and had left the Eastern Cape in the early 1820s to pursue their careers in the regions which were later to become the northern Transvaal, Botswana and Zimbabwe. Others had a more scientific inclination. Andrew Smith, a medical doctor and polymath of humble origins, after starting the South African Museum in Cape Town in 1825, travelled into Zululand in the late 1820s and into the Transvaal in 1834 making extensive observations and collections on behalf of the museum. Not only had Smith met the famous evolutionary theorist Charles Darwin, he was held in high esteem by him and other scientists of the time. However, in the history of wildlife conservation, a particularly important early visitor to the Transvaal in the early 1830s was William Cornwallis Harris. A Captain in the Indian army, Harris came to southern Africa in 1836, and for two years while on sick-leave, travelled extensively in the Transvaal, meeting not only Scoon, Hume, and Smith, but many of the African leaders and Voortrekker immigrants of the time. Harris can be regarded as the first eco-tourist in the sub-region for, unlike the commercial hunters and naturalists who preceded him, he hunted only for pleasure. His book, *Narrative of an Expedition from the Cape of Good Hope to the Tropic of Capricorn in the years 1836–1837*, published in Bombay in 1838, was followed by an English edition published in London in 1839, called *The Wild Sports of Southern Africa*, and in the next year his beautifully illustrated *Portraits of the Game and Wild Animals of Southern Africa* appeared. Harris's books inaugurated a new literary genre and publicized the opportunities for sportsmen which existed in the Transvaal. Many sportsmen followed in Harris's footsteps, often co-opting large numbers of African helpers as servants in the enterprise. These sportsmen had the financial means to travel in some comfort and belonged to the class of Englishman who would have been familiar with the strict sporting legislation of England. What they found so attractive about hunting in the Transvaal territory was the total absence of any restrictions and they happily abandoned any pretence of adhering to the hunting ethics of Europe. They revelled in slaughter and their hunting forays were shooting orgies during which they killed hundreds of animals, frequently leaving the carcasses to decay on the veld.

Had sportsmen been the only white hunters in the Transvaal, recreational wildlife conservation measures might have been enacted. But, although a large number of sportsmen were lured to the Transvaal by hunter-publicists such as Harris, it was the Boer settler ethic which came to prevail. Boer settlers did not hunt for pleasure but for trade, and early game protectionism in the Transvaal evolved from economic and utilitarian concerns.

Two Voortrekker parties entered the Transvaal at about the same time. The group led by J.H.J. van Rensburg was murdered in the eastern Transvaal, while that under Louis Trichardt made its way through the Transvaal to Delagoa Bay where most of the party died of malaria. Trichardt's journals provide the first written account of Voortrekker penetration into the Transvaal and he often referred to the wildlife he encountered. Interested in neither the scientific nor sporting value of fauna, Trichardt's focus was on wildlife as an economic resource. It provided food, domestic requirements such as leather, and items for trade.

The Boer polities which were later established in the interior were composed of Voortrekkers who had sought to free themselves from the restrictions which they believed the British government had imposed on them in the Cape Colony. They needed a viable economic base in order to assert their independence, and they found this in the rich wildlife trade. Consequently, Voortrekker views on the value of wildlife differed significantly from those of sportsmen.[6] Killing wild animals for food and domestic items spared precious livestock, and when disease carried off cattle, physical survival depended on wildlife. Organized barter with inland Iron Age communities, and trade with the markets of the Cape Colony, resulted in a measure of prosperity and enabled the Transvaal Boers not only to survive but to grow into a community of considerable power.

That community was not, however, united and once the Voortrekker spearhead of settlement had consolidated, warring factions and rival polities came into existence in different parts of the Transvaal. Five autonomous republics were declared. Potchefstroom was founded in 1838 and moved to its present site in 1842, while the settlement at Andries Ohrigstad lasted only during the 1840s. Schoemansdal and Lydenburg were founded in 1849 and Rustenburg in 1850. By 1853 a measure of fusion had come about and the name 'Zuid-Afrikaansche Republiek' was applied to the whole region. Notwithstanding this step, and the fact that liberation from British control was confirmed by the Sand River Convention in 1852, the Voortrekker settlements remained factional. Lydenburg reasserted its independence from 1856 to 1860 and civil disturbances and war continued until 1864.

During these politically anarchic years, wildlife exploitation proceeded unchecked and it did not take long for the diminution of the herds to become evident. Anxious about the adverse effect that this would have on the Transvaal economy, the Volksraad (parliament) of Andries Ohrigstad intervened in 1846 by passing a resolution on the subject of wildlife protection. In this first step towards regulating wasteful exploitation, the Volksraad exhorted all burghers to use wildlife in a responsible way by not killing more than could be used at any one time. So vital had wildlife become for the welfare of the small republic, that it was also made illegal for any foreigner to hunt, and anyone found doing so in the Andries Ohrigstad district was to be fined and banished. To a degree there was an economic reason for this, in that the burgher community did not want competition from foreign hunters, but there were also fears before 1852 that the presence of British traders among the fragmented Voortrekker groups would encourage Britain to annex the region.[7] Although the 1846 legislation was the first western conservation measure to be put into place in the Transvaal, it was extremely simple and rudimentary in comparison with the well-developed game legislation of the Cape Colony at that time. As the Voortrekkers had emigrated from the Cape Colony with the express purpose of avoiding British laws which constrained their freedom of action, it may well be that they wished also to escape from the Cape game laws.

From its inception in the Transvaal – as at the Cape – conservationist legislation was to suffer from the long-established settler attitude that destroying wildlife was not a serious criminal offence. Added to this was the fact that most Transvaal pioneers considered it immoral and unpatriotic not to exterminate wildlife, because clearing the land in this way encouraged agriculture and expedited the progress of civilization.[8]

By about 1860 the Transvaal had become divided into two distinct economic regions: settled agriculture in the south, and a hunting frontier in the north. In the southern districts, African communities had generally been conquered and dispersed, or incorporated into the labour structure of Boer society. In the north, however, many African groups fought tenaciously at this time to retain a measure of independence and used access to wildlife in order to achieve this. One way of doing this was to collaborate with whites in hunting, and the white settlers of the northern Transvaal were initially dependent on their African auxiliaries for the success of their endeavours. Neither white men nor horses could survive in the disease-ridden tropics, and a centuries-old knowledge of the environment now allied to firearms, made Africans formidable hunters. Tribute in ivory and other wildlife products was often paid to the Boer states by African clients, and Boer hunting parties usually included numerous armed 'zwarteskutters' (black shots) or 'jagtkaffers' (hunting kaffirs), as African auxiliaries were called.[9] It was a profitable and equitable partnership.

While it certainly had a beneficial impact on the material well-being of the Transvalers, professional hunting was extremely detrimental to the numbers of wild animals in the Transvaal. In 1855 it was estimated that more than 90 000 kilograms of ivory was exported,[10] as well as vast quantities of hide and horn.

It did not take long for the adverse economic effects of profligate commercial hunting to become apparent. By 1858 the economy began to suffer and in that year the first hunting legislation was passed for the Transvaal as a whole (excepting Lydenburg which was still a separate republic). It was entitled 'Wet tot het beter regelen van de jagt op olifanten en ander wild in de Zuid-Afrikaansche Republiek' (Law for the improved regulation of the hunting of elephant and other wild animals in the South African Republic). Like the Andries Ohrigstad resolution of 1846, this was based on conservation principles. Its object was to ensure a sustainable yield and thus to perpetuate the economic welfare and security of the state. However, although absent from its title, the main thrust of the law (thirteen of its nineteen clauses) was to control and restrict African access to wildlife. Blacks were only allowed to hunt if they were 'trusted servants', in possession of 'passes', and accompanied by whites who were in charge of the firearms. African ownership of guns had enabled many communities to enrich themselves on the wildlife trade, and armed bands posed a military threat to the Transvaal Boers. This the 1858 wildlife protection enactment aimed to counteract.

Perhaps not surprisingly, the law failed in its objectives, because so many whites still depended entirely on the produce of the natural environment for their existence and needed African assistance in order to exploit it. When, in 1865, an attempt was made to enforce the regulations in the Soutpansberg and fines were imposed on the most blatant transgressors, there was an outcry from the white populace who accused the government of forcing them into poverty.[11] The matter was taken no further.

The Drakensberg near Mtimba Road (White River), 1904

Trophies of Game Ranger Harry Wolhuter

Africans and whites collaborated in the nineteenth-century hunt.

View near Pretoriuskop, *c.* 1902

Africans had no constitutional means of expressing their views and their response was more violent. In 1867 the Venda, who had acquired firearms in the course of their collaborative hunting activities, destroyed the town of Schoemansdal. In the event, therefore, the provisions of the hunting law had been no more successful in achieving their aim of preventing Africans from obtaining firearms than they had been in conserving wildlife. Destruction of wildlife had led to the demise of the white hunting community, but it also played a large role in undermining the economy of African groups, who had also depended on the natural resource for their prosperity.

As time passed, the pioneering lifestyle gave way to more permanent settlement in most parts of the Transvaal. Wildlife was exterminated over large areas, farms were formally allocated and surveyed, agriculture prospered, and towns became important centres. These developments effected a change in public attitudes to wildlife. From the 1860s and 1870s a landholding and urbanized élite emerged and their views began to compete with those of the rural hunting population. Recreational hunting became predominant for this élite, and the issue of poaching became of major political importance. Landowners, even absentees, developed proprietary interests in the wildlife on their farms and established many of what would today be called private game reserves. These were advertised in the official government gazette, the *Staatscourant*, and between 1867 and 1881 some two hundred notices appeared which forbade hunters from trespassing on private farms. Scattered throughout the Transvaal, but principally in the districts of Heidelberg, Waterberg, Pretoria, Marico and Lydenburg, well in excess of three hundred farms were involved.[12] In this way, wildlife was being transformed from an economic resource available to everyone, to a commodity reserved for the enjoyment of the ruling white group. Social status, property holding and wildlife were combining to become the prerogatives of a landed gentry and to be withheld from the poorer sections of society, both white and African.

It did not take long for these emerging attitudes to take effect in a new law, Number 10 of 1870, which incorporated some of the regulations first promulgated in 1858, but extended certain aspects. It was recognized that enforcement was a problem, and state gamekeepers were to be employed. They were to police the law, with powers of arrest and the responsibility for collecting fines. While, in principle, this can be considered as a protectionist step forward, it had little effect because gamekeepers were only to be appointed when the local public in any given landdrost district demanded it. Initially, there were requests from only three districts. More restrictions were imposed on African hunters and the new legislation outlawed trapping, a measure aimed at obliterating traditional black hunters.

Although this legislation had broad public support among whites in urban and settled areas, there was sharp adverse reaction from remote rural districts. So vociferous was it, that the government was forced to back down only a year later and to repeal some of its most important provisions, thus putting the law out of action.[13] Legislation was thus ineffective when confronted by the combined pressures of a people's pioneering mentality, the belief that the supply of wild animals was inexhaustible, and the desire to accumulate capital.

In 1877, before further changes to the growing corpus of hunting legislation could be made, the Transvaal was annexed by Britain. One consequence of the annexation was an increased number of visiting British sportsmen, who added new ingredients to the changing white attitudes towards wilderness and wildlife in the Transvaal. These were a sense of self-righteousness and a degree of sentimentality.

Economic and social tradition in Britain determined that sportsmen were gentlemen.[14] Hunting by the upper classes was glorified and those who hunted commercially were scorned and vilified.[15] Killing for pleasure was also believed to be more ethical and less cruel than subsistence or commercial hunting. From a survey of sources from that time, clashing attitudes towards wildlife begin to emerge. Some European visitors recorded that Boer country folk simply could not believe that people would kill wild animals solely for amusement and waste the by-products.[16] Trophies – so important to sportsmen – were meaningless to the rural Transvaal settler who might have used horns as clothes- or saddlery-pegs, but would certainly have boiled or discarded animal heads. Africans also found it difficult to understand the motives of the sportsman. The practical nature of Transvaal hunting was thus being augmented by the notion of 'the hunt' in which ritualized and symbolic killing was a powerful idea.[17]

The period of British rule of the Transvaal was too brief for these attitudes towards wild animals to have taken substantial legislative or administrative effect. However, fish – previously ignored by the Transvaal government – were the subject of the 'Visch-bewaring Wet', Law Number 5 of April 1880. This marks the first occasion on which the word 'conservation' or 'protection' was included in a legal title in the Transvaal. The purpose of this fish conservation law was to prevent the destruction of fish by the use of dynamite and other explosives, a method of capture which was popular with mining communities which had access to such technology.

When the Transvaal War was over and the country regained its independence in 1881, burghers inundated the government with petitions demanding improved wildlife conservation laws. It had become abundantly clear that the wildlife of the region was in danger of disappearing altogether. The government, however, had more important matters to consider and only in 1884 did the issue come before the Volksraad for discussion. There, the cries of many Volksraad members, and the wider public, for stricter controls on hunting were crushed when Paul Kruger, the new president, and his Executive Council refused to make any changes and vigorously defended the efficacy of the legislation as it existed.[18]

Traditional histories of the Kruger National Park extol the year 1884 – the year in which this Volksraad discussion occurred – as being that in which President Paul Kruger made his greatest contribution to wildlife protection by declaring a state game reserve. In this view, Kruger the former hunter, becomes a heroic conservationist, a man in advance of his time. However, while it is true that in 1884 Kruger, for the first time, voiced an opinion in the Volksraad on wildlife issues, what he did was oppose a request for tighter control, contending that laws passed a decade earlier were still fulfilling their objectives. The question of a game reserve did not arise at all. Some authors, Meiring for example, in his book *Kruger Park Saga*, have contended that Kruger cherished an 'ideal from the very first year of his first term of office – to protect and conserve the flora and fauna of the Republic'.[19] This must be challenged.

The elevation of 1884 to importance for game protection in the Transvaal may perhaps be traced to the following paragraph which appeared in 1937 in *South African Eden* by James Stevenson-Hamilton, then Warden of the Kruger National Park:

> So early as 1884, President Kruger, at a meeting of the Volksraad pointed out that the game of the country was being rapidly depleted, and that it was becoming advisable to set aside some kind of sanctuary in which it might find refuge. The idea, however, did not at that time meet with support, and was dropped.[20]

Mention of the year 1884 as being crucial for game conservation does not appear anywhere before the publication of Stevenson-Hamilton's book in 1937,[21] and it seems likely therefore that his information has been used by later authors without being verified by returning to primary sources. The incorrect date appears to be a misprint in *South African Eden*, because in his personal journal of 20 May 1935, Stevenson-Hamilton described a visit to the government archives in Pretoria to investigate documents concerning the origins of the Kruger National Park and records 'the [game reserve] idea began in 1889'.[22]

Despite Kruger's contention that no new game protection laws were needed, the public was adamant that they required investigation. In 1883, the State Secretary had begun to conduct an opinion poll among Transvaal landdrosts asking for their views.[23] With the exception of those in the Waterberg, all the officials consulted agreed that the hunting law was ineffectual and sorely in need of revision.[24] The landdrosts' replies highlight generally held attitudes of the time, many of which were in the process of change. Much of the public by then held the view that only lazy and unproductive people would still hunt for a livelihood, and that poor whites would never try to improve their standard of living while they could subsist on wildlife. The landdrost of Rustenburg drew the dismal conclusion that the habit of killing any wild animal on sight was still common, and said that even people who acted responsibly on their own highveld farms reverted to hunting recklessly when they trekked with their livestock to the lowveld in winter. The landdrost of Lydenburg could not understand people who hunted for pleasure, and he blamed sportsmen on the gold-fields of Barberton for most of the destruction.

Africans, already at a severe legal disadvantage when it came to hunting, were accused by whites of much of the wildlife slaughter. Some landdrosts and many burghers indicated that African access to wildlife needed to be even further curtailed. However, there is evidence from this period which suggests that the generally unarmed, increasingly powerless, African hunters actually did little damage, and that they merely provided a convenient target for whites to use in attempts to control the game for their own benefit.[25]

The landdrosts' reports generally attest to the fact that large numbers of burghers and officials of the Transvaal in the 1880s were distressed at the tremendous destruction of game which had taken place and wanted to prevent further devastation. The government did not share this concern and new wildlife legislation was not introduced for another eight years. No doubt bureaucratic inertia played its part in the delay but it is, nevertheless, clear that the government did not consider game conservation a state priority.

But once wildlife legislation was finally updated in 1891, the matter was never again to disappear from the public agenda, and hunting restrictions were discussed at almost every Volksraad session thereafter. Some new principles were introduced, such as the need to obtain a licence to hunt in the open season, and the suggested curtailment of the rights of landowners to wildlife on their properties. The hunting privileges of landowners became an extremely contentious issue in the Volksraad as most members were farmers. The idea that landowners would need licences to hunt wildlife on their own farms was regarded as unacceptable interference in individual property rights.

Agriculture has always been a powerful political lobby and the destruction of troublesome wildlife was frequently debated by political leaders. In this respect, Africans were again put at a comparative disadvantage, because while white farmers were permitted to kill on sight any wildlife which destroyed crops, Africans had to pay for a licence before doing so.

Throughout the 1890s when hunting legislation was discussed, the issues raised or refined on every occasion included: increasing the cost of hunting licences; restricting landowners to hunting in open seasons only; shortening the open season; protecting female and young animals; identifying rare species for special protection; vituperation of African hunting; and the need for more gamekeepers and improved methods of enforcement. Although all Volksraad members seem to have been agreed that some kind of stricter control was increasingly necessary, there were always stumbling blocks related to two jealously guarded rights: that of landowners to do as they pleased on their own farms, and the long-established right of white citizens to shoot sufficient for their own consumption.

The clause which allowed whites to hunt 'sufficient for one's own consumption' had survived from the earliest legislation of 1846. The precise amount had never been specified, and this provision had therefore been a convenient loophole to hunters who would always claim when they were apprehended that they merely shot what they required to consume. In 1891 the suggestion was made in the Volksraad that clarification was needed on this score because so much illegal trading in wildlife products took place under this pretext. When the debate opened, it seemed that there was support for the stipulation of precise numbers of game which could be hunted for any individual's or party's requirements. Again it was President Kruger who interfered, arguing strongly that the clause should be left unchanged and that further restrictions were unnecessary.[26] By 1894, however, many Volksraad members were dissatisfied with the president's reactionary outlook and decided that the time had now come either to do away with the clause, or to define clearly what was meant by it. It was eventually agreed that fifteen head of large game and twenty head of small game would be an adequate quota for each hunter's own use.[27]

Yet, despite the feverish protectionist activity in the Volksraad in the 1890s, wildlife in the Transvaal continued to decrease. Very few people bothered to acquire hunting licences.[28] The law was difficult to enforce,[29] and one gamekeeper complained that even when culprits were apprehended in the very act of contravention, the lack of clarity made it impossible to lay formal charges.[30] By the mid-1890s wildlife diminution was so apparent that the possibility of the extinction of all game in the Transvaal became of real concern.[31]

This worry intensified when the rinderpest epizootic erupted in 1896. With the loss of most of the domestic stock of the Transvaal, the government was obliged to come to the aid of destitute citizens. This was done by suspending all the hunting restrictions and by allowing free public access to wildlife. The actions of the government were strongly opposed by many Volksraad members who were rich men and therefore not as adversely affected as was the impoverished rural community. The government felt justified in rescinding wildlife protection because it enabled the poor – assailed not only by the rinderpest, but also by drought and a locust plague – to acquire food. In addition, because wildlife was implicated in the spreading of rinderpest, its destruction was condoned, even encouraged.[32]

For much of the nineteenth century, wildlife conservation in the Transvaal was informed by notions of 'conservation' and the primacy of human interests. Because wildlife had a commercial value, the first legislative efforts were directed at ensuring a sustainable yield. In the 1890s, however, an influential landowning and urban lobby was augmented by sportsmen – generally visitors, but also immigrant miners, who comprised the members of the newly formed Transvaal Game Protection Association – and these underlying premises began to change. Wildlife exploitation increasingly came to be regarded by legislators as a recreational outlet, and an indicator of social status, rather than as a commercial enterprise.

From their inception in 1846, conservation laws in the Transvaal were exclusionist and regularly reduced the categories of those who were allowed to hunt. Initially, wildlife was a resource available to all, but as it diminished it was reserved first for Voortrekkers alone, then for whites, and subsequently for the wealthy or landowning white élite. The continuing extermination of wildlife in the nineteenth century bears witness that conservation legislation failed in its objectives. Professional and subsistence hunting was not terminated; landowners refused to accept the self-discipline of limiting the exploitation of wildlife on their farms; measures of enforcement were totally inadequate; and Nature herself, in the form of rinderpest and the ensuing poverty of the rural Transvaal at the end of the 1890s, conspired to reduce still further what was left of the enormous herds of the pre-colonial era. The time had come for 'preservation' to be introduced as an alternative protectionist strategy.

Even before the outbreak of the rinderpest had finally revealed how ineffective and weak Transvaal conservation legislation was, other game protectionist tactics were explored in order to save wildlife in the country. State-created reserves were implemented as an alternative strategy in 1889.

When the early government game reserves were created, the general principles governing the functions of such sanctuaries were not well established in southern Africa and it is accordingly difficult to define precisely what constituted a game reserve in the nineteenth-century Transvaal. Only two principles existed from the outset, namely, that proclaimed game reserves should comprise state, not private, land and that hunting should be restricted in some way. Matters such as the appointment of a warden, whether this official should control hunting within the reserve or forbid it entirely, or whether hunting within a reserve should be curtailed indefinitely or only for a certain period of time, were not rigidly defined and these details differed in individual game reserves. Exactly what the long-term purpose of game reserves was to be was also not defined at the time, but was left to evolve in the course of ensuing years.

It has been suggested that the establishment of game reserves marked a progressive step, and that Transvalers should be given credit for introducing what is today considered to be a 'modern' idea.[33] However, game reserves are not modern institutions at all, but have a history going back many centuries. Game reserves, as specified areas which are closed to the public, are essentially conservative and undemocratic because the land and its resources are withheld from the national weal. The principle of a national park is different, in that it is conservationist, not preservationist, and exists for the benefit of the public who have a right to enter it in order to enjoy it. Such a concept of public involvement was never intimated during the existence of the South African Republic.

The first state game reserve in the Transvaal was the Pongola Game Reserve, situated in the south-eastern corner of the country, now a part of KwaZulu-Natal. The Pongola was established in 1894 and, although it set important precedents for the establishment and management of game reserves in South Africa, it receives little attention today. This is so because successes are invariably given prominence and the Pongola Game Reserve did not prosper in the twentieth century. After about 1903 it was neglected and formal abolition occurred in 1921. The introduction of the Pongola Game Reserve in the official records of the Transvaal in 1889 marks the first occasion when the Transvaal government proposed to set aside state land for the purpose of a game reserve from which the public would be excluded and in which no hunting would be allowed. However, in taking this step, it can be seen how mixed were the motives for nature conservation, for the government was activated by current political considerations far more than by a desire to save wildlife for its own sake.

The initial suggestion for a game reserve in this area had come in March 1889 from J.C. Krogh, who was deeply involved in African affairs and

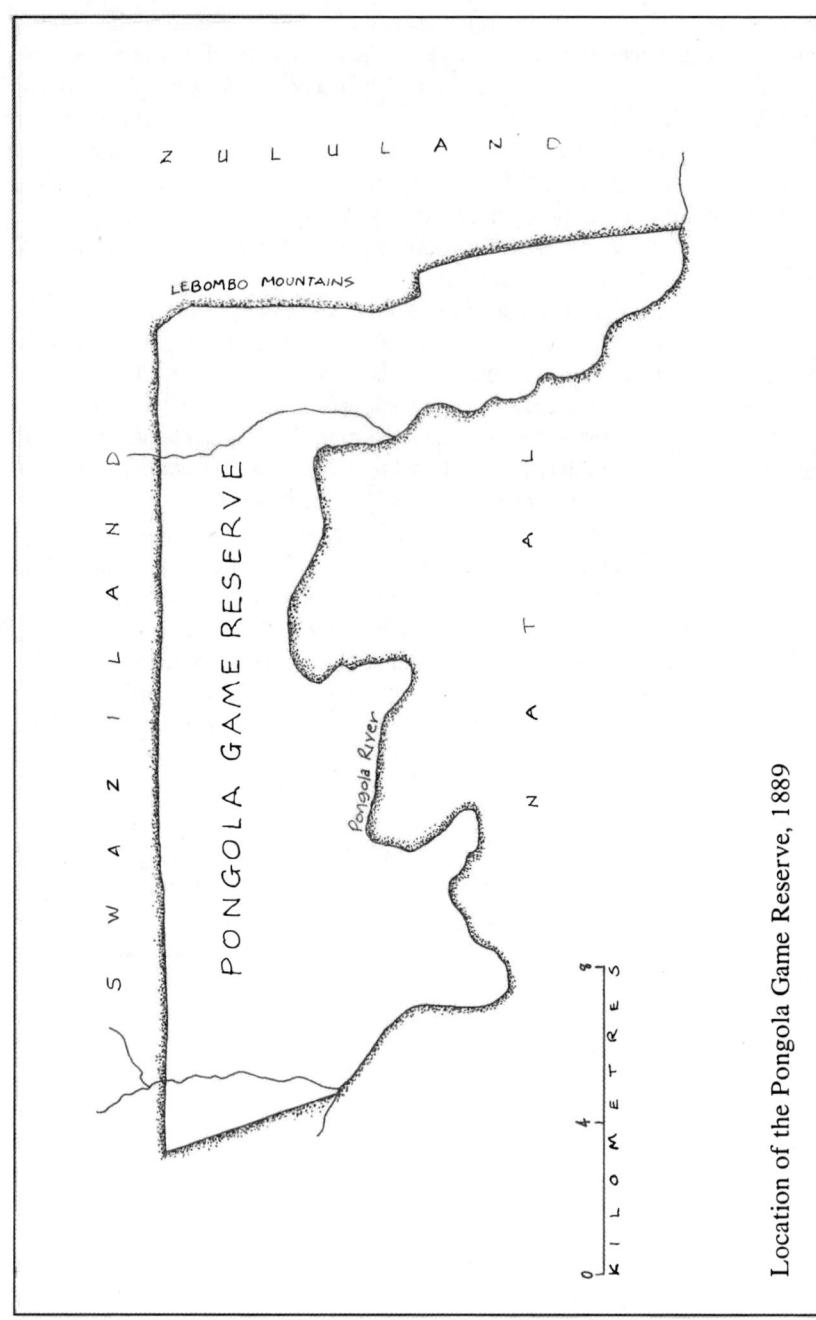

Location of the Pongola Game Reserve, 1889

matters pertaining to Swaziland, and who had been made landdrost of Wakkerstroom in 1881.[34] Although the Kruger government was not active in advocating nature protectionist legislation at that time, Krogh's recommendation came at an opportune moment when political conditions made the idea of state control in that particular district of the Transvaal extremely attractive.

The proclamation of the Pongola Game Reserve came about in the following way. At its meeting on 31 July 1889 the Executive Council – the President and members of his Cabinet – took a decision to ask the Volksraad for authority to forbid totally any hunting on certain portions of government ground in the south-eastern Transvaal owing to the 'snelle uitroeiing' (rapid extermination) of game in the country.[35] This matter was clearly extremely urgent because it was brought before the Volksraad only two days later.

In the ensuing Volksraad debate, despite the oft-stated contention in the literature that Kruger overcame great opposition in pressing for game reserves, he was, in fact, very well supported. Indeed, Volksraad member D.P. Lombard of Standerton was especially enthusiastic because he knew that the Transvaal lagged behind the rest of the sub-continent in this regard. The Cape Colony, for example, had well-established state game reserves and Lombard considered that it was 'high time' that the Transvaal followed suit.[36] Only two Volksraad members, J. de Beer of the Waterberg and D.P. Taljaard of Standerton, raised any objections and both these men represented rural constituencies in which hunting was still an important industry. In the Waterberg, commercial exploitation was still viable, while Standerton had a large destitute population which depended on hunting for survival. It was therefore not surprising that these two particular public representatives would oppose the proposition. Taljaard declared that a government which cared for its poor would not deny them the right to hunt on any state land. De Beer was, however, more concerned about giving the central government too free a hand, and he wanted the boundaries of any reserve to be defined before any decision was taken. President Kruger himself responded to De Beer, explaining that the government was unwilling to commit itself to precise boundaries, and going on to declare that 'were it not too late' he personally would favour game reserves 'over the whole country where there was government-owned land, but unfortunately the game in most areas was limited to merely a few antelope'. Kruger mentioned suitable localities for reserves; for example, the vast, unhealthy northern side of the Soutpansberg and along the Transvaal lowveld boundary with Mozambique.

But after this impressive declamation which would have transformed most of the Transvaal into a wildlife sanctuary, the President proceeded to delineate the tiny area that the government had in mind for its first game reserve. It consisted only of seven farms all situated at the poort where the Pongola River cuts through the Lebombo Mountains and at that time bordered by the Transvaal, the New Republic, Swaziland and parts of Zululand. The members of the Volksraad agreed to allow the government to proclaim these farms as a state game reserve, and only De Beer and Taljaard opposed the adoption of Article 1244.[37]

Although Kruger had indicated that the aim of the game reserve was to preserve wildlife, his reasons for choosing this small Pongola poort area had strong political overtones. It was certainly curious to outline vast areas of unallocated and unsurveyed government ground in the northern and eastern Transvaal as being suitable for game reserves and then to protect only a tiny piece of land in what was not even a particularly rich wildlife region. But one of the major tenets of Transvaal foreign policy at that time was that it should free itself from British influence by acquiring a harbour of its own. As points of coastal access were successively blocked, the strategic importance to the Transvaal of the Tongaland coast, and in particular Kosi Bay, increased.

Access from the Transvaal to the Indian Ocean in 1889 required firm occupation of the spit of land around the Pongola poort and the northern bank of the Pongola River. The international boundaries in the south-eastern Transvaal were uncertain at this time; the district was disputed and claimed by many of the communities who used it, the Transvaal, the Swazi, various Tembe–Tsonga and Maputo groups, as well as by the Zulu, white agents and numerous concession seekers. It was a disease-ridden frontier area, unattractive to white settlers, in which agents of both the Transvaal and the British governments vied with one another to obtain influence and hegemony over the Africans of the region.

The Pongola Game Reserve thus formed part of the Transvaal's strategy to stake a firm claim to the land around the Pongola poort and to give the Republic definitive legal standing in the area. This would be done because a state official – a game warden – would control the game reserve area closely. In the course of his duties the warden would control or remove African residents who might support another government and he would prevent trespassing and poaching. He would therefore be well placed to warn the Transvaal government of any untoward development. Two Transvaal agents had already been placed on the Zululand side of the Lebombo Mountains to perform a policing function and to win favour with the local chieftains. One of these agents, H.F. van Oordt, a Hollander who had been a teacher in Namaqualand and a trader, hunter and explorer before joining the Native Affairs Department of the Transvaal in 1888, was appointed Warden of the Pongola Game Reserve when it was founded in 1894.

In spite of the urgency with which the Pongola Game Reserve had been pushed through the Volksraad, proclamation took five years to accomplish. This lack of progress can be ascribed in part to the uneasy political situation, in particular to the death of Mbandzeni, the Swazi king, and to the increased power in Swazi territory of Transvaal concessionaires, as well as to vacillating British policy towards Zululand and Tongaland. The Transvaal government appointed a commission to survey the game reserve boundaries, and this added to the delay. The commissioners recommended enlarging the reserve from the seven farms proposed by the government, because they felt this to be far too small an area to be an effective game reserve. Pretoria, however, refused to reconsider its plan, thereby providing further evidence that the political purpose of holding the strategic position of the poort was more important than wildlife conservation.

In the event, the whole ploy was a failure because the harbour idea finally collapsed in April 1895 when Britain annexed much of Tongaland and the Transvaal was finally cut off from the sea. Van Oordt reportedly felt so strongly that he wanted to raise a commando against the African communities that had connived with the British.[38] From that time onwards, however, the fate of the Pongola Game Reserve was virtually sealed, for once it had no further political value, its failure as a game reserve – owing to its small size and paucity of resident wildlife – became increasingly manifest.

The administrative manner in which the decision to establish the Pongola Game Reserve was taken formed a precedent which affected all future game reserves in the Transvaal. In 1889 the Volksraad abrogated its own powers in this regard by giving over to the President the authority to establish game reserves by proclamation. Proclamations do not enjoy the same legal status as statutes in that they may be repealed at any time without recourse to the legislature. Because it allowed the President to establish game reserves in the Transvaal by proclamation, the Volksraad lost the opportunity of being the first southern African state to establish a national game reserve with entrenched legal standing.

From time to time, during the 1890s, various localities in the Transvaal were identified as being suitable for game preservation, and this decade consequently saw the birth of other game reserves in addition to Pongola. One of these was in the eastern Transvaal lowveld, between the Crocodile and Sabie rivers, which was a reservoir of wildlife because endemic diseases, such as malaria and horse-sickness, prevented prolonged occupation by humans and livestock.

The lowveld was earmarked as worthy of conservation as early as 1888, when a Bloemfontein farmer named Williams, who had some knowledge of the eastern Transvaal and had a commercial turn of mind, suggested that a game reserve be created in the Barberton area and leased out to English sportsmen at a high rent.[39] Others had similar ideas, and in November 1890 a concerted effort was made by two republican officials in the eastern Transvaal to have a portion of the region set aside as a game reserve. One was G.J. Louw, a Special Justice of the Peace at Komati, and in requesting the government to declare a game reserve between the Crocodile and the Sabie rivers, he alluded to the success of such institutions in certain parts of Europe and the Cape Colony.[40] In the same month – November 1890 – Abel Erasmus, a child of Voortrekker parents, who had grown up in Ohrigstad and who had become a feared Native Commissioner in the Lydenburg district, advocated that substantially the same area as Louw had defined be declared a 'wildkraal of reserve' (an enclosure or reserve for game) in which no wildlife could be killed without the express permission of the President. In order to tempt the government to consider his proposition favourably, Erasmus explained that only Africans and no whites resided in the area of the proposed reserve and that the enterprise would involve expense only in the region of £420 per year.[41] The government did not react to these requests, not even bothering to reply to either official.

The matter lapsed for five years and then, in 1893, G.P.J. Lottering of Bethal raised it anew.[42] Again the government let the matter lie without response in the files. Two years later, in 1895, H.T. Glynn, a gold-miner at Lydenburg, and F. Streeter, the customs official at Komatipoort, wrote to the State Secretary in the same vein. The government at last took heed of these entreaties and asked for an opinion from Abel Erasmus and Van Oordt. Both men agreed that a second game reserve in the Transvaal would be highly desirable.[43]

Because it became evident from the delay that the government was not accommodating the significant public interest in a game reserve between the Crocodile and Sabie rivers, two Volksraad members – R.K. Loveday (Barberton) and J.L. van Wijk (Krugersdorp) – decided in September 1895 to act unilaterally. They introduced into the Volksraad a motion which directly instructed the Executive Council to establish a game reserve in the eastern Transvaal. The exact circumstances surrounding their action are not altogether clear. It has been suggested that President Kruger was behind the idea, having converted Loveday to the protectionist cause.[44] For various reasons this is an unlikely explanation. In the first instance, Kruger, as President and Chairman of the Executive Council, had the power at any time to proclaim any area of the Transvaal to be a game reserve in terms of the authority granted to him by the Volksraad in 1889 – it merely had to appear in the *Staatscourant*. But despite separate requests over a long period from Louw, Erasmus, Lottering, Glynn and Streeter, the President did nothing about proclaiming a game reserve in the eastern Transvaal. Moreover, Kruger and Loveday were political opponents, the latter being English-speaking and an outspoken member of the opposition. It is improbable that Kruger would have used one of his most vociferous political adversaries to introduce legislation on his behalf. In addition, from the time of his election to the Volksraad in 1891, Loveday, a keen sportsman and prominent member of the Transvaal Game Protection Association, had been a strong proponent of stringent hunting regulations. Support for a game reserve in his own constituency was thus very much in keeping with Loveday's long-held views on the matter.

On 6 September 1895 Van Wijk and Loveday informed the Volksraad that they intended to submit a motion the following week which would instruct the Executive Council to proclaim a game reserve in the Lydenburg district. Three days later this motion came up on the order paper and the Volksraad agreed to discuss it, the decision to do so being taken by a very narrow majority: twelve to eleven.[45] Debate on the Van Wijk-Loveday motion subsequently took place on 17 September 1895. Surprisingly – bearing the close vote of 9 September in mind – there seems to have been no discussion at all and no counter-proposal was made. In the final presentation, Loveday proposed the motion with Van Wijk as seconder, and the Volksraad enthusiastically adopted ('bij acclamatie werd aangenomen') the resolution that the Executive Council be directed to proclaim a government game reserve in the eastern Transvaal. No tally of votes was published, but that the decision was not unanimous is evident in the requests of three members to have their negative votes recorded.[46]

This decision of the Volksraad did not immediately make the Sabi Game Reserve,[47] as it was later to be called, a reality. Because it did not have the power to do so, the Volksraad could only ask the Executive Council to proclaim the reserve and, therefore, it was the government which was required to take the initiative further. However, nothing was done.[48] In February 1896, dismayed by the lack of action, Loveday wrote to W.J. Leyds, the young Hollander who was State Secretary of the Transvaal and Kruger's closest political adviser. Apologizing for worrying him when the greater issues of the Jameson Raid and its aftermath were on his mind, Loveday told Leyds that because a great deal of hunting was taking place, the game reserve must be proclaimed urgently and an official placed in charge in accordance with the Volksraad decision.[49] By the end of November 1897 – more than two years after the initial Volksraad request – still no proclamation had been issued. Loveday wrote again, this time in a less conciliatory manner, and demanded to know why the express wish of the legislature was being ignored by the executive.[50] On 29 December 1897, the Executive Council at last discussed the matter at a meeting,[51] and the necessary proclamation was issued three months later, on 26 March 1898.[52]

It transpired, however, that this proclamation merely initiated formalities regarding the establishment of the game reserve rather than finalizing them. One such formality was to ask both Dr J.W.B. Gunning, the Director of the State Museum in Pretoria, and the Mining Commissioner in Barberton for their opinions.[53] Later in the year, when visible progress had still not been made, Loveday decided to raise the question once more in the Volksraad. There he publicly berated the government for deliberately ignoring the Volksraad decision and his own numerous subsequent approaches, and explained the anxiety of the lowveld residents over the continuing unrestricted hunting.[54] Then on 6 September 1898 the Executive Council finally agreed that a warden should be appointed at a salary of £250 per annum and that four African policemen should assist him in his duties.[55] Nonetheless, as late as August 1899, no appointment to the post had been made. In that same month, the Mining Commissioner in Barberton advised Leyds that the game reserve was 'at present nothing other than a proclaimed hunting ground for the benefit of blacks and lawless whites who do not care for any law' and that almost every day gunshots could be heard within the boundaries of the reserve.[56]

The matter of who was appointed the first warden of what was later to become the nucleus of the Kruger National Park has become contentious. An official history of the Kruger National Park has asserted that one of the policemen at Komatipoort, I.C. Holtzhausen, was given charge of game conservation in the area of the Sabie and Crocodile rivers between 1890 and 1899 and that after 26 March 1898 he was assisted by Paul Bester. This evidence comes from an interview conducted many years later with an aged Holtzhausen and with Bester's daughter.[57] However, no confirmation of these appointments has been found in the official records. In 1892 when Field-Cornets and Native Commissioners were appointed *ex officio* gamekeepers, the men responsible for this district were N.H. Versfeld (Komati) and D.J. Schoeman (Crocodile River). There was a rumour that Commandant G.J. Louw, the Special Justice of the Peace who had initially advocated the establishment of the reserve, had been placed in charge of the reserve, but this proved to be unfounded.[58]

Because of its subsequent history as the nucleus of the Kruger National Park, the Sabi Game Reserve has received a great deal of attention and it is not generally known that it was only one of many preservation schemes inaugurated in the Transvaal at that time. Two other game reserves were suggested in 1895, even before the question of the Sabi Game Reserve was raised in the Volksraad. One of these was located on the Springbok Flats in the Waterberg district, and it owes its origin to H.P. van der Walt, a local farmer. It seems that a number of farmers had established private game reserves in the vicinity, and Van der Walt suggested that twelve government farms be set aside for a similar purpose.[59] In this case, the Executive Council acted swiftly, establishing the reserve without consulting the Volksraad. The local Volksraad member for the Waterberg, De Beer, had strong objections to a game reserve in his constituency and he raised the matter in the Volksraad. De Beer argued that as it was Africans who perpetrated most wildlife slaughter and as they would not respect game reserve boundaries, the measure would have no effect as a conservation strategy. The Volksraad was swayed by De Beer's entreaties and agreed that the Waterberg reserve should not be established, but it had no power in the matter, this being in the hands of the Executive Council alone.

Despite the Volksraad objections, the Executive Council went ahead and proclaimed Van der Walt's game reserve in April 1898.[60] A warden was appointed and all hunting was prohibited for a five-year period. Again De Beer went to the Volksraad, which on this occasion did not support him. He therefore approached the State Secretary directly on 16 May 1898 and won Leyds over to his point of view. Although the reserve was not abolished, the regulations were relaxed considerably.[61]

The other game sanctuaries in the Transvaal which were established at this time were not discussed by the Volksraad at all, but were created by the Executive Council by simple proclamation. One of these comprised the townlands of Pretoria and the adjoining farm of Groenkloof (1895), which was closed to hunting for three years at the instigation of the Transvaal Game Protection Association.[62] Others were the government-owned land and forests in the districts of Piet Retief and Vryheid (1896).[63]

After the rinderpest and the accompanying extermination of wildlife, the Executive Council proclaimed many tracts of government ground closed to hunters for five years. By 1898 these included the townlands of Belfast, Nylstroom and Wakkerstroom, and all state land in the wards of Marico, Hex River, Elands River and Zwagershoek. In 1899, similar provisions were applied to the townlands of Middelburg and Potchefstroom, and to the northern section of the Soutpansberg district.[64]

Although these numerous game reserves were formal realities in the Transvaal before the South African War, the only one for which regular records survive before 1900 is the Pongola Game Reserve. There Van Oordt took his job seriously as informer for the government and submitted a comprehensive report for each of the four years he was employed. These record the hostility of the local Africans to the game reserve, details of the smuggling of firearms across the border, and reports of British movements in Zululand.[65] Van Oordt had a reputation for harsh dealings with Africans, and he claimed that the punishments he meted out to trespassers, including hard labour and lashes, had curtailed poaching and that game was becoming more numerous – although not as abundant as it was in Hluhluwe and Umfolozi, the newly established game reserves of neighbouring British Zululand.[66]

In the final years of the existence of the South African Republic there was therefore a shift in emphasis away from protecting game through countrywide legislation to the protection of game in certain special sanctuaries created for this purpose. This meant the abandonment of the conservationist principles of sustainable yield and the introduction of rigorous preservation in areas from which the public was excluded. Although game reserves had come to be seen as the more effective protectionist structure, they had the effect of removing the wildlife resources of certain areas from the economy, an issue which was to become important in later decades. But at the turn of the century, because those resources were so depleted and because agriculture had not yet developed to a degree which made the profitable exploitation of the game reserve areas possible, such removal does not seem to have produced any visible ill effects on the Transvaal economy.

Imperialists and Sportsmen 1902-1910

The new government, after the South African War, not only initiated changes in nature protection principles, but also brought the Transvaal into the international conservation movement. The British colonial administrators, who replaced the officials of the Transvaal Republic, had a long history of European game conservation measures associated with a strong nineteenth-century wildlife protection ethos. Augmenting the enthusiasm for wildlife was the fact that the sporting lobby in Britain was extremely powerful, manifesting itself in the Society for the Preservation of the Wild Fauna of the Empire, an organization with considerable political leverage.[1]

The imperial administrators of the Transvaal were also influenced by the literary work of 'penitent butchers' – former sportsmen such as Edward North Buxton, President of the Society for the Preservation of the Wild Fauna of the Empire, Henry Bryden, renowned athlete, traveller, hunter and author, and Frederick Courteney Selous, whose reputation as a great African hunter was virtually unchallenged[2] – who deplored the decline of wildlife on the grounds that it was 'a precious inheritance of the Empire'.[3] The strong movement against cruelty towards animals in Victorian Britain brought with it revulsion against trapping and commercial hunting, particularly, as Bryden put it, 'slaying the game for the paltry value of their hides'.[4]

After 1900, almost everywhere throughout the Western world, protectionist issues became prominent in matters of government, although the nature of the debates varied. Approaches to conservation differed considerably between the European imperial powers and the United States, for instance. In North America conservation was highly politicized and the public divided. The opposing points of view were represented by John Muir, who had been influential in founding some of the American national parks, and Gifford Pinchot, chief of the Forest Service. Muir, Transcendentalist and Romantic, favoured preservation, believing that intact ecosystems engendered an experience of spiritual harmony. Pinchot favoured utilitarian, controlled exploitation, arguing that natural resources should be sustainably used for the public good. President Theodore Roosevelt – himself an African wildlife hunter of some stature – took Pinchot's part, thus elevating conservation to a national policy platform.[5]

While not as antagonistic as they were in the United States, these two streams of protectionism were evident during the London conference of April 1900, when, for the first time, European powers acted in concert on matters of wildlife conservation. Interestingly, the impetus for the London conference did not come from Britain, but from Germany, which had extensive colonies in wildlife-rich East Africa. International agreements were much in vogue at the turn of the century and high-level delegates from all European countries with interests in Africa attended. On 19 May 1900, a formal convention was signed and the contracting parties bound themselves to a series of complicated restrictions on wildlife exploitation. However, the complexity of circumstances in Africa, the economic interests of settler communities, and rivalry between the colonial powers made this convention a dead letter from the outset. Good intentions foundered on the question of control of the international trade in wildlife products – particularly ivory – which formed the economic base of the East African colonies in particular. Negotiations to have the colonies ratify this treaty dragged on until the outbreak of the First World War, when the project was finally abandoned.[6]

Given the international protectionist interest at the time, British concern over the southern African indigenous fauna was considerable. In June 1900, the month in which Pretoria was occupied – two years before the end of the South African War – wildlife protection regulations were published.[7] The issuing of such a proclamation in the midst of a devastating colonial war is an indication of the high importance which wildlife conservation was to enjoy in the new colony of the Transvaal.

When the South African War ended in 1902, both forms of protectionism were maintained and placed in separate government departments. Responsibility for promulgating hunting legislation was given to the Colonial Secretary's Department, while game reserves were, interestingly, put into the portfolio of the Department of Native Affairs. This was headed by Sir Godfrey Lagden, who had risen from the ranks of the junior civil service to become the Administrator of Basutoland and Swaziland in 1881, and had been transferred to the Transvaal after the war.

New game legislation was promulgated by Ordinance 28 in October 1902. This law, like its nineteenth-century predecessors, generally remained based on class and race distinctions. However, in terms of hunting privileges, it treated all landowners equally, whether white or African. Thus, for the first time in the Transvaal, African landowners had hunting rights. This did not suit the interests of the Transvaal Game Protection Association, which became an important pressure group and, sensing the fervour of the new authorities for the wildlife cause, acted as advisers to the government on game matters. Most of the members of the Game Protection Association were affiliated to the Transvaal Land Owners' Association, composed of 'the most important land-owning companies in Johannesburg',[8] which also controlled a major proportion of the rural Transvaal, principally for speculative and mining purposes.[9]

In an effort to protect their sport and their rights as landowners, throughout the period 1902 to 1910, these associations attacked two principal targets, subsistence and commercial hunters. Despite laws which put ever harsher restrictions on African hunting (for example, by controlling African ownership of dogs), whites often sounded warnings that the total extinction of wildlife would result from African game 'slaughter'.[10] Initially, the colonial administrators shared the colonists' concern, and instituted an enquiry. This, in the event, demonstrated not only that Africans did not destroy great numbers of wildlife, but that on the contrary,

> the over protection of game in some parts [of the Transvaal] has resulted in the most disastrous consequences to the Natives who had in many cases lost their whole crops . . .[11]

Preventing Africans from hunting had less to do with the reduction of game, than with the desire by employers to prevent African subsistence hunting, because in eking out a living from the veld, Africans were being 'indolent and lazy . . . loafing their time here doing nothing'[12] and staying independent of the labour market. This was a matter which was crucial to the post-war and modernizing Transvaal. As the Game Protection Association expressed it:

> . . . the destruction of game by the natives . . . enables a large number of natives to live by this means who would otherwise have to maintain themselves by labour.[13]

The other campaign was waged against professional Boer hunters and strict legislation was instituted to put a stop to this method of making a living: sport was the only acceptable hunting motivation. By selling biltong, impoverished whites continued to make a profit from the hunt and, to wealthy sportsmen, selling wildlife products in order to secure a livelihood was anathema.

Today it is accepted that all wildlife has an ecological niche and is worthy of protection. However, at the beginning of the century, species now regarded as rare and beautiful were actively eradicated as 'vermin'. Some species, like crocodile, were despised because they were 'an animated trap, something lower than the meanest of reptiles' which made one's 'flesh creep',[14] while hyaena were 'a hideous family'.[15] The list of verminous species was considerable and included lion, leopard, cheetah, wild dog, crocodile, jackal, hyaena, birds of prey and many reptiles. These animals were considered to be evil because they could endanger either human life or domestic stock, but principally because they ruined the enjoyment of sportsmen by preying upon the dwindling numbers of antelope species. The aim was to protect only mammals desirable from a sporting perspective.

Game reserves were the other principal method of wildlife protection, and in the Transvaal after the South African War the British inherited the state-owned game reserves. The British administrators were familiar with the preserve concept, and game reserves had already been established in other British colonies, for example, in Australia in 1879, in Canada in 1885, in Kenya in 1897, in the Cape Colony in 1856, and in Zululand in 1897.[16] In addition, locations for other game reserves in southern Africa had frequently been mooted, Mashonaland being considered in 1894, the Kalahari in 1892, and the Cape Flats and Bushmanland before 1898.[17]

Three of the Transvaal game reserves were re-proclaimed after the war – the Sabi, the Pongola and the Pretoria townlands and the adjacent farm of Groenkloof. Two new reserves, the Singwitsi Game Reserve (the northern part of the eastern Transvaal lowveld) and the Rustenburg Game Reserve (on the Bechuanaland boundary between the Groot Marico and the Matlabas rivers) were established. The Sabi and Singwitsi were later to form part of the Kruger National Park, while the Rustenburg Game Reserve, the personal project of Colonial Secretary Jan Smuts, lasted only from 1909 to 1914.

During the life of the Transvaal Republic no definitive statement had ever been made on the function of game reserves and this was remedied in the colonial Transvaal. It was decreed that game reserves were for sportsmen and that reserves would eventually contribute to the economy when the numbers of antelope increased and the sanctuaries could be opened to those who would pay for the privilege of hunting.[18] The existence of the Sabi Game Reserve was known to the British military authorities even during the South African War. Indeed, it seems that the establishment of a vast reserve in this district was suggested independently at that time by Abel Chapman, a man with wide experience of hunting throughout the world and a keen game protectionist. In December 1900 he detailed a proposal for what he called a 'National Game Reserve' along the entire eastern boundary of the Transvaal, from either the Sabi or Crocodile River in the south, to the Olifants or Limpopo River in the north, and bounded by the Drakensberg on the west and the border of Mozambique on the east. These approximated the boundaries of the modern Kruger National Park. The area was ideal for a sanctuary, Chapman argued, because it was a 'tract of country, which is, has always been, and always must remain, of no practical value or utility to man'.[19] The military administration asked Gunning, still at his post as the Director of the State Museum, to comment on the proposal. Gunning was not as enthusiastic as Chapman, and responded that it would be excessive to take the reserve boundary as far north as the Limpopo. He suggested that only the southern portion between the Sabi and Olifants rivers should be proclaimed a reserve and that it should be placed under the control of his museum.[20] In the event, the government heeded the advice neither of Chapman nor of Gunning and, when the war ended, merely re-proclaimed the small original reserve between the Sabie and Crocodile rivers.[21]

Reports of British interest in the game reserve travelled quickly and Arthur Glynn, a Lydenburg farmer and hunter, applied for the post of warden in October 1900.[22] Nothing came of Glynn's application because at that time the lowveld was still under Boer control. By 1901, however, the British had occupied most of the eastern Transvaal, and Tom Casement, the Mining Commissioner at Barberton, became involved, expressing his concern to Pretoria that hunting occurred regularly within the boundaries of the Sabi Game Reserve.[23]

Casement's complaints were taken seriously in Pretoria, and in May 1901 general orders were issued to all military personnel not to shoot game. While most obeyed this injunction, there was in the lowveld an irregular unit called Steinaecker's Horse, which flagrantly flouted it. Steinaecker's men had spent the duration of the war harassing Boers along the road to Delagoa Bay and had, at the same time, taken every opportunity to hunt wildlife in the area. The unit had not only hunted for food and sport but had even entered the trophy market, supplying other army units with curios to take back to Europe.[24] Captain H.F. Francis, a member of Steinaecker's Horse who had been a hunter-trader before the war and who had collected for many museums, reported this to Casement. In due course he was rewarded with an appointment as 'Game Inspector' of the Sabi Game Reserve, the creation of which post had first been agreed upon by the Pretoria authorities.[25] Francis's term of office as the first Warden of the Sabi Game Reserve was, however, very short: he was killed in action just a month after having been installed, at the end of July 1901.[26] Another officer of Steinaecker's Horse, Lieutenant E. 'Gaza' Gray, who had spent

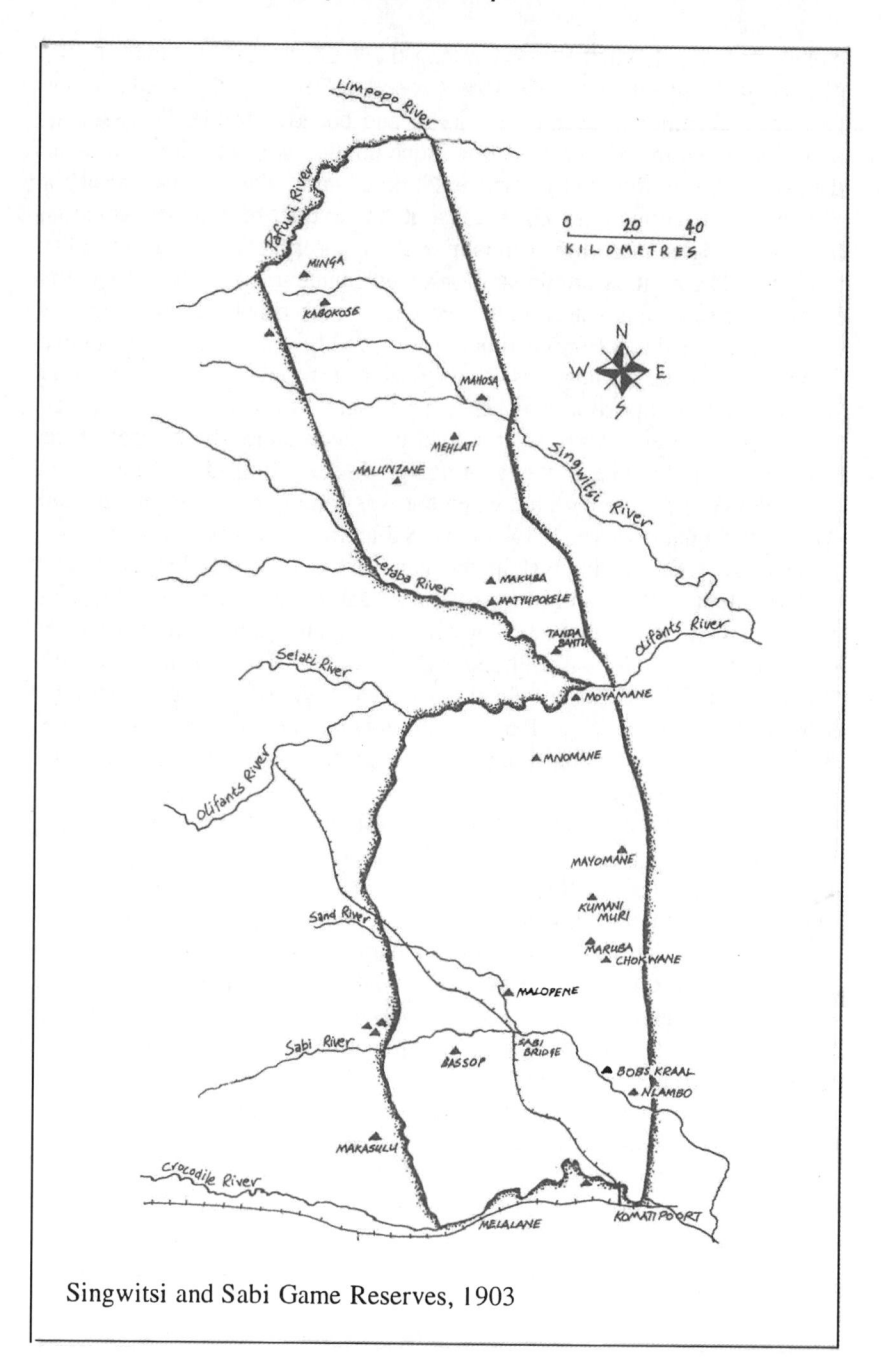

Singwitsi and Sabi Game Reserves, 1903

many years in the lowveld, asked whether he might replace Francis, but Casement did not consider him a suitable candidate.[27]

Casement instead suggested to Pretoria a 'reliable' man of his acquaintance. This was W.M. Walker, a former prospector from Moodie's diggings who, during the war, had joined the Imperial Light Horse and later the British Intelligence Service. He was 'well acquainted with the low country and [spoke] Dutch and Kaffir fluently'.[28] Walker was duly appointed as second Warden of the Sabi Game Reserve on 24 October 1901, but was a dismal failure in the post.[29] In view of the dangers to which he would be exposed, he was to receive what was then the large annual salary of £480. Walker discharged his duties in a desultory fashion: he continued to live in Barberton, he visited his new charge only once, by rail, and did not even leave the security of the railway line on this occasion. Walker refused to move into the game reserve because he disliked the unhealthy climate, the unsettled nature of the place, the 'scattered Boers' and the lack of suitable accommodation.[30] Such an unadventurous and timid man was clearly unsuitable for the warden's position. Needless to say, his superiors believed that they were not receiving value for their money, and Walker was dismissed at the end of January 1902.[31]

There were numerous applications to replace Walker.[32] The qualities which the authorities were seeking in a game reserve warden were those which Chapman had summarized in his report as belonging to 'a practical British "Head Ranger"'.[33] The successful candidate was James Stevenson-Hamilton,[34] a man who was greatly to influence the course of South African wildlife protection, and who was to remain in his post until 1946. An officer in the Inniskilling Dragoons, Stevenson-Hamilton was seeking a civilian position at the end of the South African War. After several fruitless enquiries at the beginning of June 1902, Stevenson-Hamilton was introduced to Godfrey Lagden on 11 June, hoping that the Native Affairs Commissioner would be in a position to appoint him either as a boundary commissioner, or to the administration of Barotseland, an area he had come to know from extensive travels there in 1898 and 1899.[35] However, when Stevenson-Hamilton met Lagden again on 22 June he observed that on this occasion Lagden mentioned that 'they were going to start a game reserve in the Eastern Transvaal and would I take the post of ranger?' Later Stevenson-Hamilton was disappointed to learn that it was 'rather a subordinate position . . .'[36] But despite his misgivings, Stevenson-Hamilton accepted the post in July 1902, and could look forward to, as Lagden expressed it, a 'very interesting and sporting job', especially for a man 'brim-full of pluck and resource'.[37]

Although, unlike Walker, Stevenson-Hamilton was not very familiar with the eastern Transvaal, he had been in South Africa before, when his regiment had been stationed in Natal in the late 1880s. He did not speak Dutch or any African language, but he possessed other qualities which suited him for the task before him and which were to become apparent in the years ahead. He was administratively efficient, imbued with military discipline; he had built up a good deal of immunity to disease and privation, was intelligent, articulate, observant, unmarried and a leader. In addition, and importantly for a member of the Native Affairs Department, he understood the 'treatment and control of natives'.[38] Although one of the books he was later to write was dedicated to 'the guardian spirit of the Lowveld',[39] Stevenson-Hamilton was not a mystic or a pantheist, but essentially a practical imperialist. Like many others engaged in nature conservation at that time, Stevenson-Hamilton was a Scot. He was heir to large estates near Glasgow, and had been educated at Rugby and subsequently at Sandhurst. Stevenson-Hamilton was a forceful character, small of stature, outwardly confident, even arrogant.[40] He loved the wilderness and was unhappy in urban surroundings;[41] and from his writings one learns that he welcomed physical hardship. Despite this, photographs of his home in the Sabi Game Reserve reflect all the accoutrements of a colonial gentleman.[42]

The new Warden did not regard wildlife conservation as a long-term career option at the outset, but he was nevertheless punctilious in the exercise of his duties. Even in the course of his first decade as Warden, Stevenson-Hamilton gained a reputation as a highly knowledgeable naturalist. He also canvassed public support for the game reserve and influenced white public opinion on conservation matters. A competent author, Stevenson-Hamilton wrote numerous articles for journals such as the *Transvaal Agricultural Journal*,[43] *The Field*,[44] *Blackwood's Magazine*,[45] the *Journal of the South African Ornithologists' Union*[46] and the *Journal of the Society for the Preservation of the Wild Fauna of the Empire*.[47] By 1910 his wide reputation as a leading naturalist of the Empire had gained him access to the officials in Britain of the Zoological Society, the Society for the Preservation of the Wild Fauna of the Empire, and the Royal Geographical Society, and he befriended many influential international wildlife leaders.[48]

Although Stevenson-Hamilton had had private reservations about his career in the Sabi Game Reserve, by 1910 he had become convinced that the area had an important future and his manifesto in *Animal Life* gives an idea of the changes which were taking place in conservationist thinking in the Transvaal at the time. As a dedicated Victorian imperialist, Stevenson-Hamilton insisted that wildlife was 'a heritage', and that 'the fauna of an empire is the property of that empire as a whole, and not of the small portion of it where the animals may happen to exist'.[49] But there were other reasons for protecting wild animals: they must 'remain available for the investigations of naturalists, the legitimate aspirations of sportsmen, and the visual gratification of the public of another generation'. Stevenson-Hamilton made a distinction between a 'sanctuary' which enjoyed absolute legal inviolability in that no hunting whatsoever was permitted within the defined area, and a 'preserve', which was 'an area wherein animals are preserved for the use of a privileged few'.[50] He came increasingly to consider that state game reserves should be regarded as 'sanctuaries' rather than 'preserves'.

With these aims in mind, Stevenson-Hamilton strove to ensure that the species he wanted to protect had sufficient space in which to breed and roam freely, without interference from poachers, hunters, predators or agricultural development. No sooner had he taken up his post in the Sabi Game Reserve and explored the region, than he sought ways of expanding the conserved area. Three months after accepting the wardenship, he saw the value of extending the reserve northwards to the Olifants River and westwards to the Selati railway line. Lagden was offered three inducements to agree to the scheme: 'the country itself is unfit for the ordinary white man to live in during the greater part of the year',[51] it was 'much the finest game district in the Transvaal . . . although the big game is but a shadow of what it was a few years ago, I still have no hesitation in saying that more exists here than in all the rest of the Transvaal put together, and that after a few years of careful "nursing" we shall have a Reserve which cannot be beaten, if not in the world, at all events in South Africa,' and 'the land has been prospected again and again, and nothing workable in the mineral line has been brought to light'.[52] Lagden accepted the idea unhesitatingly.

By April 1903 official arrangements for enlarging the game reserve were well under way.[53] But there was a disadvantage, in that more than half the land was not crown land, but was privately owned, principally by companies such as the Transvaal Land and Exploration Company. Stevenson-Hamilton approached all these owners, persuading them to waive their hunting rights as landowners and to allow him to administer and police their farms for a period of five years.[54] This proved to be a far easier negotiation than Stevenson-Hamilton had anticipated;[55] the landowners had nothing to lose and much to gain by accepting the arrangement. Speculation in land was widespread in the Transvaal after the South African War and companies often acquired farms in remote regions at such low prices that there was no necessity to obtain a short-term return on their investment. Owing to the incidence of malaria, the farms to be incorporated within the game reserve were useless for all practical purposes, and their administration by Stevenson-Hamilton and his rangers represented a saving of expenditure. African squatting, or trespassing and poaching were considerably reduced by putting the Warden in charge.[56] In April 1903 the Executive Council considered the proposed extensions and in August of that year it formally altered the boundaries of the Sabi Game Reserve.[57]

A further development at this time was the establishment of an extremely large, new game reserve in the northern part of the eastern Transvaal. In December 1902 a resident of the Soutpansberg district, Leonard H. Ledeboer, had proposed the idea with support from the Native Commissioner at Pietersburg. From a Natal family, Ledeboer had first fought on the Boer side in the South African War, but had changed his allegiance and became an intelligence officer for the British in the northern Transvaal. He had become involved in some of the escapades of the Bushveld Carbiniers and gave evidence at the courts martial of some of the officers in this detachment. Once again, Lagden was quick to agree to the scheme,[58] and as a result, in May 1903 the Singwitsi Game Reserve was proclaimed.[59] This included the area between the Letaba River to the south and the Levubu (or Pafuri) River to the north, bounded on the west by a line running between these two rivers and on the east by the border of Mozambique. Having had no hand in its proclamation, Stevenson-Hamilton explored the Singwitsi during September and October 1903. He expressed himself delighted with it, and found it, despite its small amount of game species, 'well worth protecting'.[60]

The proclamation of the Singwitsi Game Reserve meant that, apart from the triangular-shaped area between the Letaba and the Olifants rivers, all the eastern Transvaal lowveld from the Crocodile River to the Levubu River was a game reserve. As his territory expanded to its full extent Stevenson-Hamilton required staff to assist him in his duties. His headquarters were established in the southern part of the reserve at Sabi Bridge, now called Skukuza, the post which Steinaecker's Horse had manned during the South African War. Major A. A. Fraser, a Scot and a retired Indian Army officer, was brought from his post as Warden of the Pongola Game Reserve to become the Warden of Singwitsi. Stevenson-Hamilton organized the administration of the reserves along efficient paramilitary lines, dividing the area into sections and placing a white game ranger, assisted by a number of black 'police', in each. The first employees were '"Toothless Jack", an old hunting boy of Glynn's who agrees to come along as guide', 'Nicholas Reneke, who is a half-caste Cape . . . John, a Free State Basuto youngster . . . then there are two waggon boys, leader and driver, both Basutos'.[61] A month later two rangers were employed – Rupert Atmore, an intelligence officer whose period of service lasted only a few months, and Harry

James Stevenson-Hamilton, 1899

Warden's annual trek, c. 1910

Ranger Leonard Ledeboer

Warden's quarters at Sabi Bridge, 1907

Wolhuter, who had been a farmer and storekeeper in the eastern Transvaal and, during the war, an officer with Steinaecker's Horse. Wolhuter was to remain a game ranger until his retirement in 1946. 'Gaza' Grey who, with Wolhuter, had been a member of Steinaecker's Horse, and the man Casement had earlier rejected as being unsuitable for the post of Warden of the reserve, joined Stevenson-Hamilton without pay on the understanding that he could have free grazing there for his cattle.[62]

During the course of the decade, other rangers were employed: Thomas Duke, of Irish extraction, in 1902, Cecil de Laporte, in 1903, and Tim Healy, another Irishman, in 1908. Their tasks were to control the Africans resident in their sections, arrest poachers, patrol regularly and to report generally on game matters. Stevenson-Hamilton believed that the position of ranger carried some responsibility, but had a low opinion of most of the men who worked for him, declaring that every lowvelder was a 'wrong 'un' and that 'all the flotsam and jetsam apply to me; I suppose they think it will be an easy life with not much to do except drink and so will suit them'. Stevenson-Hamilton was thus at first disappointed in the capabilities of his rangers: Wolhuter, for example, omitted to have a group of Africans, who were charged with assaulting the African police, properly identified and the case fell away. But even when the rangers discharged their daily duties competently, according to Stevenson-Hamilton, they could not be entrusted with real authority.[63]

Part of the difficulty in attracting suitable candidates was no doubt the extremely small budget within which Stevenson-Hamilton had to operate. In June 1902 the allocation for the Sabi Game Reserve was increased from £2 150 to £4 000 per annum.[64] No increase was granted after the enlargement of the reserve,[65] although Stevenson-Hamilton had asked for one.[66] If it is borne in mind that the total budget of the Native Affairs Department for 1904 to 1905 – excluding game conservation – was £91 182 4s 4d,[67] it will be realized that, despite the rhetoric of many officials and the alacrity with which game reserves were established, conservation was low on the list of financial priorities. On the other hand, the fact that it drained the treasury of so little may have been a reason for the continuing existence of the reserves. A few schemes – such as rearing ostrich chicks for the feather industry – were explored to enable the game reserves to generate at least a portion of the revenue they needed, but these met with no success.[68]

Although he was a junior civil servant, Stevenson-Hamilton enjoyed a great deal of personal freedom and power in the execution of his authority, much of it owing to his distance from Pretoria. Anyone wishing to enter the reserve had first to obtain a permit from him and he was therefore aware at all times of who was within the reserve boundaries. Stevenson-Hamilton was appointed Resident Justice of the Peace as well as a Native Commissioner and, at the beginning of 1903, he arranged that the regular police vacate the reserve and hand over their powers to the Warden and his rangers. In March 1903 he was able to prohibit the movement of stock across the reserve, thus ensuring that members of the Department of Agriculture could not interfere in his domain. Both mining and prospecting were also forbidden within the reserves.[69] Consequently, throughout the period from 1900 to 1910 all applications for prospecting permits in the game reserve were refused, although treasure hunters in search of the fabled 'Kruger millions' were occasionally permitted to enter it.[70]

Stevenson-Hamilton's titles and powers could well have become meaningless, but a test case provided him with an early opportunity to demonstrate his authority. In August 1903 he brought a charge against two senior officers of the South African Constabulary, a Major Urquhart and Captain F.W. Jarvis, for shooting a giraffe and a zebra within the game reserve boundaries. Stevenson-Hamilton had become anxious that his authority would be undermined, particularly when the public of the eastern Transvaal began 'hinting that officers of the Constabulary enjoy immunity when they break the Game Laws'.[71] Jarvis defended himself by stating that the evidence

> taken by Major Hamilton from his natives is such an absurd fabrication of misstatements ... [Stevenson-Hamilton] ... is entirely unacquainted with what is going on some 100 miles away and dependent on the natives he employs who do nothing to stop other natives hunting in this district as much as they like.[72]

The case against Urquhart and Jarvis created a stir in the Transvaal, and eventually involved the Transvaal Game Protection Association, the Chief Staff Officer of the South African Constabulary, the Lieutenant-Governor, and the High Commissioner's Office. Because Stevenson-Hamilton had been convinced that the case would be 'a travesty of justice' and 'enough to make one chuck one's job', he was relieved when the two men were in fact convicted, although he considered that the fine they received in lieu of a prison sentence was a light one.[73]

Stevenson-Hamilton's independence of action was important to him: 'I hope the Department will back me up and let me run things in my own way; in which case I think the show will be a success, but interference from outside will be fatal.' One obstacle concerned his superior, Lagden. Having initially held a high opinion of him, by November 1902 Stevenson-Hamilton considered him to be 'an old woman' who 'won't push things ahead'. Stevenson-Hamilton wrote, too, that Lagden had begun life 'in the London Post Office' and 'lately conveys to me the idea that he thinks he can treat me, who am quite independent of my present employment, and only work for the love of the thing, as if I were a junior clerk'. In fact, by 1904 Stevenson-Hamilton had concluded that all officialdom in the Transvaal was composed of 'a lot of blackguards' and 'low class dogs posing as Englishmen'.[74]

The existence of the game reserves impinged upon the interests of numerous government departments and Stevenson-Hamilton and his game reserves bore the brunt of inter-departmental jealousies, particularly between the Departments of Lands and Native Affairs and the Office of the Colonial Secretary. Stevenson-Hamilton complained generally of a lack of support from Lagden, especially when anything controversial was at stake. Indeed, Lagden's own political career in the Transvaal appears at times to have been precarious: an indication of this can be seen by the way in which game reserves were removed from the Native Affairs Department's jurisdiction in July 1905, without Lagden's knowledge or consent, and allocated to the Colonial Secretary's Office.[75]

More inimical to the game reserves than governmental acrimony, was the general modernization of the Transvaal. As the decade progressed the view that wildlife existed only for sporting pleasure gave rise to several comments from agriculturalists that recreational considerations should not be permitted to interfere with resource development. The question of the under-utilization of crown land was also being raised. While disease and climate acted as deterrents to white settlement in the lowveld, the continued life of the game reserves was assured. But the rinderpest of 1896 had exterminated the dreaded tsetse fly, the vector of nagana or sleeping sickness, and as early as January 1904 it was becoming clear that the lowveld was not as unsuitable for settlement as it had been in the nineteenth century.

Not only did the game reserves encounter opposition from those who promoted the economic development of the colony, but they were even attacked by sportsmen — the very group whose interests they were designed to serve. From the outset of his appointment, Stevenson-Hamilton was disappointed at the extreme selfishness of sportsmen in the Transvaal. When the suggestion was made that sportsmen should assist the game reserve staff in killing 'vermin' within the reserve, Stevenson-Hamilton was against the idea, claiming sarcastically that he knew all about 'sportsmen',[76] who merely wanted an excuse to kill the antelope the Warden was so assiduously protecting.

'Vermin' control proved a handy weapon for sportsmen to use as a means of gaining entrance to the game reserve. At that time it was believed that the numbers of predator and prey were directly related. Thus, the increase in game species which Stevenson-Hamilton was nurturing was considered to have led to an increase in the number of lion, which farmers alleged were threatening domestic stock outside the reserve. Stevenson-Hamilton, however, argued that the presence of game within the reserve 'tends to keep the carnivora within the district and not drive them out'.[77] Lagden supported Stevenson-Hamilton in this instance and wrote, 'As regards the Lions, it seems a very unsporting thing to countenance their utter destruction and I am not in favour of that.'[78]

The issue of the over-abundance of lion was raised at a meeting of the Transvaal Game Protection Association on 14 January 1905 by F. Vaughan-Kirby, a prominent member of the Lydenburg branch of the association, a declared enemy of Stevenson-Hamilton, and later a game warden in Natal. Vaughan-Kirby raged about the issue and stated that

> . . . in certain inhabited parts of the district, lions, leopards, and other wild animals were getting altogether out of hand, owing to the inadequate measures in operation for their extinction by the Reserve. These animals were a positive danger to human life, and one native had already been killed by a lion: in addition to that, stock was frequently destroyed. As a matter of fact, the Sabi Game Reserve was simply a Government lion-breeding concern, and not a protection for game.[79]

Importantly, game reserves were a point of interaction between colonial officials and rural Africans. In 1902 Stevenson-Hamilton wrote scathingly about exploitative whites:

> Great fuss in Johannesburg papers about the native question; it is said they are being treated all wrong; fulminating heavily about "Colonies having their way". Actually the scarcity of native labour is at the bottom of the talk. The natives made so much during the war that they won't work and also they are now busy planting. The J'Burg gold bugs want compulsory labour introduced although of course they don't put it quite like that. In everything connected with the native every single white man wants to have a finger in the exploitation pie![80]

Although Stevenson-Hamilton did not align himself with 'gold bugs', his own actions and attitudes towards Africans were those common to his age. The Western protectionist ethic of the time considered any human habitation within a game reserve to be inappropriate; thus one of Stevenson-Hamilton's first actions was to force African residents to vacate the Sabi Game Reserve. However, he soon revised his opinion, considering that the ideal game sanctuary 'should contain as few native inhabitants as possible. (Complete absence of the latter is rather a disadvantage than otherwise.)'[81] Two reasons can be advanced for this change of heart: he came to appreciate that Africans did not exterminate wildlife and that as tenants on crown land they provided labour and paid rent.

When the Sabi Game Reserve was re-proclaimed in 1902 it had been decided that all resident Africans were to be evicted. Stevenson-Hamilton initially attempted to execute the removal with some consideration for the needs of the people involved, suggesting for example that they should be relocated at a time suitable for the cultivation of crops.[82] However, some months later he was accused of setting fire to huts in order to force people to move, although his superiors in the Native Affairs Department insisted that it was only huts which had already been evacuated that were being burnt.[83] By August 1903 some two or three thousand people had been moved out of the Sabi Game Reserve,[84] while as late as 1906 a group of Africans living on the perimeter complained that 'the government wants to drive them away from the low veld so as to include these parts in the game reserve'.[85] Thus, from their formal inception, game reserves have been regarded by neighbouring African groups as a threat to both their agricultural interests and their access to land.

When it was established in 1903, the Singwitsi Game Reserve was also the home of numerous African communities. Stevenson-Hamilton did not advocate expelling them, possibly because he appreciated by then that without firearms, 'the damage they do in a year will not equal that done by a few Boers in a week'.[86] A further expedience may have been that Stevenson-Hamilton relied on locals to inform him and his rangers about poaching violations.[87] In May 1905 it was decided that the considerable number of Africans in the game reserves should, like other squatters on crown lands, be subject to the payment of squatters' rents. From this date onwards Africans who resided in game reserves were a source of considerable revenue.

African residents opposed game reserves not only for alienating land, but also because they were unable to protect themselves against dangerous animals. Although their presence in the reserves was exploited for labour and income, Africans were not allowed to carry firearms. When an application was received by the Native Affairs Department from chieftain

Mpisane to allow his messengers to carry assegais when they travelled in the game reserve, Stevenson-Hamilton was quick to conclude that Mpisane's request was unreasonable, being 'only an attempt to give his kaffirs an excuse for going about armed, which I take it is not desirable'.[88] In 1907 the Native Commissioner of the Northern Division supported chieftains Makuba and Mhinga in wanting to own a number of rifles for self-protection, much to the ire of Stevenson-Hamilton[89] who, in any event, did not like Mhinga. He complained that the chieftain was offensive: 'I think he ought to be put right on the subject of manners towards white men, quite apart from their being officials of the government.'[90]

Many Africans were not only evicted from their homes and forced to live outside the game reserves on 'native reserves' or 'locations', but they were also, of course, denied access to game as a means of subsistence. As the task of the game reserve officials was to build up numbers of game species, the Warden and his rangers were diligent in seeking out and apprehending poachers. Africans, in particular, were arrested merely for 'being in possession under suspicious circumstances of [game] meat'. Suspected poachers frequently resisted arrest, which was not surprising in view of the severity of the punishments they received. Nevertheless, resistance does not appear to have been concerted or organized: on occasion Africans informed upon one another and chiefs co-operated with game reserve staff in apprehending poachers.[91]

By 1910, the main aim of the Transvaal game reserves – to provide 'a nursery for the propagation and preservation of the South African fauna'[92] – had been accomplished. According to Stevenson-Hamilton's observations, in 1902 there had been no black rhinoceros, elephant, eland, hartebeest or ostrich in the area; there were about fifteen hippopotamus, five giraffe, eight buffalo, twelve sable antelope, two roan antelope, five tsessebe, forty blue wildebeest, one hundred waterbuck, thirty-five kudu and numerous impala, reedbuck, steenbok and duiker.[93] By 1909 he recorded twenty-five elephant, seven or eight rhinoceros, fifty or sixty buffalo, numerous hippopotamus and eland, and large herds of roan antelope, hartebeest, kudu and many other species.[94]

To a very great extent, this had been the personal accomplishment of Stevenson-Hamilton. By concentrating power in the office of the Warden, he had prevented various government departments from turning the vast game reserve into either a 'native reserve', or a prospecting and mining area, or even a locality for white settlers. In achieving this, he was greatly assisted by the disadvantageous tropical climate of the area and the prevalence of malaria. By building up a reputation as a man who had great knowledge of wildlife, his opinion persuaded the authorities not to allow

Transvaal sportsmen to invade the reserve. By disciplining and training his staff, he succeeded in patrolling the extensive reserve boundaries effectively and in increasing the probability that offenders who flouted the game regulations would be apprehended. And by expelling Africans, or by closely controlling the lives of those who remained within the reserves, Stevenson-Hamilton curtailed African subsistence hunting.

Although he encountered opposition from many quarters, his most important ally – the legislature of the Transvaal – never deserted him. The Legislative Council supported all his endeavours, one member bravely going so far as to compare the reserve with Yellowstone National Park in the United States and deeming it 'the duty of the Government to take this matter in hand, and make these preserves something in the nature of a national institution'.[95] By 1910 Stevenson-Hamilton had reached substantially the same conclusion. He began publicly to express the view that game reserves should remain strictly preservationist in perpetuity and never be opened to sportsmen as had been the original intention.[96] A fresh outlook was coming into prominence with the formation of the Union. And with new politics, was to come a new era in wildlife conservation.

Creating a National Park 1910-1926

Although wildlife conservation culminated, in the mid-1920s, in the foundation of the Kruger National Park, the Transvaal game reserves had initially lost considerable support when the Union of South Africa was established in 1910. With Union, a two-tier system of central and provincial government was introduced, and responsibility for nature protection was given to each province. But the allocation of state land was the task of the central authority and this led to conflict between the two levels of government over the game reserves in the Transvaal.

The waning of enthusiasm for game reserves after 1910 owed much to a general commitment to the economic development and modernization of the newly formed national state. Mining was followed by secondary industry and commercial farming, and South Africa was set on course to become an industrial society in which medieval-type game preserves such as the Sabi and Singwitsi had little place.

In the popular literature, the prelude to the National Parks Act of 1926 is frequently depicted as a contest between the forces of 'good' (those in favour of national parks) and 'evil' (those antagonistic to or apathetic about the idea). Stevenson-Hamilton compared the passing of the act to a fairy-tale with a happy ending, in which the game reserve 'Cinderella' became the national park 'princess'.[1] Simplistic interpretations of this kind beg closer examination and a more objective and critical explanation is needed, one which takes cognisance of the complexities of the South African political economy.

The creation of national parks – anywhere in the world – can only be understood in the context of the time and place in which this occurred. In a nutshell, what was accomplished with the Kruger National Park was not so much the acceptance that the principle of a national park was morally correct, as the acceptance by white South Africans of the philosophy that the viewing and studying of wildlife constituted a legitimate, and economically viable, form of land use and that state land and finance should be allocated for this purpose.

Many circumstances intertwined to make the national park a reality. Its foundation took place at the same time as clear demonstrations of an aggressive, though perhaps still nascent, Afrikaner nationalism, and a search for a white South African national identity. Among others, these manifestations included a new South African flag, the adoption of Afrikaans as an official language, the revival of interest in Voortrekker traditions, the resurgence of republican sentiments, and the loosening of ties with imperial Britain. At that time, too, there was increasing state economic intervention and national industries, such as the Electricity Supply Commission, were founded. These outbursts of political and economic nationalism coincided with the end of the attitude that wildlife was a utilitarian commodity – at least for whites – and with the entrenching of a growing sentimental, romantic and aesthetic view of nature.

This nationalistic interpretation of wildlife conservation in the 1920s accords with the reasons why countries such as the United States and Australia established their national parks. For example, in the United States, ideas about the preservation of areas of scenic beauty were mobilized to promote American national feeling.[2] In Australia, too, the sentiment of nationalism both fed upon and encouraged the romanticization of the Australian frontier experience.[3] National parks appear to be connected to a certain stage in a country's cultural evolution and serve to weld together different groups within it. That this is true of South Africa in the mid-1920s can be seen in the groping for a common identity between English-speaking and Afrikaans-speaking whites. Their collaborative creation of a national park played a role in the process of unifying these two culturally different, but economically converging, groups. But in their search for common ground, whites totally excluded Africans. The establishment of national parks thus constitutes yet another strand in the consolidation of white interests over African.

Before the 1920s, the time was not ripe to expand wildlife conservation programmes. In fact, after 1910 there came direct challenges to game reserves. The first casualty in the Transvaal after Union was the abolition of the Rustenburg Game Reserve. When Jan Smuts had been Colonial Secretary of the Transvaal in 1909 he had established this reserve on his own personal initiative.[4] It included private as well as state land and after Union the landowners were anxious to withdraw from the scheme so that they could pursue progressive agricultural systems. The Warden, P.J. (Hans) Riekert, who had been a personal friend of Smuts, was not a credit to his post, for not only was he involved in fomenting trouble with the neighbouring Tswana groups in Bechuanaland, but he was himself an active poacher and gun-smuggler. In 1914 he was an active participant in the rebellion of that year and Smuts removed him from his Warden's post and put him in jail with his two rebel sons. He died shortly afterwards and soon the Rustenburg Game Reserve was forgotten.[5]

Official neglect of the Pongola Game Reserve in the south-eastern Transvaal had begun in 1902 and continued after 1910; neither a warden nor game rangers were appointed and funding for the reserve ceased entirely. Although nominally still responsible for the Pongola Game Reserve, by 1910 Stevenson-Hamilton had lost all interest in it, and occasionally the Magistrate of Piet Retief or a member of the Native Affairs Department paid it a cursory visit.[6] Although this reserve had lacked white supervision for many years, wildlife protection measures had been carried out by voluntary black rangers. After they had been retrenched when funding of the reserve had ceased, two rangers, 'Nondwaai' and 'Majwaba Tipia', remained in the reserve and acted against poaching and trespassing infringements in an honorary capacity.[7] Moves to do away with the reserve were initiated in October 1920, when the Minister of Lands asked the Administrator of the Transvaal if the Pongola Game Reserve might be used for the settlement of demobilized soldiers. He argued that finding state land for settlement was a higher national priority than the continued existence of an ineffective game reserve. In the lack of discussion on the abolition of the game reserve, and the promptness with which the instrument of deproclamation (Proclamation 1 of 1921) was drafted and published, one can almost sense the relief in provincial circles at having, at last, a sound reason for vacating the area.

Although referred to as 'sacred ground',[8] even the Sabi and Singwitsi Game Reserves were not spared the effects of post-Union circumstances which so detrimentally affected both the Rustenburg and Pongola Game Reserves. As Union loomed, Stevenson-Hamilton had been warned that wildlife protection would became a party-political issue and that agitation to reduce the size of the reserves would intensify.[9]

In 1911 the first move in this direction came from white farmers who cast covetous eyes upon the grazing potential of the south-western part of the Sabi Game Reserve. A petition was presented to the Provincial Council asking that this portion of the reserve be deproclaimed and opened for grazing. The Council discussed the matter and referred the petition to the Executive Council.[10] Reluctant to alienate the farming vote and also mindful of the drought conditions which prevailed at the time, J.F.B. Rissik, the surveyor of the Witwatersrand gold-fields who had become the first Administrator of the Transvaal, agreed to allow the grazing concessions in the game reserve, although he did not countenance deproclamation.[11]

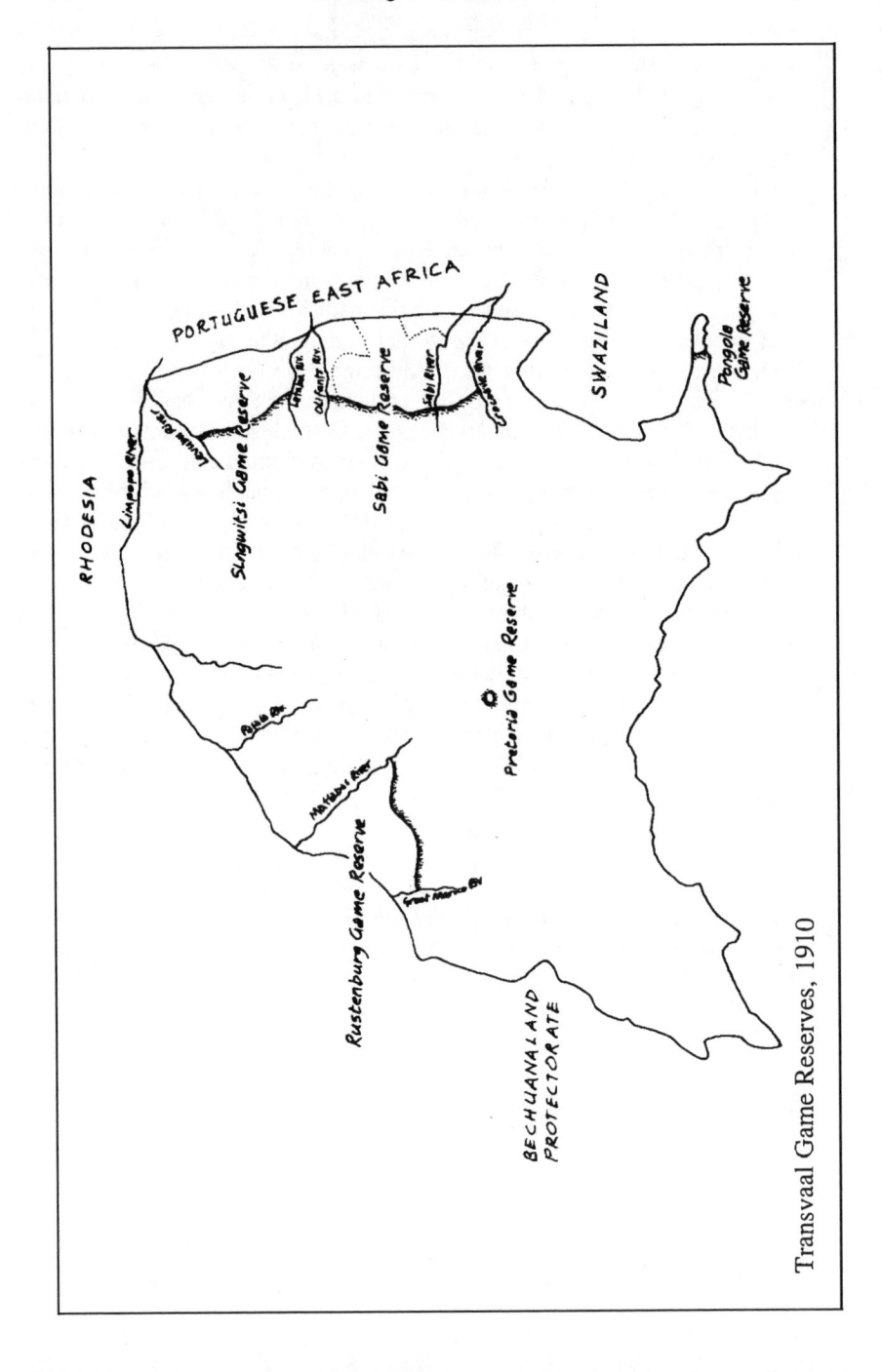

Transvaal Game Reserves, 1910

Denser settlement by whites of the rural areas of the province had been a prime objective of successive Transvaal governments. After Union the central government, searching for suitable land, considered the Sabi Game Reserve. The completion of the Selati railway line had given access to a part of the eastern Transvaal hitherto poorly served by communications, and in 1913 the Department of Lands asked the Transvaal provincial authorities to excise the portion of the game reserve adjacent to the railway line. The province refused the request because it considered that using the railway line as a game reserve boundary would make any conservation regulations impossible to enforce.[12] In 1916 the Department of Lands tried again, but was rebuffed once more.[13]

Another central government department which considered that the game reserves were merely 'sentimental objects' which were far too large,[14] was the Department of Mines. There was some debate within this department as to whether valuable minerals were in fact to be found within the reserves: some argued that there was nothing other than coal or copper which were abundant elsewhere.[15] While agreeing that the existence of game reserves should not be permitted to interfere with the exploration for and exploitation of mineral resources,[16] the provincial administration felt that to open the reserves for mining was not yet warranted.

Capitalist farming interests were also antagonistic and provided a powerful lobby for reducing the size of the reserve. The landowning companies, whose ground had been included within the boundaries of the extended game reserve in 1902 and 1903, began to reconsider their position. As time passed and circumstances changed, these owners contended that they were prevented from exploiting their farms because of the agreements they had signed when handing them over to be administered by the game reserve authorities. The contracts had initially covered a five-year period and were extended for a further five years in 1908. When the expiry date of 31 March 1913 drew near, the Transvaal Land Owners' Association began to put pressure on the provincial government to end the arrangement between them. In 1913 the agreements between the parties were renewed for just one year, during which time the province promised to formulate a definite policy as far as the future of the reserves was concerned.[17]

By 1916 the province had made no progress in this connection, and the Transvaal Land Owners' Association suggested an exchange of land with the government so that the game reserve could become wholly state-owned.[18] Stevenson-Hamilton had little sympathy with what he regarded as selfish capitalist interests, declaring in 1913 that he did not 'think we need to be at a lot of worry and trouble to please people who really have never done anything except acquiesce in our looking after their property for them'.[19]

Many of these threats to the game reserves were defused by a growing change in white public attitudes to wildlife. Commerce or sport as a rationale for wildlife conservation was being replaced by a shift towards sentimental and scientific views. At an annual general meeting in November 1911, the Transvaal Game Protection Association announced that the aim of saving game was no longer to pander to the selfish pleasures of sportsmen, but that wildlife should be preserved for posterity to see and appreciate.[20] Two years later the President of the Association, E.F. Bourke, a prominent Pretoria businessman and Transvaal landowner, stressed again that wildlife should exist for the benefit of future generations, adding that it was necessary for 'scientific' purposes as well.[21]

With its long history of internal dissent, unanimity among members of the Transvaal Game Protection Association was difficult to achieve when this new principle became prominent.[22] Some sportsmen, being farmers and landowners, wanted access to game reserve land. The Lydenburg branch of the Transvaal Game Protection Association, for instance, complained at an annual general meeting that the western boundary of the Sabi Game Reserve was inaccurately demarcated and difficult to follow, and asked that this portion be opened to sportsmen.[23] On hearing of this view, Stevenson-Hamilton immediately wrote to the Provincial Secretary urging him to refuse the Association's request.[24]

Despite these demands to reduce the size of the Transvaal reserves, before the outbreak of the First World War the boundaries of the Sabi and Singwitsi Game Reserves were in fact extended rather than contracted. The reserves were not contiguous: the northern boundary of the Sabi Game Reserve being the Olifants River, and the southern boundary of the Singwitsi Game Reserve being the Letaba River, there was a substantial gap between them. Although Stevenson-Hamilton had the authority to protect wildlife in the intervening region, the area did not formally become part of the reserves until the situation was rectified by proclamation in 1914.[25] When the amalgamation was first mooted in February 1913, the Department of Lands refused to permit the extension.[26] Evidence no longer exists in the records of what efforts were made behind the scenes to persuade the Minister of Lands to change his mind, but by December 1913 he had agreed.[27]

If economic interests appeared antagonistic to the Sabi and Singwitsi Game Reserves, natural circumstances appeared to conspire to reinforce them. Between 1912 and 1916 recurrent drought and the consequent lack of breeding habitats for the vectors of horse-sickness and malaria created the impression that game reserves were indeed agriculturally viable and not as 'worthless' as had originally been thought.[28] In addition, the fact that some whites lived permanently in the lowveld also seemed to indicate that the region was not climatically impossible for white occupation.[29]

More importantly, however, an outbreak of nagana in Natal evoked an over-reaction in the form of calls for the destruction of all wildlife in South Africa. Nagana had disappeared from the Transvaal and Natal with the outbreak of rinderpest in 1896, and leading entomologists had speculated that because so much wildlife had died from the rinderpest, it was the lack of a game host which had been the critical factor in eradicating the tsetse fly. When nagana recurred in Natal after an absence of more than a decade, the burgeoning numbers of wildlife within the Natal game reserves were held to be responsible.[30] Both the provincial and central governments assisted agriculturalists in eradicating almost all the wildlife of Zululand to curtail the nagana epidemic and massive slaughter occurred. In Swaziland, too, game reserves were abolished and wholesale extermination of all wildlife encouraged.[31]

Stevenson-Hamilton was extremely worried about the effect that the situation in Natal would have on his reserves and wrote to Selous in 1911: 'This . . . is a most hazardous time for big game . . . the sleeping sickness has aroused a kind of panic even in regions where the appearance of the disease is outside practical politics . . . many [will] take advantage of this panic and turn it to their ends of game extermination.'[32] His fear ultimately proved to be unfounded, for the disease did not break out in the Transvaal.

It has been said of the American national parks that tracing their genesis is 'like nailing jelly to the wall',[33] and this remark applies also to the South African situation. Over the years certain individuals, particularly Paul Kruger, have been given the credit for introducing to South Africa the national park. However, as is the case with the origins of many institutions, it is impossible to pinpoint the precise moment of inception. Much of the difficulty lies in defining precisely what constitutes a national park. On the one hand, if a national park is a reserve proclaimed by the highest legislative body of a country, then Natal achieved this in 1907 when the Legislative Council established the Drakensberg park.[34] On the other hand, if the aim of a national park is to serve a large region, to attract tourists and in other ways to bear some comparison with the national parks in the United States, then, it seems, the concept was first aired publicly in the Legislative Assembly of the Transvaal in 1907 when A. Woolls-Sampson, the Reform Committee member who had founded the Imperial Light Horse during the South African War, mentioned that the Transvaal game reserves could, one day, become like Yellowstone.[35]

Stevenson-Hamilton claimed that he had initiated the national park idea and that he had raised the question of the nationalization of the Sabi and

Singwitsi Game Reserves at the time of Union in 1910,[36] but he did not refer to the incident in his journal at the time. He certainly broached the subject with the Provincial Secretary in February 1913, writing of a wholly state-owned, 'permanent game sanctuary',[37] and he also corresponded privately with the Administrator about the matter. It is clear from the latter correspondence that Stevenson-Hamilton thought that his suggestion for the nationalization of the game reserves was 'premature' and that it was more likely that the reserves would 'remain as an asset of the Transvaal province' than that they would pass into the hands of the national state.[38]

Other voices joined Stevenson-Hamilton in these years in calling for the establishment of a national park. In 1912, the Witwatersrand branch of the Transvaal Game Protection Association proposed the nationalization of the Sabi and Singwitsi Game Reserves and the motion was carried in January 1913.[39] The Transvaal Land Owners' Association also favoured the proposal, and had put out feelers in this connection to the provincial authorities believing that they, too, were 'generally in favour of nationalization'.[40]

While the officials of the province may well have been so, their views were not, it seems, shared by all of the elected legislators. The question of a national park was raised in the Transvaal Provincial Council in June 1913, when the member for Soutpansberg, T.J. Kleinenberg, announced that the 'the time has arrived when the Sabi and Singwitsi Game Reserves should be nationalized and that the Union government be urged to take the necessary steps to accomplish this'. He suggested that the central government be asked also to 'consider the advisability of forming National Reserves in other parts of the Union to preserve South African Fauna for the benefit of future generations' and that 'a Commission of Enquiry be appointed to investigate the matter thoroughly and recommend areas suitable for this purpose'. His colleagues in the Provincial Council were unenthusiastic. After a short debate the matter was adjourned until the following day but, although the motion appeared on the agenda at every subsequent meeting during the rest of the session, it was never discussed again. When the session was prorogued in September 1913, the national park issue was dropped without any further ado.[41]

The outbreak of the First World War delayed further progress in respect of national parks, although the Transvaal Game Protection Association made a public statement in 1915 that it still favoured nationalizing the game reserves.[42] It was, however, an antagonist who was responsible for initiating the next move: S.H. Coetzee, the member for Lydenburg, forced the issue in the Provincial Council in March 1916 by introducing a motion asking the Administrator of the Transvaal to urge the Union government to reduce the area of the Sabi Game Reserve. An amendment to Coetzee's motion requested the Union government to hand over the state land within the reserve to the Provincial Council.[43]

As the tier of government ultimately responsible for land allocation, the central government was becoming increasingly involved in the Transvaal game reserves and, as early as 1914, the matter of national game reserves was being informally discussed at high levels of government. In May 1914, Smuts, then Minister of Finance and Defence, had asked to be kept informed of game conservation matters in the Transvaal,[44] and in November he had written directly to Rissik:

> ... there appears to be a grave risk that the future of the Reserve may at any time be imperilled by the establishment of cattle ranching in that area ... it would be a thousand pities to endanger the existence of our South African fauna. It has been suggested that the best way of obtaining the object in view would be to constitute a portion of the existing reserve as a National Sanctuary on the lines of similar institutions which exist in the United States and in other parts of the world, and set it aside for all time for the purpose ... If you agree generally with my views, I think the first course to adopt is to appoint an impartial commission to go over the ground ...[45]

The Provincial Council dealt with the matter fully on 6 April when G. Hartog, the member for Parktown, asked that a commission of inquiry be appointed into the game reserve, to which the Council agreed. In June 1916 members of the commission were appointed[46] and the report was published in August 1918.

That such a commission was held during war-time indicates the importance of the interests which were affected by the existence of game reserves. Taking each of these in turn, the commission concluded that pastoralists needed additional land and that the system of issuing grazing licences in the game reserve should continue. The commission sympathized with what it called the 'public-spirited attitude' of the land companies in allowing their land to remain within the reserve for so long, and recommended that the government acquire these farms and compensate the companies accordingly. The commission also considered the effect of the 1913 Natives' Land Act on the issue of land for African settlement: the Native Affairs Administration Bill had allocated the infertile Singwitsi Game Reserve for this purpose.[47] The Game Reserves Commission did not visit the Singwitsi Reserve and, apart from remarking that the area was probably unsuitable for any human settlement, it considered that a thorough inspection of the region was needed before a final conclusion could be drawn.

The most significant outcome of the Game Reserves Commission, however, was on matters of protectionist philosophy. In this respect, the commission was 'not a little struck by the uselessness of having these magnificent reserves merely for the *preservation* of the fauna', and advocated a more conservationist stance – in fact, the 'creation of the area ultimately as a great national park'. For the first time, the objectives of and arguments for a South African national park were spelled out in some detail:

> We think that . . . greater facilities should be offered to scientists, naturalists, and the general public to make themselves acquainted with a portion of their country which should be of the greatest natural interest for the following reasons:
>
> (i) Here one may view and study conditions once generally obtaining throughout large areas of the Union, but which, owing to the advance of civilization, are now rapidly disappearing and must eventually disappear altogether.
>
> (ii) As a training ground for the scientific student, whether in botany, zoology, or other directions, the area is unequalled.
>
> (iii) It is becoming more and more difficult for the town dweller to gain knowledge of the natural conditions of the country, and with the gradual extinction of game and other animals that is steadily going on, even to see the fauna of the country other than in the sophisticated surroundings of a zoological collection.
>
> (iv) Here and nowhere better can the natural surroundings and habits of South African fauna be really studied, unaffected as the animals are by the instinctive dread of the huntsman, which in other parts of the country tend completely to alter their habits.[48]

This manifesto of the commission expressed some novel principles as far as South African game reserves were concerned. What was new, was firstly, the principle that the wildlife in the reserve should be exploited by visitors and students and, secondly, that the natural habitat of wildlife was as much an aesthetic experience for humans as it was vital to the existence of the animals themselves.

The publication of the *Report of the Game Reserves Commission* came at the end of the First World War. Many officials of the Sabi and Singwitsi Game Reserves had been on active service and the administration of the reserves had all but collapsed. When Stevenson-Hamilton had joined the

Advertising poster designed by Stratford Caldecott, c. 1928

Stevenson-Hamilton and Mr and Mrs A.J. Crosby of the Transvaal Land and Exploration Company, c. 1925

Stevenson-Hamilton's office, 1914

Jan Smuts, Julius Jeppe and John Rissik (L. to R.) at the warden's home, Sabi Game Reserve, 1912

South African Railways publicised the Sabi Game Reserve in the 1920s.

Minister of Lands, P. Grobler, 1926

Paul Selby promotional literature, 1926

army in 1914, ranger De Laporte acted as Warden. But when De Laporte himself had joined up, no ranger except the elderly Fraser, still Warden of the Singwitsi Game Reserve, had been prepared to take the post. Fraser's administration was disastrous, Stevenson-Hamilton said that it would have been comic had it not affected the game reserves so seriously. Fraser apparently considered office work 'undignified' – he wrote no letters or reports and kept no legal or climatic records. He fell out with all the government officials in the district. His twenty-five dogs ran amok in the Warden's house and the African staff were confounded when he persisted in sleeping throughout the day and in doing his chores throughout the night.[49]

Stevenson-Hamilton returned to South Africa only in 1920, and was depressed at what he considered to be a chaotic situation, complaining that:

> The system of control, carefully built up since 1902, has been seriously impaired since I left in 1914. In that year we held an excellent command of the natives and of the reserves generally, and administration proceeded by routine perfectly and easily . . . on the whole the impression I receive [in 1920] is that there has been a general retrogression, bringing the state of things now obtaining back to about the position occupied in 1904.[50]

Stevenson-Hamilton was disappointed in more than the circumstances in the Sabi and Singwitsi Game Reserves at this time. He wrote that it was generally a time of 'a "slump" in faunal preservation, a condition which may in part be attributed to the general slackening of the fibres of civilization due to the late war'.[51] Wildlife conservation in South Africa certainly did seem to be under attack from many quarters. Game reserves were deproclaimed in three of the four provinces of the country, in Namaqualand in 1919, Gordonia-Kuruman in 1924, and Umfolozi in 1920.[52]

The tide was about to turn in the Transvaal, however, with fresh political circumstances after the First World War. In 1919 the Transvaal Game Protection Association, whose activities had been largely in abeyance during the war, supported the recommendations of the Game Reserves Commission,[53] and in the same year, the Transvaal Land Owners' Association took the initiative by meeting the Administrator and asking him to exchange the private land within the reserves for state land elsewhere.

Despite the enthusiastic statements of its own commission, it took the provincial authorities almost a year to react to the demands of the Transvaal Land Owners' Association, and then, it seems, they only did so under pressure from the central government. In September 1920 the Provincial

Secretary formally advocated the nationalization of the game reserves and prepared a memorandum for discussion by the Executive Council.

The most serious stumbling block was the large number of privately owned farms included in the Sabi Game Reserve. The Game Reserves Commission had recommended that landowners be compensated if their farms were to become part of a national park, either by way of suitable financial recompense or by an exchange for farms in other localities within the province.

The difficulties raised by central government interests were threefold. Firstly, the Native Affairs Department sought land for African occupation. The question of African habitation and white access to labour in the eastern Transvaal had become critical after the war due to increased white agricultural activity and settlement in the White River district. Africans who refused to work on white farms in the vicinity demanded land of their own, while white settlers resented the fact that Africans were able to withhold their services by living, albeit clandestinely, in the game reserves. Secondly, the province had to contend with the Department of Mines which now desired to exploit the coal deposits in the Sabi Game Reserve and, thirdly, with the Department of Lands which wanted game reserve territory for white settlement. There was no way out of the impasse but to hold a meeting of all the interested parties so that these issues could be 'definitely and finally' resolved.[54]

This conference took place on 25 February 1921. There was no opposition to the idea of a national park in the eastern Transvaal and, without exception, all delegates considered the existing area of the game reserves to be too large. Even Stevenson-Hamilton conceded that the western part of the Sabi Game Reserve could be taken over by the Native Affairs Department, there being 'no great objection from a game preservation point of view'.[55]

Ultimately, the conclusion reached by the meeting was that the Sabi Game Reserve should be contracted on the western side. Some land would be allocated for African settlement and many of the private farms that had hitherto been part of the reserve would be excluded thus reducing the number of exchanges or sales. The Department of Lands would accordingly acquire all the remaining privately owned land in the reserve, so that the 'area of the game reserve [could] be defined by statute and . . . taken over by the Union Government as a permanent national game sanctuary'.[56]

The way to the national park was not yet clear, because the private landowners put obstacles in the way of exchanges and sales. They saw the opportunity to make a substantial financial profit from the government out of their lowveld properties and there was 'a good deal of difficulty in arriving at a satisfactory arrangement . . . owing to the question of the value those owners attached to their land'.[57] By February 1922 this issue was still unresolved, and the delay meant that the national park issue could not come before Parliament that year,[58] but by November a compromise seemed assured. Prime Minister Jan Smuts then announced his firm intention of introducing legislation for the establishment of 'a National Park and Game Reserve' during the next parliamentary session.[59]

However, when Smuts wished to conclude matters with the Transvaal Land Owners' Association in December 1922, he discovered that the Association still had reservations about the level of financial compensation for game reserve farms, and that there were objections to the proposed boundaries. It was therefore agreed that an inspection of the area would have to be made by both land surveyors and the Minister of Lands himself,[60] and faced with the delay this would entail, Smuts had no option but to postpone the introduction of legislation.[61] However, in readiness for the scheme, in 1923 the name of the two reserves was changed to the Transvaal Game Reserve, and considerable land on the western side was excised as a 'native area'.[62]

Having delayed the promulgation of legislation in 1923, the landowners were confronted a year later with a change of government and a new Minister of Lands, the staunch Afrikaner nationalist and former rebel of 1914, P.G.W. Grobler. It seems that Grobler was able to take a firmer stand with the landowners:[63] although he was concerned that insufficient finance would be available for exchange he, nevertheless, managed to locate suitable unoccupied land in the Transvaal which the landowners finally accepted at the end of 1925.[64] It may well be that the landowning companies realized that the Pact government, with its lack of sympathy for Johannesburg business interests,[65] would not negotiate any further and that expropriation was a possibility.[66] It has also been suggested that some land companies, particularly the Transvaal Consolidated Lands Company (which was the principal private landowner in the game reserve), were disillusioned with the Smuts government and happier to co-operate with the National Party.[67]

Although public opinion in Johannesburg appears at first to have favoured landowners,[68] whites generally seem to have been amenable to the idea of the creation of a national park.[69] Many politicians capitalized on this attitude, and when the establishment of a national park seemed probable, they began to participate in the project. Support from Smuts was not new, his involvement in wildlife conservation having been evident early in the century. The public association of other national politicians with the cause can be explained by the growing aggressiveness of Afrikaner nationalism culminating in the election victory of J.B.M. Hertzog's National Party in 1924 and the formation of the Pact government.

Interest in Voortrekker culture became widespread in the mid-1920s. This was epitomized in the struggle to have Afrikaans recognized as an official language, in the elevation of Voortrekker leaders to the status of national heroes, and in celebrations of Voortrekker festivals.[70] Recently it has been convincingly demonstrated that Afrikaner nationalism at this time was being provided with an historical context and that romanticized notions about Voortrekkers were being manipulated to form a national mythology.[71]

Reverence for this Afrikaner past, which was being constructed, grew apace in the 1920s. Although not a supporter of Hertzog, Deneys Reitz, who was Minister of Lands from 1921 to 1924, provides an example of the trend. Reitz had close connections with the former republics of the Orange Free State and Transvaal and had a sentimental attachment to the pioneering history of the Afrikaner. He idealized the national park proposal as the realization of 'Paul Kruger's dream'[72] and stated that it was a national duty to preserve the landscape of the park 'just as the Voortrekkers saw it'.[73] A politician who was an active Afrikaner nationalist, and who had even closer connections with the Transvaal Republic, was Grobler, the new Minister of Lands. Grobler declared that 'it is due to the farsightedness of the late President Kruger that we are today able to establish a park'.[74] Grobler was related to Paul Kruger and had been brought up in the president's household: he was thus proud to be associated with what he considered to be the high ideals of his forbear.[75] Politically this was advantageous for him: as was pointed out 'the scheme can only give him [Grobler] popularity'.[76] Grobler, in fact, later claimed that the Kruger National Park had been founded on his initiative alone.[77]

In addition to enfolding wildlife protection within an Afrikaner cultural tradition, the Voortrekker past was manipulated by National Party politicians in order to gain the support of 'poor whites', and the national park issue served to unite factions and classes within Afrikaner society in the years after the First World War.

Many English-speaking protectionists – many of them sportsmen – made deliberate use of these Afrikaner sentiments to lobby for the creation of a national park; a particular case in point being the issue which centred on the naming of the proposed park. In December 1925 Stevenson-Hamilton wrote to a Transvaal politician that the 'Kruger National Park' would be an excellent name 'and would carry an atmosphere with it [that was] attractive and highly popular'. He asked whether this suggestion could be relayed to Grobler.[78] Privately, Stevenson-Hamilton was less tactful:

> The man who *really* was responsible was R.K. Loveday . . . but the "Kruger stunt" is I think of priceless value to us, and I would not for the world do aught but whisper otherwise . . . I wonder what the old man, who *never in his life* thought of wild animals except as biltong, and who, with the idea that it did not matter much one way or the other, and in any case would not affect any one except the town sportsmen, gave way under strong pressure exercised by Loveday and one or two others and allowed the reserve to be declared. I wonder, I repeat, what he would say could he see himself depicted as the "*Saviour of the South African game*!!!"[79]

How the name of the proposed park was publicized was also politically loaded. The name 'Kruger National Park' had been the formal suggestion of Judge J.A.J. de Villiers, later Chief Justice of the Union, and was put forward at a meeting of the National Monuments Commission[80] (of which he was a member) in December 1925. Some English-speakers were not appreciative of a politically opportunistic name for the park, preferring the title, 'South African National Park'. The comment was even made that 'if any person's name is to be used, a "National Milner Park" would be more appropriate',[81] for Lord Milner had been responsible for the proclamation of the Sabi and Singwitsi Game Reserves after the South African War. Grobler, of course, had no reservations on this score,[82] and advised the Senate that 'in proposing to give the name of Kruger National Park to the reserve, Hon. Senators will agree with me that it is the right thing to connect President Kruger's name with the institution'.[83] Invoking the name of the president certainly touched the right emotional chord at the right time. Not only was the Hertzog government keen to re-establish a republic, but the name was also consistent with the Afrikaner view of saluting national heroes by naming monuments or institutions after them. For the English-speakers, the matter of the name was not seen as an important issue, except in so far as it served to whip up support for the establishment of the park itself.[84]

Stevenson-Hamilton could not ally himself publicly with the national park campaign because neutrality was required of him as an official of the provincial government.[85] However, in Stratford Caldecott, the Paris-trained landscape artist who then lived in Cape Town, and who had no personal vested interest in the national park, Stevenson-Hamilton found a mouthpiece and a staunch ally. The two men had met when Caldecott had visited the Sabi Game Reserve in August 1925 to produce posters of wildlife to publicize railway tours of South Africa – one of which incorporated a trip through the game reserve.[86]

In an article in November 1925, Caldecott linked the names of an 'English gentleman' (James Stevenson-Hamilton) and 'the great Afrikander' (Paul Kruger) suggesting that both had had an equal hand in creating a national park in South Africa.[87] Associating these two men demonstrates the utility of the national park as a scheme to merge English-speaking and Afrikaans-speaking South Africans in striving towards a common ideal and in this way putting a divided past behind them. The *Cape Argus*, noting that 'South Africa first' was one of the mottoes of the government, declared that the national park plan offered a good opportunity to put this ideal into practice.[88] The *Rand Daily Mail* claimed that the national park question was not a party political but a 'national' question.[89] Thus the English-speaking pursuit of unity and the Afrikaner pursuit of a separate, historical identity coincided to advance the same wildlife protection goal. On one occasion rivalry between the two groups surfaced when Afrikaners felt that the English-speakers were getting too much of the credit for initiating the idea of a national park. In order to overcome this problem, which threatened to jeopardize the campaign, Stevenson-Hamilton suggested to Caldecott that

> It might do good to point out that we wanted to get the help of both races, but whereas we knew the Dutch-speaking people were *already* with us on account of their knowledge of requirements and tradition of the Park, we felt that the English-speaking section required information and enlightenment and that also it was among them that our principal opponents might be expected, especially the J'burg element. I think [once] worked out the above might do us good, and there is a lot of truth in it; all our opposition so far has been from the English speakers, private and official.[90]

All the daily newspapers in the country welcomed the formation of a national park and even vied with each other to be the scheme's greatest supporter, stressing the common heritage and values which wildlife represented for whites and how these could strengthen national unity. At the same time it was acknowledged that the park would gain international recognition for South Africa and 'enhance and invigorate our prestige in foreign lands'.[91] It was pointed out, too, how the South African 'character' had to some extent been moulded by the wildlife of the region,[92] while the protection of a 'fairyland' in which 'spiritual regeneration' could take place was important.[93]

Caldecott, almost singlehandedly, orchestrated a massive national press and publicity campaign in order to consolidate public opinion on the side of the national park. If anything, his efforts erred on the side of idealistic over-enthusiasm, and Stevenson-Hamilton at one time warned him not to 'exaggerate too much' or people would tire of the propaganda and actually be repulsed.[94] Once the ball was rolling, however, publicity was self-generating. Newspapers and periodicals gave the national park issue extensive coverage,[95] while organizations such as the Boy Scouts lent their weight to the project. Because of their regional rivalries, game protection associations were less effective publicly than might have been anticipated.[96] Despite this, they played their part in marshalling sportsmen behind the national park and, in the event, the national park issue led to the federation of regional associations into a national conservation society.[97]

The involvement of Caldecott, an artist, in the park campaign illustrates, too, how themes of nature were beginning to permeate South African aesthetics. Afrikaans nationalistic poetry of the time dealt with the landscape more than wildlife, but poetry which celebrated the external influences on the Afrikaner character naturally also evoked to some degree the sentiments which facilitated the creation of the Kruger National Park. Having been dominated by the European indoor tradition, the visual arts were being increasingly influenced by the South African landscape and wildlife photography made its serious début during these years.

The practical and financial advantages of a South African national park augmented the sentimental, aesthetic and nationalistic arguments which were put forward. Aware that his party needed the support of rural Transvalers, Grobler stressed that national park land was agriculturally unproductive. Far from retarding development, the creation of a national park would encourage economic growth in the lowveld.[98] Tourists were crucial to the financial success of the venture, and it was never doubted that visitors would materialize in large numbers, provided that an infrastructure could be created to 'enable the South African and overseas public, under conditions of great safety and comfort, to view wild life as it existed in the sub-continent previous to the arrival of the white man'.[99] It was calculated that if ten thousand Americans visited each year the revenue to the park would be in the region of £1 million, 'a sum which should appeal to all South Africans'.[100] Other economic arguments suggested that the national park would facilitate the domestication of elephant and eland, and would also lead to an increased supply of venison.[101]

Science was also to benefit from the creation of a national park in that extinctions of species, such as that of the quagga and blue antelope, would be prevented in future.[102] However, scientists in South Africa were the one group which came out publicly against the park. Opinions came mainly from veterinarians who linked the existence of wildlife with diseases of domestic livestock. Stevenson-Hamilton was particularly worried by this because he was unable to convince certain entomologists that nagana did not occur in the Transvaal game reserves.[103] The Warden was suspicious, however, of the motives of these entomologists and veterinarians, contending that they were merely using the park question to jostle for higher positions in various government and provincial departments.[104]

In a show of solidarity, the National Parks Act was passed unanimously by both Houses of Parliament in May and June 1926.[105] The debate consisted largely of adulatory comments on the roles that Paul Kruger and James Stevenson-Hamilton had played in the inception of the park, and gratitude was also expressed to 'Providence that we have been given that locality to establish a national park in the interests of the preservation of our fauna'.[106] In giving his blessing to the bill, Smuts, the Leader of the Opposition and always the expansionist, expressed the hope that the park would eventually extend as far north as central Africa.[107]

While the politicians were congratulating themselves on the national park, the idealists – particularly Stevenson-Hamilton and Caldecott – were apprehensive, and Caldecott wrote to the Warden:

> I understand that you have no stomach to see the place full of rubberneck waggons and tourists, but it was vulgarization or abolition, I suppose, and it was at that price only that the animals could be saved. Perhaps a time of finer living and thinking is coming for those who will follow us and they will be thankful for that beauty saved for them.[108]

As well as reflecting conditions in the mid-1920s in South Africa, in that the name 'Kruger' in the title was indicative of the cultural and class heritage which was being given expression in establishing the park, and the description 'national' being synonymous with 'white', the foundation of the Kruger National Park also heralded changes in environmental thinking. The vague ideas which had underpinned the management of the game reserves were now made explicit: the concept of a national park was not preservationist, but conservationist. Henceforth, the area would be managed for the benefit of white tourists and not purely in the interests of increasing the numbers of animals.

In addition, for the first time the physical environment was given consideration, and not just the wildlife which inhabited it. Ecological thinking had still to evolve further, but in 1920 Stevenson-Hamilton, for example, began to feel repugnance towards destroying some of what were then regarded as vermin species, particularly lion. He remarked, 'now I think the nearer to nature the better in a reserve, so when I see a lioness with her children, I feel like saying, "good luck to you" . . . I think that the ideal should be to show the country and the animals in it to the public as God made both.'[109]

It was envisaged that visitors would come to the park in order to see wildlife in its natural habitat, and would thus experience to some degree the frontier or pioneering past. It seems, therefore, to be true that in South Africa, as in other countries, national parks were used as fantasy worlds, enshrining the olden-day values of romantic nature by which society as a whole could no longer afford to live.[110] In many respects too, they may be considered to be tokens of atonement for the profligate killing of wildlife which had occurred in the past.[111]

In exploring the idea that whites romanticized their past through the natural landscape and its wildlife, it is imperative to take cognisance of the fact that whites chose to disregard the role that Africans had played in that past. African attitudes and interests were ignored or over-ridden. One can, however, argue in this respect that what the national parks did accomplish as far as Africans were concerned was to deny them access to a large portion of the Transvaal; a portion which was not agriculturally useful at the time, but which could nevertheless have supplemented the very small area of land which the Natives' Land Act of 1913 had allocated for their settlement. In South Africa it appears that the considerable African resistance to the game reserves may actually have accelerated the formation of the national park precisely because tighter central administration was considered to be a deterrent to African occupation of the area under consideration. The new park must therefore be seen as a means of providing more effective control over both neighbouring Africans and the few who still resided within the park.[112]

The establishment of the Kruger National Park came at a time when African and white attitudes to wildlife had polarized. Important though this observation is, it is possibly more significant in the final analysis that creating the national park provided tangible evidence of the unity of whites on nature conservation for the first time. The divisions of opinion which had previously been so apparent, between sportsmen, the landed and monied classes and 'poor whites', had been publicly resolved by declaring wildlife to be culturally and sentimentally important to all whites and recreational viewing to be a legitimate form of resource exploitation. This protectionist conviction was generally moulded by the industrialization of the country, the improved material circumstances and urbanization of whites and the lack of opportunities for sport or commercial hunting on state land. Consequently, the foundation of the Kruger National Park represents a measure of the adoption by the white lower classes – those former biltong and subsistence hunters – as well as sportsmen, of the views which were those of the élite. In this way, the establishment of the national park manifests an advance in political expediency as much as progress in conservation strategy.

Politics and the Park after 1926

The National Parks Act of 1926 did not bring into being immediately all the features of the Kruger National Park as we know it today. The new legislation provided for numerous changes of principle and practice but many of these took years to manifest themselves. Most obviously, the structure of administrative management altered. A Board of Trustees was appointed and the hitherto undisputed authority and freedom of action of the Warden was curtailed by bureaucratic controls. The game reserve policy of allowing wildlife to live undisturbed by the prying public was altered. The imperial preservationist ethic – to nurture 'game' species for the later delight of sportsmen – was replaced by a more encompassing appreciation of the value of all wildlife, together with the landscape which contained it. The national park was opened to visitors and they became the chief beneficiaries of the national park and, indeed, its very reason for existence. The landscape of the game reserves was transformed as access roads, bridges and camps were constructed for the visiting public.

But one crucial attribute of the national park could also not be manufactured overnight – its symbolism for the South African public. Legislation stipulated that the Kruger National Park was a 'national heritage', but who exactly constituted the 'nation' and whose heritage was to be enshrined in the park? English-speaking sportsmen? Afrikaner biltong and commercial hunters? African subsistence hunters? Those seeking luxury, or those escaping from urban comforts? Was the 'heritage' to be an imported one, perhaps from the United States of America, where national parks had originated? Or was it to be forged in collaboration with other countries also newly inclined towards national parks?

Establishing the Kruger National Park did not automatically create a national park philosophy: what the park would ultimately become had to evolve with the passing of time. In the ferment of the political and socio-economic circumstances of South Africa in the 1920s, national park ideology could be moulded by whatever interest group had sufficient power and influence to do so. The park had obtained legal security, but was culturally, politically, and even ecologically, adrift.

The process which culminated in entrenching the present ideals of the Kruger National Park – indeed of the now considerable network of South African national parks – was a long one, and probably peaked only in the 1970s. The National Parks Act took wildlife conservation out of the hands of sportsmen and old-style game wardens and projected it into the mainstream of South African politics. Those politics were distinctly white, and the socio-political culture of South African national parks was consequently shaped by white interests. While provincial game reserves were fringe affairs, enjoying only minority support, national parks offered a new and more universal symbol, and one which was to become increasingly meaningful to the South African white public.

Political developments intertwined with the national parks' organizational structures to create those qualities which have now come to be associated with the Kruger National Park. How this came about is the concern of the present chapter, which examines the role of the National Parks Board and its employees (in particular the Warden of the Kruger National Park), the contribution of the visiting public, and, most crucially, the impact of national party politics. Although the contribution that rural Africans have made and the impact that they have had on the evolution of wildlife conservation legislation in the Transvaal have formed a thread running throughout this work, racial segregation and apartheid attitudes after 1926 were so important a determinant of national park strategy, and impinge so greatly on its future, that they warrant particular attention. Chapter 5 thus explores the relationships between the Kruger National Park and black South Africans, and analyses how many criticisms of national park policy have come into being.

Bureaucratic structure has played a decisive role in the evolution of a national park ethos in South Africa. Placed under the general supervision of the Minister of Lands, national parks were not constituted as a government department, but were placed under the control of the National Parks Board of Trustees, a statutory body representing state, provincial and private wildlife conservation interests. The Board was admonished to 'control, manage and maintain' all aspects of South African national park policy,[1] and consequently had considerable power. Although the National Party was in power at the time, because the national park issue was directly related to the fusion of the two white groups, the composition of the Board showed considerable variety in personality and approach. The first chairman was Senator W.J.C. (Jack) Brebner, a leading National Party politician and very close associate of Hertzog, then Prime Minister. Another National Party member of the Board was Oswald Pirow, Cabinet Minister from 1929 to 1933 and from 1938 to 1939, and pro-German founder in 1940 of New Order, the Nazi-sympathizing political organization. Some Board members were politicians from the opposition party. Deneys Reitz, the former Minister of Lands, was one. So was H.B. Papenfus, a man well known for his promotion of conciliation between Afrikaner and English South Africans, and R.A. Hockly, the Member of Parliament for Fort Beaufort in the Eastern Cape. Three members were appointed for their particular knowledge of wildlife and the lowveld. They were Sir Abe Bailey, Transvaal mining magnate and landowner, and a sportsman prominent in the Transvaal Game Protection Association, W.A. Campbell, a wealthy Natal and eastern Transvaal landowner, and Dr A.K. Haagner, who had succeeded Gunning as head of the Pretoria Zoological Gardens. Haagner's position was as representative of the Wild Life Protection Society of South Africa. A.E. Charter, the Secretary, was the nominee of the Transvaal province. The appointment of the last member of the team, Gustav Preller, provides an important early clue to the political direction the Board would take. Preller was not a wildlife enthusiast, but a determined publicist for Afrikaner nationalism, a state historian, journalist and active promoter of Voortrekker history. He was put onto the Board in order to provide a cultural dimension to South African national parks.

At the time of their appointment, there was no opposition to any of these Board members, indeed, Stevenson-Hamilton had been expecting an entirely Afrikaner nationalist complement and was thus pleasantly surprised by the range of interests which were represented.[2] Members were appointed to the Board for a five-year term, but some of the initial appointments were short: Bailey, Charter and Haagner each served for only one year. The Wild Life Protection Society's representative thereafter was Paul Selby, a mining engineer, keen sportsman and early wildlife photographer, but the other two were replaced by politicians W.H. Rood, Member of Parliament for Barberton, and T.C. Stoffberg, Chairman of the National Party in the Transvaal and 'a dedicated Afrikaner'.[3] Politicians thus came to dominate the Board and membership became a form of political reward.

The National Parks Board was an intermediate authority, sandwiched between its master, the government, and its servants, its employees. Both relationships were pivotal to the success of national park strategy. In the Board's dealings with its employees, the initial most crucial link was between the Board and the Warden of the Kruger National Park. In 1926 this was still James Stevenson-Hamilton, but at the time, he was not at all sure that he wanted to continue in his post, which – in any event – had to be re-created. This was so because he was employed by the province and the post fell away when the game reserve was nationalized.[4] Stevenson-Hamilton was well aware that tension between Afrikaners and English-speakers in South Africa was running high. His loyalties were to the British camp, and he believed that the National Party government would persecute English-speaking civil servants and that he would probably be replaced by an Afrikaner. Having become used to taking decisions without reference to higher authority, the Warden also disliked the idea of having to report to a Board which he considered would become increasingly interfering and dictatorial.[5]

As he was then sixty years old and almost at retirement age, Stevenson-Hamilton returned to Britain to reconsider his position, taking up employment with the Zoological Society in London. While he found it interesting, Stevenson-Hamilton also found his work of publicizing the Zoological Society and its associate, the Society for the Protection of the Fauna of the Empire, involved little excitement compared with what he had become accustomed to in the eastern Transvaal. In the game reserves, as he recounts in *South African Eden*, he explored unusual and remote parts of the lowveld on horseback, often accompanied only by African servants. He had unrivalled opportunities to encounter wild animals in their natural state and to study their habits closely. He turned this privilege to good effect, by carefully recording his observations in publications which were designed to inform and educate others. By the 1920s he enjoyed a considerable international reputation as a knowledgeable wildlife expert and his many articles and books, particularly *Animal Life in Africa*,[6] were both influential and highly regarded by world standards.

At his job in London, by contrast, Stevenson-Hamilton found himself in a urban environment teeming with people, 'the city of the dreadful night', he called it.[7] Although he revelled in the museums and educated society which Britain had to offer, he hated the 'greyness' of it all, and found that the damp weather had a depressing effect on his spirits. Therefore when the National Parks Board asked him to re-accept the position of Warden, Stevenson-Hamilton was keen to return, but he wanted to do so only on his own terms. He agreed to come back only for one year, on condition that he had 'a written guarantee . . . to the effect that all internal administration of the Park . . . and in fact all matters outside of financial control and general advertising work, shall be left entirely in my hands without interference . . .'[8] The Board telegraphed its agreement in principle, apart from being unable to 'divest itself of obligations imposed on it under Act'.[9]

In the event, Stevenson-Hamilton could not, of course, have total liberty, because he was directly responsible to the National Parks Board, and he had to abide by its decisions. He disliked this intensely, for he came to think that the Board interfered too much in the minutiae of his job. To a large extent this was true, because Board members were not qualified to provide any general nature conservation direction, and consequently busied themselves with administrative and petty detail.[10] Stevenson-Hamilton could have resigned his position at any time, and had, in fact, frequently considered doing so, either to return to Scotland to run his family estates or to seek employment elsewhere in the world. But the lowveld came to enthral him, and after 1927, he confided to his journal that more and more 'my fate binds me indissolubly to this place'.[11]

In 'binding' him to the Kruger National Park, Stevenson-Hamilton's own personal circumstances at the time also played a large part, for he had married in 1930 for the first time at the age of sixty-three. His wife, Hilda Cholmondeley, undoubtedly assisted him to cope with his enforced and increasing subservience to the National Parks Board. Hilda was young – twenty-nine – enthusiastic and totally in love with the wild. Despite (perhaps owing to) her urban English background, she delighted in her role as the Warden's wife and in being able to enjoy the freedom and adventure which it offered. A competent artist, she made a name for herself as a specialist in wildlife subjects and also became expert at making wildlife documentary films. However, Stevenson-Hamilton's marriage compromised both his own employment and retirement options, for after a long solitary and independent lifestyle, he now had a wife whom he loved deeply and who cared passionately for the game reserve. He also had to provide financially for a growing family: three children were born of the marriage, of whom two survived infancy.

The struggle between Stevenson-Hamilton and the National Parks Board opened in 1927, when the Warden asked whether his title could be altered from 'Warden' to 'Director', bringing him in line with the United States National Parks Service. The Board could not agree to this, but Stevenson-Hamilton was not especially perturbed, for he considered that the Board was still finding its feet.[12]

By the mid-1930s, his attitude was less generous, recalling Board meetings that he considered to be 'dreadful', and Board members who combined ignorance with arrogance. He recounted personal jealousies and even 'wars' between Board members, and an atmosphere of 'lies and scandals'. He detected coteries which were either 'on his side' or 'against him', and often gained the impression that had he resigned as Warden many Board members would have been delighted.[13]

There is no doubt that from Stevenson-Hamilton's point of view, Board members could certainly be troublesome. They had no defined portfolios and many of them simply enjoyed dabbling in wildlife issues when they felt like it. Attendance of Board members at meetings was irregular: by 1935 Gustav Preller had attended only eight of the fifty meetings which had been held. Not until 1942 was every Board member present at the same meeting.[14] All, however, enjoyed what was the highlight of the Board's year – the annual tour around the Kruger National Park in the company of the Warden. The Board also had access to the rangers' daily journals of their activities and wildlife sightings. This seems to have been a popular perquisite, to the extent that one Board member complained that the journals were becoming a little tedious to read and that rangers should be instructed to include every lively detail and amusing or interesting incident.[15]

Stevenson-Hamilton did not merely invent his persecution, even the chairman of the National Parks Board admitted in 1941 that 'there was a deliberate attempt to get rid of' the Warden.[16] The seasoned politician Reitz also sympathised with Stevenson-Hamilton, writing 'there is apparently an undercurrent of intrigue which it will be hard to counter, and I can only say I am very sorry indeed to see the way in which the good spirit of the Board has deteriorated of late'.[17] The Warden considered certain Board members to have been an 'argumentative nuisance', 'weakness itself' and even 'pompous, stupid, prejudiced, ignorant and hostile'.[18] He resented being obliged to carry out instructions from people he did not respect and despised 'amateurs who know all about wildlife,' accusing Board members of often talking 'fatuous rot'.[19] He did not like being ignored or brushed aside and was angered, for example, when he was informed, not by his superiors but through the press, that he had been appointed a member of various commissions.

Even the Board's representatives from the Wildlife Society of Southern Africa were not necessarily allies of Stevenson-Hamilton, being generally ineffectual members of the public, rather than astute politicians like some of their fellows. There was particular animosity between Stevenson-Hamilton and H. S. van Graan,[20] who became the Board's secretary and who tried hard to increase his own power at the expense of the Warden.[21]

The unresolved question of supreme command within the Kruger National Park in Stevenson-Hamilton's time impacted on the game rangers as well as their Warden. The lack of harmony between Stevenson-Hamilton and the Board was known to the rangers, some of whom exploited the situation by by-passing their direct superior and going directly to the Board behind his back.[22] They also had disagreements among themselves which the Warden was at times hard pressed to resolve.[23] Right from the start in 1902, as has been mentioned, Stevenson-Hamilton had had a low opinion of most of his rangers, considering them to be 'flotsam and jetsam'.[24] It was, however, only to be expected that such a job would be more attractive to the mavericks of society than to the average ordinary citizen, because it had appeal for solitary, perhaps even misanthropic, characters with a penchant for adventure and often a lack of a strong sense of responsibility. Stevenson-Hamilton thought that while some of them began their duties well, they subsequently slacked and did very little or took to alcohol abuse.[25] It is quite possible, though, that their responsibilities were hard to define, and it was difficult to check up on their daily activities as they were stationed in remote parts of the Park far from the Warden's eye.

As the years went by Stevenson-Hamilton's particular personality seems to have engendered in him a fierce desire, amounting to stubbornness, to remain at the Warden's post, for, in truth, it had become his whole life and his all-absorbing interest. He just could not imagine himself without the Park or the Park without him.[26] And even while recognizing that his mental and physical capabilities were deteriorating in the 1930s, he could not bear to let go, resisting all the strong hints from the National Parks Board that he ought to retire.[27] Despite Stevenson-Hamilton's personal objections, the Board's plan was that he should retire in about 1939 or 1940, once a suitable successor was found,[28] but when the Second World War broke out Stevenson-Hamilton was given a few additional years of public service as no younger man could be spared for the job. Once the war had ended, however, the Warden had to accept the inevitable and left the Park's employ, refusing any valedictory celebration, amid 'all intriguing and bad feeling'.[29]

While most of this intrigue had to do with differences of politics and nature conservation philosophy between Stevenson-Hamilton and the Board, some of it was no doubt created by the fact that the Warden tried hard to perpetuate his methods, philosophies and influence, by leaving copious instructions, notes and lists of ideas about what he had tried to achieve and how he had gone about it. He detailed especially what qualities were needed in a warden and game rangers and what ideals lay behind nature conservation and efficient administration.[30] Stevenson-Hamilton's enforced retirement – even at the age of almost eighty – caused him great distress because he believed that he was being 'pushed out'.[31] He confided in his diary his unhappiness that for the first time since 1888 he was out of the public service, and how much he would have preferred to have 'died in harness'.[32] Stevenson-Hamilton died only in 1957, and while he certainly had periods of great contentment in his retirement on his White River farm, he found it difficult to be merely an ordinary citizen, shopping, collecting the post or visiting friends, and he resented his increasing infirmities and lack of commitment to a clearly defined goal.

The frequent tension between the National Parks Board and Stevenson-Hamilton in the twenty years of their mutual dealings never became public knowledge. In the 1930s the Warden felt secure because of his high reputation, and there would have been a public scandal had he been told to leave. At that time he was still fêted and famous, appearing as a hero in many publications and receiving many honours. However, the strain and disagreements between the parties are well documented both in the official records of the Board and in Stevenson-Hamilton's personal journals and correspondence. Probably part of the conflict was a classic case of a strong personality with a taste for immediate action, strong lines of authority and belief in the opinion of 'the man on the spot',[33] confronted by a large committee more inclined towards careful, even tedious, discussion and a preference for ponderous bureaucracy.

The power struggle between Stevenson-Hamilton and his Board had its origins in the fact that the National Parks Act did not define the precise organizational responsibilities and administrative structure of the parties involved. When the Kruger National Park was in its infancy, Stevenson-Hamilton and his small staff could cope adequately with visitor and wildlife management affairs. Later, however, when the success of the Kruger National Park was demonstrated by the many thousands of visitors who demanded sophisticated facilities, and when other national parks were established, some kind of head office and formal administrative bureaucracy was required. This Stevenson-Hamilton resisted, and while he was in command, his experience and stature ensured that the enterprise ran fairly smoothly. After his retirement, however, neither his successor, the Board, nor the head office in Pretoria, could cope adequately, and by the early 1950s there was increasing evidence of mismanagement and corruption at the highest levels of the national park authority. The government stepped in to investigate these allegations. A detailed inquiry into the Board's affairs was instituted, known as the Hoek Commission, whose report resulted in changes to the organizational structure and to lines of managerial responsibility. A full-time Director was appointed and control was centralized in Pretoria. This meant the final victory for bureaucracy and the end of the era of the cult of the 'game warden hero'. Such an outcome was inevitable — indeed desirable. The 'one-man band' with its para-military style of ruling was inappropriate in the post-war world. Younger men and fresh ideas were not necessarily detrimental under these conditions.

Visitors were critical in determining the success of the Kruger National Park and their requirements shaped to a large degree how the area would evolve. Because the era of the private motor vehicle had arrived in South Africa, the first emphasis was on sight-seeing. Consequently it was recreational, rather than educational, facilities, which were first needed. The tourist public was delighted with what it experienced in the Kruger National Park from the moment that one section of the Park first opened in 1927. Mrs Wolhuter, the game ranger's wife, was amazed at the 'crowds of motor cars out this winter, as many as four in one day!'[34] In that initial year, tourist revenue amounted to £3, the following year it was £179, and in 1929, £850, when Stevenson-Hamilton reported the rest-camps to be overflowing with more than thirty cars. By 1930 more than nine hundred cars arrived and great pressure was put onto the five hundred kilometres of new tourist roads.[35]

Tourist regulations evolved in response to practical circumstances. At the outset, no visitors could be allowed into the northern part of the Park owing to the lack of roads and amenities. The threat of malaria and the fierce summer thunderstorms led to the decision in 1931 that the Kruger National Park would open only during the winter months and not throughout the year. In 1932, Shingwedzi camp opened when a good road from Letaba to Punda Maria was constructed. By that time, the rest camps were quite inadequate as visitors poured in by car and by rail. There was no administrative machinery to take bookings and therefore no means of knowing how many visitors would arrive to demand accommodation and services. There were only a few huts, so most people camped in tents and did their own catering. Sometimes game rangers offered accommodation in their homes to tourists who were hard-pressed. At the camps, bad behaviour was frequent: drunkenness and loud noise from gramophones and radios spoilt the wilderness experience for many. Caldecott had warned Stevenson-Hamilton of 'vulgarization . . . rubberneck waggons and tourists',[36] and when a tourist used one ranger's personal toothbrush on a visit to the Park,[37] vulgarization seemed a most appropriate way of describing the process. When the visitors left each year Stevenson-Hamilton was glad to have some peace.[38] Despite incidents of bad behaviour – particularly rudeness to African game guards[39] or getting out of vehicles to walk in the bush – the majority of tourists made the most of the Park and appreciated what it had to offer in the way of African wildlife.

With each passing year, visitors arrived in ever-increasing numbers and some wrote books and articles extolling its wonders. Through publications such as Edith Prance's *Three Weeks in Wonderland*, the enchantment and excitement of a visit to the park was clearly communicated. Prance described how much she had 'ardently desired . . . to see the great Game Sanctuary' and had plunged into Wonderland in the Transvaal when she chanced to visit the Kruger National Park. She was thrilled to see the 'fascinating denizen[s] of the Sanctuary'. Chief in providing visitor

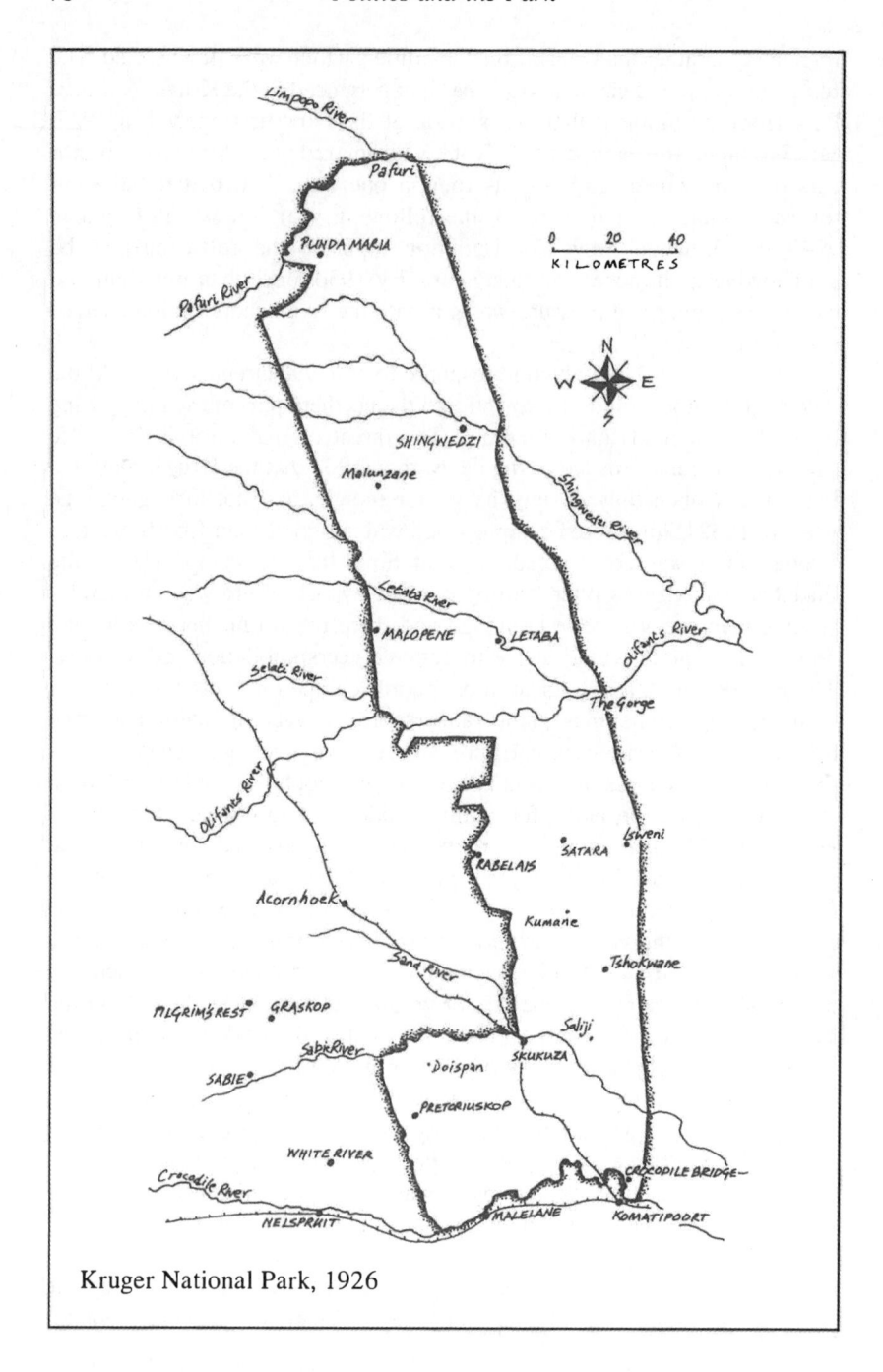

Kruger National Park, 1926

excitement was, of course, the lion, seen 'picking out pleasant spots for the day's siesta after a gorgeous meal'. Smaller creatures, such as steenbok which 'live alone because they prefer it', also gave amusement and interest. Prance stayed at a number of camps, referring to Skukuza with its post office, store, kitchens and bathrooms, even at that time as being a 'metropolis' more than a camp. Despite having huts and tented accommodation for some seven hundred people, many had to sleep in their cars in the 1930s.[40]

Another woman visitor to write of her experiences was Mrs M.E. Wood, the wife of the Union Astronomer. In 1935 she explained how the adventure began fifty miles outside Pretoria where the tarred Great North Road ended and the dirt began. The Woods slept in their car at Warmbaths and were delighted by the nearby sound of 'native drums'.[41] Proceeding from Johannesburg along the main eastern Transvaal road, the journey was much the same as T.C. Sinclair's in 1932. The tar ended at Benoni and from there, his Baby Austin 7 battled its way to Pretoriuskop. At the camp, the bustling of bats and the roaring of lion kept the Sinclairs awake at night; during the day they drove along the narrow and winding roads, no more than 'tracks in the grass' and crossed the Sabie and Letaba rivers by pontoon. They walked in the veld, too, for there was no restriction on leaving one's vehicle to take a stroll and get closer to any wild animal.[42]

The huge number of visitors necessitated a growing infrastructure to provide for them. The staff at the Park was unable to manage all aspects of visitor care, and experiments with private contractors, the employment of gate officers and ticket formalities, the construction and design of rest-camps and accommodation, were made. Complicating any permanent development strategy was the fact that most of the Kruger National Park was open only during the winter season when there was less likelihood of flooded roads and rivers and of malaria. It was thus difficult to offer permanent employment, and to take care of accommodation facilities when there were no visitors.

At first the National Parks Board tried to avoid any responsibility for the tourism operation and invited the South African Railways to take over the tourist management in the Kruger National Park which they did for some years. But when this arrangement ended, private contractors tendered for the provision of stores and gate commissions. In the 1930s there were numerous complaints about the actions of store-keepers.[43] Often they did not have necessities for tourists and the National Parks Board was obliged to consider the employment of its own gate-attendants and tourist officers. But the shortage of funding for development stood in the way of this, for although visitors were numerous, charges were minimal, and visitor revenue had not met the high expectations which had been initially raised. The government was reluctant to step in and assist because it considered that, with a major attraction such as the Kruger National Park to exploit, it should not be too difficult for the National Parks Board to be self-supporting.

Stevenson-Hamilton was also responsible for retarding visitor services. He was determined to provide a wilderness experience for visitors to the Kruger National Park and he fiercely resisted any attempt either to upgrade accommodation or to provide entertainment, even of an educational nature. In 1930 he was appalled that Board member Papenfus could suggest allowing 'dancing and gramophones at the rest camps if you please!'[44] and he even dismissed the showing of instructive wildlife films and lantern slides at the rest camps as unnecessary 'entertainment'.[45]

The arrangement with the South African Railways, which lasted for some years, was that the SAR undertook to provide transport, publicity and catering and pay the Board a percentage of their charge, which in turn would pay for roads, rest-camps, guides and protection. The first three camps were at Skukuza, Satara and Pretoriuskop. The pressure of visitor numbers ensured that whatever accommodation was provided was filled continuously and to capacity in the season. The perennial shortage of money meant that the provision of accommodation usually lagged far behind visitor demand and there were frequent complaints of overcrowding, a lack of facilities and poor conditions of hygiene.[46] Because he held the view that the Kruger National Park was not a recreational outlet, Stevenson-Hamilton considered that camps should be functional, efficient and minimal, the main aim being to provide the ambience in which to savour wildlife and nature.[47] 'Luxury' mattresses, for instance, rather than coir ones, were not stocked even in 1939, and electric light at Pretoriuskop was also regarded as unnecessary because too many improvements would 'over-civilize' the Park.[48] No stranger to physical hardship himself, Stevenson-Hamilton wrote that all tourists wanted was comfort at night with adequate catering and camp arrangements; 'the scenery and general lay-out [of the rest-camps] to all excepting a very small minority of artistic and highly cultured people, are purely secondary considerations.'[49] Despite these inadequacies, most visitors were neither deterred nor dissatisfied: in 1940, at the beginning of the war, more than 22 500 came to the Kruger National Park.[50]

To enable visitors to travel with ease around the national park, road-making was a major consideration, and this meant a great deal of work for game rangers and labourers. Each summer brought with it storm damage to roads and river crossings and these had to be repaired before the following tourist season. Eventually, rules and regulations for travel within the Park were devised, usually in response to poor behaviour. Soon no travelling was permitted at night, tourists had to keep on the roads and not drive off into the veld, they were obliged to return to a rest-camp each evening and only to erect tents in strictly demarcated areas.

After Stevenson-Hamilton had retired in 1946, under a new Warden development of the park accelerated and it became altogether more comfortable. Although also from a military background as Stevenson-Hamilton had been, J.A. Sandenbergh was of another generation and recognized that 'the public are more and more expressing a desire for greater comfort and convenience in the camps. I think the spirit of roughing-it in the Park is dying off rapidly and is today confined to the older lovers of the Park . . . I think it would be futile to fight against this public tendency.'[51] Sandenbergh also wanted to encourage tourists to remain for longer periods in the Park. New camps were established, the old ones enlarged and provided with better facilities, particularly by way of furniture, electricity, kitchens and ablution blocks. Not everyone welcomed these changes. An article which appeared in a popular magazine lamented the new atmosphere as pandering to the interests of visitors first and neglecting the appreciation of wildlife. Tourists ought to be honoured guests, happy to 'rough it' for the sake of what the Park had to offer. Luxury huts only brought more of the wrong kind of visitor, and with them noise, dust and superficial and tawdry tourist literature.[52]

As part of being a national park, the principle of allowing public access to everyone was entrenched. But by 1953 the Park was bulging with people, camping on every available space in the rest-camps, and in that year a limit was placed on the number of visitors – three thousand – who might be accommodated at any one time. It was even suggested that school holidays in South Africa should be staggered to ease pressure on the Kruger National Park.[53] At this time, too, the Park took over the catering, trading and garage services and ran these on its own account, and organizational diversity became increasingly necessary. The various functions of game rangers, tourist officers and maintenance and administrative staff were separated and clarified. Thus, from about the mid-1950s, the Park had changed from a remote 'wonderland' where the denizens of the wild roamed freely in an environment in which man was the transgressor, to become the abode of big business, managed principally with the comfort and convenience of visitors in mind.

In their rush to visit the Kruger National Park, probably not many early visitors appreciated the political direction in which the Kruger National Park was moving. With hindsight, however, it is now quite plain to see that it was being deliberately appropriated by Afrikaner nationalism. Given the strong British imperial tradition behind the origins of South African game reserves, the international links of Stevenson-Hamilton, and the democratic impulse of the national park movement in the United States, it is interesting to analyse how increasing exclusionism, instead of internationalism and inclusion, should have become the hallmark of the Kruger National Park until very recent times. One newspaper article has summarised this as the 'Kruger Culture ... Afrikaans ... the culture's chief tongue ... Boereparadys De Luxe ... [where] even your card-carrying Seffrican Engelssprekend could feel like an outsider, to say nothing of a Finn or a Japanese or – unthinkable – a Disenfranchised.'[54]

The 'Afrikanerization' of national parks generally went unchallenged by other white South Africans, the major reason for which may lie in the intense overtones of moral goodness which have come to be associated with nature conservation. After the almost total destruction of wildlife in the late nineteenth century, the twentieth introduced an almost religious belief among whites in the 'goodness' of conservation and the inherent 'evil' in any other point of view. As encapsulated in the title of a popular history of the Wildlife Protection Society of Southern Africa, there are only two camps, *The Conservationists and the Killers*. Consequently, to question any aspect of a national park was considered tantamount to attacking the conservationist ethic in its totality. A further reason for the lack of opposition at the time was the desire for reconciliation between English- and Afrikaans-speaking South Africans and the former thus accepted what was happening with little demur.

The National Parks Board was to become extremely closely aligned with the rise of Afrikaner nationalism and this millstone around its neck may prove difficult to shake off. Although the nineteenth-century wildlife conservation history of the Transvaal, outlined in an earlier chapter, demonstrated no strong conservation impetus from Afrikaners in particular, after the Kruger National Park became successful, Afrikaners sought to take the credit for it and to maximise its political utility. This was achieved by hitting on the ideal vehicle: 'Kruger', the name of the park. The direct connection between the name of the republican president and the national park was first invented and then exploited and manipulated.

Initially the National Parks Board did not capitalize on the Paul Kruger-conservation connection. On the contrary, even in 1938 National Parks Board member Gustav Preller, the custodian of Afrikaner culture, wrote a biographical film script of Kruger in which he depicted the President, not as the 'saviour of wildlife', but as 'forever eating biltong. Through the story this incessant biltong-eating comes out.' Quoting it as a source of pride and machismo, Preller's script shows Kruger to have been a biltong

Travelling conditions for the first tourists in the Kruger National Park

Tourists camping out in the Kruger National Park, *c.* 1930

Satara supply store, *c.* 1930

Skukuza rest camp, *c.* 1929

Balule rest camp for Africans, 1930

Gustav Preller and guests at Skukuza, 1930

Punda Maria rest camp under construction, 1933

Unveiling the plaque to Paul Kruger, 1933. Piet Grobler speaking, flanked by Hilda Stevenson-Hamilton and Judge Brebner

The first meeting of the newly established National Parks Board, 1927

connoisseur who could determine from a single bite the wild animal species from which the biltong was made. Preller describes in some detail many of Kruger's hunting adventures, but makes no mention at all of any contribution by Kruger to nature conservation.[55]

The identification of the personality of Paul Kruger with nature conservation is a myth but, like all myths, it was designed to serve a specific purpose. Like all myths too, it contains elements which conflate truth, semi-truth, distortion and fabrication. A successful myth needs a simple anecdotal story, forces of 'good' opposing those of 'evil', opposition overcome by a strong hero ahead of his time, an appeal to patriotism or nationalism, and evidence of a direct unchanging link between the past and the present.[56] After the 1948 elections brought an Afrikaner Nationalist government to power there was a need for the Kruger-wildlife conservation myth and, accordingly, it came into being. Historians debate whether 1948 is a watershed in South African history. One opinion stresses inherited legislation and public attitudes, while the other emphasizes degrees of discontinuity. As expounded from the mid-1940s onwards, the official history of the Kruger National Park contains elements of both points of view: portions of the mythology certainly existed before 1948 but were altered substantially thereafter. After 1948 the myth became successful because it had particular political advantage for the National Parks Board and for the government.

The most complete expression of the myth in its full modern form can be found in *The Kruger Park*, a book written in about 1970. The author R.J. Labuschagne, was a former Dutch Reformed Church social worker, who headed the Information and Education Sections of the National Parks Board after 1953, and was later its Deputy Director. The Foreword, contributed by the then Prime Minister, B.J. Vorster, exhorts, 'We, the heirs of Paul Kruger, have been given the task of preserving this paradise intact' for the following reasons as explained by the Board:

> On March 26, 1898, President Paul Kruger signed the proclamation establishing . . . a wildlife sanctuary between the Sabie and Crocodile Rivers . . . This act marked the end of a fourteen-year phase in which the President himself fought tirelessly for an idea that often involved him in bitter controversy. In 1884, a year after his election as Head of the State, no one could foresee that the threat of extinction would soon confront wild-life in the game-rich Transvaal. But President Kruger's remarkable courage, conviction and foresight enabled him to overcome every difficulty. His victory over opposition was all the more noteworthy because it was achieved when gold was being mined

in the vicinity of the area and when there was alarming unrest and disorder, deputations of gold miners demanding more rights, an uncontrollable influx of all kinds of adventurers and undesirable elements, the Jameson Raid, clashes with Native tribes; events which led, barely eighteen months after the establishment of the game sanctuary, to the Anglo-Boer War. One can only guess what would have happened if the President, in those critical times, had regarded the proclamation as of minor importance and delayed its promulgation. For fourteen years Kruger propounded the idea of the wildlife sanctuary. In all the debates . . . he emerged as a fanatical conservationist . . . and won more "converts" to his point of view. One of them . . . was R. K. Loveday. For President Kruger it was a personal matter, and, if he had had his way, the Kruger Park would have been proclaimed in 1884. Then it would have become the second of its kind in the world . . . The whole concept of the Park assumed poignant significance in the venerated statesman's life when he went into voluntary exile and cast his eyes over the region as his train rolled slowly to the frontier . . . The wild figs and thorn trees cast bowed shadows to form a guard of honour and the animals stood silently listening to the rolling wheels.[57]

As will be recalled from earlier chapters, developments in wildlife conservation strategies in the nineteenth-century Transvaal did not occur in this manner at all. There was no fighting 'tirelessly for an idea', no 'bitter controversy', no 'victory over opposition', no 'remarkable courage, conviction and foresight'. Kruger was not a 'fanatical conservationist' and there is no evidence at all of any game reserve idea in 1884. The Transvalers were, in fact, behind their times in wildlife conservation.

How then did the Kruger myth originate? Ironically, two English-speakers were responsible for raising Paul Kruger's protectionist profile. One was Stevenson-Hamilton himself, whose popular autobiographical account of the park, *South African Eden* (1937), linked Paul Kruger, the Sabi Game Reserve and the date 1884, as has been explained. In the same year, Marjorie Juta – a keen wildlife protectionist herself – wrote the first sympathetic biography of Paul Kruger in English, and made explicit many of the elements of the myth for the first time. Written in an anecdotal style, Juta invented 'live' conversations and, without providing any sources, devoted three pages to Kruger's views on the game reserve. One fictitious conversation is between Kruger and Volksraad member Stoffel Tosen, meeting on a 'frosty morning in May . . . enjoying a cup of coffee . . . on the stoep of the presidency'. Despite evidence in the formal records that

Tosen was deeply concerned about the extermination of wildlife in the Transvaal,[58] he is depicted by Juta as a hardened wildlife killer, requiring conversion by the ever-patient Kruger.[59]

In 1951 all elements of the story were brought together in an easily accessible source. In 1946 and 1947 a series of three articles on the history of wildlife conservation by journalist H.P.H. Behrens was published in *African Wild Life*,[60] the new journal of the predominantly English-speaking Wild Life Society of Southern Africa. Behrens related the wildlife protection story through anecdotes in the lives of three men: President Paul Kruger, Warden James Stevenson-Hamilton and game ranger Harry Wolhuter. Behrens followed this up in 1951 with a contribution on 'Paul Kruger – Wildbeskermer' which appeared in the popular Afrikaans magazine, *Huisgenoot*. Taking his cue from Marjorie Juta, in this version Behrens berates Afrikaans biographers for not honouring Kruger for his innate love of wildlife, which Behrens believed he held to such a degree that despite the political travails of his republic, he gave dedicated personal attention to nature conservation over many decades. 'With triumph in his eyes', Behrens explains, Kruger listened to Van Wijk (the English-speaking Loveday is not mentioned) in the Volksraad on the subject of the Sabi Game Reserve, now the 'great' Kruger National Park.[61]

While sensationalism and emotion form part of the journalistic repertoire, Behrens's unreliable account was taken further by the National Parks Board and uncritically and unquestioningly accepted by senior officials and eminent scientists within the Board's organization.[62] Doing so proved most useful to the Board in developing its close bonds with the Nationalist government after 1948. It was valuable to point to historical evidence of early direct state intervention and support because this provided a precedent for the Board to demand similar support from the government in power. The Board hailed contemporary politicians for following in the footsteps of Oom Paul. In an important official publication, the Board claimed that 'since 1948 the National Parks Organization has received tremendous support and attention from the Government', singling out for special mention in this regard, J.G. Strijdom, then Minister of Lands, as well as J.B.M. Hertzog, Piet Grobler, Hendrik Verwoerd, C.R. Swart and B.J. Vorster, all prominent Nationalist politicians holding high public office.[63]

In elevating these contemporary political figures on the basis of their support for nature conservation, more myths were created. An example of this concerns Strijdom, the Minister of Lands mentioned in laudatory terms above. But in terms of nature conservation concerns, far more important to South Africa than his support for the National Parks Board was Strijdom's abolition of the Dongola Wild Life Sanctuary in 1949. This seldom-mentioned national park in the northern Transvaal comprised an extremely large tract of land along the Limpopo River west of Messina, and it was entrenched by legislation of the Union parliament in 1947, just as the Kruger National Park had been in 1926. The Dongola issue was highly politicized: it was fiercely supported by Smuts and his cabinet and just as strongly opposed by the opposition. Because, however, the Dongola Sanctuary was a project close to the heart of the Smuts government during the war years, the National Parks Board, composed almost entirely of Nationalists at that time, refused to accept Dongola into the official national park fold. The proposed name of the Dongola area, the 'Smuts National Park', was anathema to J.F. Ludorf, the staunch Nationalist then chairman of the National Parks Board. But there were other factors in the National Parks Board's refusal to add Dongola to the growing list of national parks. Its proclamation also involved expropriating white farmers whose votes were needed by the National Party.[64] Thus, the abolishment of Dongola was an important election platform of the National Party in 1948 and soon after its assumption of power, the law which had created the sanctuary was repealed.

The intimate relationship between the government and the National Parks Board after 1948 was mutually beneficial. The Board received greatly increased financial and other state support,[65] and its part of the bargain was to endorse government policy. This it did by manipulating the symbol of Paul Kruger.

One seminal policy of the incoming government – indeed a reason for its electoral success – was to minimize the international and imperial connections. Former premier Smuts was thus vilified for concentrating on international statesmanship rather than promoting Afrikaner interests at home. And in opposing the Dongola Wild Life Sanctuary the National Party had focused on the 'undesirable' international connections which might arise between Dongola and Rhodesia and Bechuanaland. Literature emanating from the National Parks Board emphasized that no international agency had influenced Kruger when the Sabi Game Reserve was established – it was an achievement of the President, acting quite alone. So, although there is abundant evidence that he loved nature and supported many protectionist projects, Smuts stood accused of considering the Sabi Game Reserve to be 'a waste of time', and, personally, of irresponsible land-use.[66]

Stevenson-Hamilton was also a target for those who needed to elevate the personal role of Paul Kruger. First, he was ignored, and in a prominent National Parks Board publication, Stevenson-Hamilton's important account of his wardenship of the Park, *South African Eden*, is not even mentioned, although it was the only book about the Kruger National Park in print at that time.[67] Second, the first Warden was vilified as being unsuitable for his task: 'it would have been difficult to conceive of anyone seemingly more ill qualified for the job. He was a Scottish aristocrat and trained British officer.' It is even alleged that Stevenson-Hamilton met Paul Kruger in 1890, and 'On the stoep of the Pres. Kruger's residence . . . before the first game park in the Transvaal had been established . . . they became engrossed in a discussion of South Africa's game and the necessity to preserve it. Stevenson-Hamilton had already lost his heart to the Bushveld where he had found so much beauty distracting his mind that he sometimes forgot to shoot game.'[68] Records reveal that the two men never encountered each other, nor had Stevenson-Hamilton visited the lowveld by 1890.[69] The naïve Stevenson-Hamilton thus becomes Paul Kruger's disciple.[70] Thirdly, Stevenson-Hamilton was removed completely from the wildlife conservation arena in South Africa. After his retirement, he had been appointed a member of the National Parks Board on 31 May 1947, and after a brief term of just over a year, was removed without explanation.[71] For an international conservationist of his high reputation, this was certainly a slap in the face, and the Wild Life Society's representative on the Board commiserated: 'I am afraid it is the start of a series of changes, and all the Park appointments will gradually be replaced each year. I am sorry you were the first one, and I do feel that in your case an exception could have been made, even by the Nationalists.'[72]

It was also important for the Board to denigrate Stevenson-Hamilton's achievements as Warden – indeed, it was useful to establish an Afrikaner as holding this post. The existence of Walker, the first official Warden of the Sabi Game Reserve had been mentioned by Stevenson-Hamilton in his book *South African Eden*, and details of his appointment can be found in the Transvaal Archives. However, National Parks Board accounts have chosen to ignore this man completely, and in the 1950s, as has been explained earlier, park officials found dubious evidence of two previously unrecorded former wardens during the time of the Transvaal Republic.[73]

Although evidence of Broederbond involvement is notoriously difficult to locate, many incidents which Stevenson-Hamilton perceived as 'difficulties' can probably be traced to what was at this time becoming 'an immense informal network of influence' reflected frequently in cultural concerns.[74] A major goal of the Broederbond was Afrikaner affirmative action, and in promoting this within the National Parks Board it was extremely successful. A stumbling block after 1948 was English-speaking Sandenbergh, Stevenson-Hamilton's chosen successor. The removal of

Sandenbergh, was, however, fairly easy, because he was a failure as Warden and even a disappointment to Stevenson-Hamilton who considered that he had compromised the accomplishments of many years of hard work.[75] Not only did it become increasingly evident that Sandenbergh's talents as an administrator were over-estimated, but he also became enmeshed in political machinations and accusations of corruption and drunkenness which the Hoek investigation of 1952 raised.

Indeed, although full details of Hoek's inquiry were never made public – despite it being very much in the public interest to do so – its findings were used to transform the administration of the National Parks Board into an all-Afrikaner one.[76]

Sandenbergh refused to resign in response to political pressure, but in 1954 he was dismissed and replaced by Louis Steyn. Steyn was one of the first Afrikaans-speaking game rangers to have been appointed to the Kruger National Park in 1929, and for many years he had coveted the Warden's job. Steyn was well known for his extreme anti-English opinions; his daughter, for example, would not attend a function held at the predominantly English-speaking club at White River fearing her father's wrath at fraternising with 'Engelse'.[77] Stevenson-Hamilton had never trusted Steyn, regarding him as the 'unpaid spy' of Nationalist agents such as Preller, who were only too keen to be supplied with gossip about the internal workings of the Kruger National Park and to use it to their advantage.[78] Although Steyn was a disturbing influence, and his behaviour on occasion totally inappropriate to his office,[79] his long record of service and his family connection to a National Parks Board member – made him a certainty for the Warden's job in the 1950s as Afrikaners consolidated their hold on the civil service.

Environmental conservation came to enjoy worldwide endorsement after the Second World War and with this endorsement came the opportunity of promoting Afrikaner values in international circles. The National Parks Board, aware of South Africa's increasing isolation by the world community on account of her racial policies, strove to give the country a place within the nature conservation community, and did so also by invoking the Kruger story. The Kruger National Park was described as the 'show window which displays South Africa to the rest of the world'.[80] The opinion expressed by Stevenson-Hamilton in 1903 that 'game laws are . . . so much waste paper [to Boers] . . . they have no sporting instincts and no sense of honour' – one widely echoed by other writers at that time[81] – was countered by portraying Kruger as an early conservationist, and (incorrectly) the founder of the second oldest national park in the world.[82] Kruger's 'world lead' in nature conservation was an avenue to international respectability and 'saintly countries' and 'sanctimonious critics overseas' were cautioned to take cognisance of Afrikaner South Africa's moral rectitude in this connection, even though they vilified its racial policies. To bring home the point to foreign visitors, and to dilute the memory of Stevenson-Hamilton after whom a rest-camp (Skukuza) and a library had been named, there were plans for an immense commemorative sculpture of Paul Kruger in the Kruger National Park, which were eventually scaled down to the bust which stands at the Kruger Gate today.[83]

The National Party's tendency to eschew internationalism while also trying to avoid total ostracism, formed part of its principal goal of establishing a republic. Here the National Parks Board could help the government considerably because the Kruger myth was of direct relevance to republican ideals. Harking back to republican times and commemorating traditions of the past (Kruger Day was made an official public holiday in 1950) demonstrated political continuity between the old republic and the new, but it also engendered a fresh spirit of cohesion and patriotism.[84] Present South Africans were all the 'heirs of Paul Kruger'[85] whose national park was founded for the 'benefit of the nation'.[86] Equating 'the nation' with 'Paul Kruger' meant that patriotism and support for republicanism, Afrikaner traditions, apartheid and ultimately all policies of the government in power, came to coincide.

The question may well be raised as to why English-speaking South Africans, particularly those with imperial connections, so readily accepted this propaganda. To some degree it can be accounted for by the fact that the Board officials responsible for it were well-qualified scientists and administrators and their stature added weight to their historical pronouncements. But it also stems from the common perception that wildlife conservation is a 'non-political' matter. The public notion that nature conservation falls outside the national political arena makes the national park common cause between English- and Afrikaans-speakers, and thus a locus where fraternal relationships, more difficult on matters of hard politics, can blossom.[87]

In its publications of the 1960s and 1970s, the National Parks Board infused a strong Christian element into Kruger's love of nature, another important platform of National Party policy, as church, state and party became forged into a single entity.[88] Whereas Stevenson-Hamilton had referred to 'the Guardian Spirit of the Lowveld' or 'Mother Nature',[89] a more personal relationship between man and the God of the Voortrekkers is suggested after 1948. The Chief Director of the National Parks Board believed, for instance, that 'the word of God reaches us nowhere more manifestly than it does in nature',[90] while Public Relations Director

Labuschagne suggested that 'exalted personages of the past have ever fled to nature for medidation [sic] and solitude: Christ climbed the Mount of Olives . . . Solomon repeatedly exhorts mankind to return to nature; President Kruger spent three days on the Magaliesberg in silent meditation . . . It is for this reason that the South African nation undertakes the yearly pilgrimage to the Kruger National Park.'[91]

Although 'nature as God made it' was to become the popular hallmark of the Kruger National Park, after 1948 the area became increasingly controlled by a growing team of scientists and efficient bureaucrats. For many years, scientists had yearned for more influence within the park, but Stevenson-Hamilton had fiercely resisted their overtures fearing that scientific interference would spoil the wilderness experience, remove any element of fantasy and turn the national park into a zoo.[92] In time the national park was fenced, regular censuses of wildlife conducted, a culling programme begun, wide-ranging wildlife research projects conducted, the landscape managed through a controlled fire regime, and more tourist facilities provided. Modern society has a great respect for 'science', believing it to be both 'objective' and 'neutral', and this is why the 'history' of the Kruger National Park when presented by people with higher academic scientific degrees – even members of the Royal Society of South Africa[93] – is widely accepted as 'true'.

Elevating the person of Paul Kruger as the central theme of the Kruger National Park since 1948, has had important consequences. The cluster of self-reinforcing myths[94] has positioned national parks, and wildlife conservation generally, directly inside the Afrikaner republican moral, historical and political arena, thereby denigrating the imperial sporting tradition and alienating African popular opinion to a considerable degree. Many South Africans still see Kruger's legacy in the National Parks Board, an organization generally without significant African participation and dominated by Afrikaans scientists and bureaucrats.

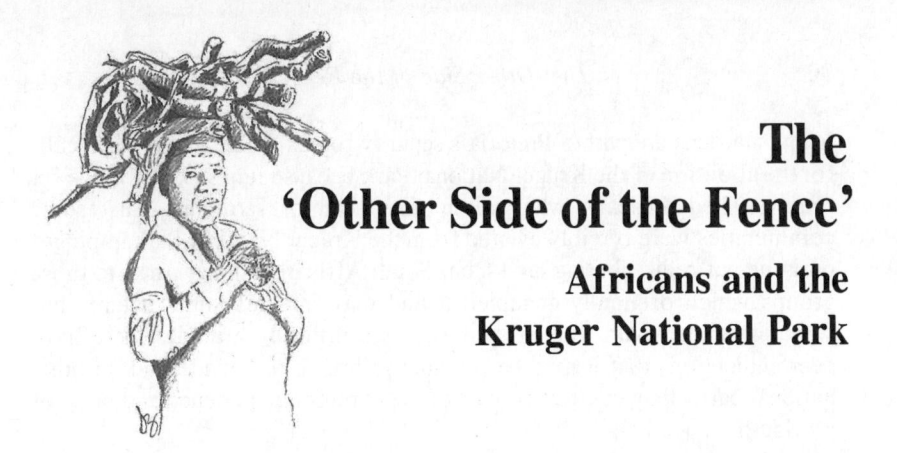

The 'Other Side of the Fence'
Africans and the Kruger National Park

As has been elucidated in the previous chapter, in South Africa the close relationship between the state and wildlife protection has associated game reserves and national parks closely with the government in power. Until very recently, a major concern of all governments has been to exclude Africans from the political process. From 1652 onwards, white domination and racial segregation have permeated all aspects of South African life: by extension it has been an underlying principle of wildlife protection.

The white public of South Africa has come to regard its national parks with a considerable degree of pride, and these areas have come to symbolize the morality of protecting the wildlife heritage of the nation. The general reluctance to dwell on the less romantic aspects of wildlife conservation is therefore understandable, for these may well taint the virtue of the exercise as a whole. Moral altruism, however, merely obscures the political and economic reality of conservation issues and unless the 'other side' of conservation is appreciated, understood and taken into account, there may be little left to conserve – even within national parks. This is so because 'on the other side of the fence' from the relatively intact protected ecosystem with its lush grassland and abundant wildlife, live impoverished communities, desperate for land and for access to natural resources.

The emergence of a substantial African middle class which might have had the money and leisure to join whites in enjoying the Kruger National Park was blocked by repressive social and economic legislation. Africans were forced to live in overcrowded, degraded and unattractive rural and urban environments. In general, any appreciation of the aesthetic elements of the landscape has consequently been sacrificed to land-hunger and poverty. For a large proportion of Africans, the Kruger National Park – far from being a symbol of national pride – is perceived as part of a governmental structure from which they have been systematically excluded. National parks have been manifestations of 'apartheid repression' and 'game wardens are part of Pretoria's security forces'.[1] There have been calls for the abolition of the Kruger National Park because it has no relevance for impoverished Africans who are in dire need of farmland. That some communities were forcibly evicted from the Kruger National Park impinges on issues of redistributing land from South African national parks to those groups which originally occupied it and may threaten some nature conservation endeavours. But in spite of these differing attitudes there have been indications that it may be possible to bridge the divide and, in time, national parks may come to be part of the common experience and pride of all South Africans.[2]

In published accounts of early white travellers and settlers, Africans are usually portrayed as intruders in and ravagers of an environment which deserved European custodianship.[3] This is certainly a curious point of view, because those same accounts provide illustrations of an abundance of wildlife and a stable ecological balance. While pre-colonial societies certainly made use of the natural environment of the sub-continent, before white occupation of South Africa there were factors which circumvented any tendencies to exterminate wildlife.

Whites brought to Africans an increased access to markets and firearms, and thereby introduced powerful incentives for large-scale commercial hunting. As has been shown, for some decades after Voortrekker settlement of the Transvaal, the economy was based on indiscriminate wildlife hunting in which Africans and whites actively collaborated and prospered from the trade. When this mutually advantageous partnership degenerated into a power struggle over the diminishing herds, whites felt sufficiently confident to exclude their collaborators and to corner the trade for themselves. Thus began a process of alienating Africans from wildlife which has continued to exist until very recent times. There is considerable substance to the African attitude that game reserves and wildlife protectionist legislation have from the start been detrimental to African interests. Not only was wildlife conservation legislation itself discriminatory against Africans, but there were also restrictions on trespassing, firearm and dog ownership and a ban on all trapping of wildlife.

Preventing Africans from hunting was not merely an economic strategy, it was embedded in white cultural perceptions. Whites generally regarded Africans as 'savages' or barbarians, and thus unable to 'appreciate' European refinements such as notions of 'cruelty' or 'pleasure hunting'. The sportsman William Cornwallis Harris was explicit in his disparagement of Africans: he compared the physical features of the Khoikhoi with those of the bushpig, and those of the San with those of the baboon.[4]

Not only were Africans compared with certain undesirable wild animal species in terms of physique but also in behaviour. In the mid-nineteenth century there was a common belief that a staple diet of venison was unhealthy for 'civilized' people. It was alleged, however, that Africans were able to eat any animal, even the unpalatable zebra.[5] In his survey of historical English attitudes to animals, Thomas considers that the injunction against gluttony has its origin in the view that over-eating, and absorption with the question of procuring food, are bestial traits.[6] Thus in taking a delight in consuming large quantities of food, Africans demonstrated their 'inferior humanity' to sportsmen and thus forfeited their right to hunt.

The issue of 'cruelty' was frequently raised in order to stop Africans from hunting. However, people who hunt from necessity usually have no evil intent towards the animals they kill, only practical considerations of food or profit. Hunting is a prelude to eating or selling rather than an end in itself. For this reason cruelty and sentimentality have a place only when pleasure is the aim. Upper- and middle-class European values such as the acceptability of shooting for sport and the condemnation of the cruelty of snaring for food, were imposed on Africans, whose values were the opposite: killing for sport was wasteful, and snaring was an appropriate utilization of a natural resource.

The blame for exterminating the wildlife of the Transvaal in the nineteenth century was generally laid upon Africans. With hindsight it can be appreciated that Africans had very little to do with this, and that the greatest destructive influences relate to the agricultural transformation of the countryside and to the modernization and industrialization of the Transvaal. But in addition to these broader processes, it seems that even white market hunters and sportsmen killed more than did Africans at that time. Even Abel Erasmus, the Native Commissioner in the eastern Transvaal who was renowned for his harsh treatment of and unyielding hostility to Africans, appreciated that whites were far more destructive.[7] Africans were subject to far stricter legal limitations and, possibly in consequence, within African 'locations' plenty of wildlife survived. There were even reports of active African conservation intervention in 1894.[8] However, by the early twentieth century, the most powerful reason for legislation designed to prevent Africans from being able to subsist on wildlife, was to force them into wage labour, either in urban areas or on white-owned farms.[9] Wildlife conservation thus played a role in creating a proletariat as the industrialization of the Transvaal commenced.

How whites in the Transvaal viewed African hunters after the South African War was made clear in statements made by the Transvaal Game Protection Association.[10] In 1902 the new Transvaal colonial administration introduced wildlife protection legislation in which African landowners were treated equally with whites, a move which was abhorred by the sporting fraternity, most of whom were employers of African labour.[11] Sportsmen seemed unable to appreciate any attitude towards wildlife except their own, and over-enthusiastic trout fisherman were responsible for a law prohibiting the catching of any species of fish in the Transvaal between May and September each year, thus depriving rural people of protein during the winter months. It took two years for the hardship that this law created to be brought home to the lawmakers and only in 1906 did Ordinance 5 allow the capture of certain indigenous fish species throughout the year.[12]

Game reserves also fitted into the pattern of general exclusion of Africans from wildlife and extended opportunities for white domination. A major rationale for the Pongola Game Reserve was to control and subjugate Africans in what was then known as 'Sambaan's Land'. Warden H.F. van Oordt had a wide reputation for his ruthless treatment of Africans, and he evicted many from the small reserve. So did Stevenson-Hamilton, when the Sabi Game Reserve was re-established in 1902, a move which gained him the African name of 'Skukuza', he who scrapes clean.[13] But despite the assertion in a popular account, that Stevenson-Hamilton had removed 'all the black squatters . . . settling them closer to their traditional tribal chiefs in adjacent areas',[14] the Sabi Game Reserve did not lose its resident African communities. As has already been mentioned, when the reserve was extended from the Sabie to the Olifants River in August 1903 by including private and crown land, and when the Singwitsi Game Reserve was declared in May 1903, more people were incorporated. They did not have to vacate their homes because the colonial authorities had by then come to appreciate that Africans could be useful to the conservation effort by providing both labour and funding.[15]

Consequently, the policy of removing Africans from the game reserves was reversed. After May 1905, the almost three thousand African residents, like all other tenants on crown lands, were subject to the payment of rent either in the form of cash or labour.[16] The three-month compulsory labour period for the approximately four hundred dues-paying tenants proved extremely profitable, as did rents in cash.[17] Tenants were, in exchange, allowed to tend crops and livestock within the boundaries of the game reserve, provided that wildlife regulations were not infringed.

Like all tenants on crown lands, they resented this control. They would often 'disappear' when their labour was being sought.[18] On the other hand, game reserve labour seems to have been less onerous than farm labour and the reserve was accused of providing a refuge for those avoiding it.[19] White game rangers disliked the work of overseeing tenants and did not enjoy having to listen to 'troubles and indabas', but accepted the duty because it had the advantage of consolidating control over Africans.[20]

From the beginning, Africans fiercely resisted being controlled by game reserve authorities, and poaching was one way of demonstrating this. However, as far as resident Africans were concerned, game reserve officials were pleasantly surprised at how little wildlife they killed.[21] The absence of poaching seems to have been due primarily to the fear of losing their land and being forced into so-called African 'locations' or into having to labour for white farmers. In 1911, for example, Stevenson-Hamilton reported that 'Although the ranger [Fraser] has not initiated any prosecutions, he states that in the case of several kraals which he strongly suspected [of poaching] but could get no evidence about, he managed, in co-operation with the local police and other authorities, to get them removed from the reserve. In many ways the fear of this acts, it is found, as a better deterrent than either fine or imprisonment.'[22]

Hunger and drought conditions invited poaching. By 1913 desiccation of the land was so severe that many game reserve residents were dying of starvation,[23] but they were not, by law, permitted to hunt wildlife in order to survive. However, by 1918 the continuing food shortage, possibly coupled with the realization that owing to the First World War, the number of white staff in the reserve had been reduced, encouraged Africans within the reserve, particularly those south of the Letaba River, to embark on what Fraser, then Acting-Warden, called 'a wave of insubordination'. Africans living on the private land within the game reserve were also 'becoming increasingly difficult to deal with'.[24]

While residents seem to have poached only sporadically, Africans living outside the reserve on the southern bank of the Crocodile River, being desperate for food, engaged in considerable poaching activities at this time.[25] In addition, Mozambicans had taken to killing wildlife on a large scale. Armed and hungry people made deep forays into game reserve territory, and police posts were established on the Mozambique side of the border in order to prevent illegal border crossings.[26] This step appears to have been unsuccessful: in 1915, Fraser reported poaching so widespread that he considered the situation uncontrollable. Poaching parties from Mozambique were large, well organized and accompanied by many dogs. They also had firearms, unlike Transvaal Africans who were not permitted to bear arms, and the African staff of the game reserve, carrying only assegais, was powerless against them.[27]

While there can be no question that poaching was a means of protesting against white domination, it is equally clear that game was essential for subsistence when destitute rural dwellers were faced with starvation. In conditions of drought it must have been very tempting for people to avail themselves of the expanding numbers of game close at hand. Moreover, if whites were unsure at that time of the ultimate purpose of game reserves, how much more confused must Africans have been to see a valuable food resource going to waste.

Although poaching received prominence in every annual report of the game reserves, it seems that this activity was actually not responsible for very much game destruction. But what was important was the demonstration of white authority over Africans, Stevenson-Hamilton believing that the policing duties of his staff were essential to law and order in the lowveld.[28] Thus poaching seems to have been detested by game reserve officials not so much because of the danger it presented to wildlife populations, but because it represented freedom of action on the part of Africans and therefore a corresponding lack of white supremacy. A game warden in Natal confirmed that Africans used poaching in game reserves to express their 'outstanding grievance' – the fact that they had been deprived of land which they considered to be their 'rightful inheritance'.[29]

Suspected poachers in the game reserves frequently resisted arrest, which was not surprising in view of the severity of the punishments they could receive.[30] Penalties imposed on Africans were more severe than they were for whites. For instance, an African hunter who had killed a duiker received a month's imprisonment with hard labour without the option of a fine, while a group of three whites who had killed four reedbuck, two duiker, a steenbuck and a korhaan, were sentenced to a fine of £5 or seven days' imprisonment.[31] Punishments were inflicted on youths who caught small creatures, such as cane rats and tortoises, and even chasing lion off a kill was regarded as a poaching offence.[32]

The wide publicity given to African poaching in the reports of the Sabi and Singwitsi Game Reserves entrenched the view among middle-class whites that Africans living within or near parks could not be trusted to take care of wildlife.[33] Before 1915 figures for the numbers arrested in connection with illegal acts in the Sabi and Singwitsi Game Reserves were provided in the reports without specific offenses being itemized. In 1912, for example, there were 201 arrests of Africans, in 1913 there were 330 and in 1914 there were 244. Only when detailed figures were given – for the first time in 1915 – does a picture emerge: in that year there were only 27 arrests relating to game, but for other offenses, principally trespass, there were 493 arrests. The following years show the same pattern; in 1916 there were 91 convictions under the game law and 763 convictions for other offenses, and in 1918, 37 and 408 respectively.[34] Given the small size of the staff of the game reserve, particularly during the war years, it is remarkable how many arrests were in fact made. But one does not have to seek far to find the reason why so many criminals were apprehended.

An African policeman apprehends a poacher.

Pretoriuskop entrance gate, 1928

Ranger J.J. Coetser and African police, October 1922

Kumane picket, 1906

African police in the northern section, 1909
Maksine, Nompolo, Sajine, Watch 1, Watch 2

African police quarters at Sabi Bridge, 1911

Witwatersrand Labour Association bus and passengers *en route* to the gold mines

Ranger Duke with African tenants using the railway trolley, 1908

From the time of the establishment of game reserves, reserve officials had considered the interests of any industry to be inimical to game conservation, with one exception, the mining industry. The Witwatersrand mines required large contingents of unskilled labour and in the provision of manpower game reserves co-operated with the mines. The Witwatersrand Native Labour Association was allowed to construct a road through the northern section of the game reserves in 1918 so that labourers recruited in Mozambique and elsewhere could make their way easily to the mines. The miners were effectively supervised as they traversed the reserve and no cases of poaching occurred.[35]

Although co-operation with the Witwatersrand mines did not afford labour directly to the game reserves, indirectly it did so in the way that it attracted illegal immigrants into South Africa, particularly from Mozambique. The system which seems to have operated in the game reserves was that the illegal work-seekers were either arrested or reported themselves as trespassers to the Warden, as the Special Justice of the Peace, and then consequently received a fortnight's imprisonment, this being the appropriate sentence for the offence.[36] When their sentence ended, the men received what was known as a 'pass' – permission which entitled them to seek work in the Transvaal. These prisoners were not incarcerated while serving their sentences, however, but laboured instead in the game reserves 'on road making or anything else', at the same time receiving rations 'supplemented by meat obtained by them from game killed by lions'.[37]

This casual system of labour was on occasion abused. In 1919 the Department of Customs complained about Fraser's behaviour as Acting-Warden,[38] and the Department of Justice expressed concern about the laxity which attended the keeping of criminal records at Sabi Bridge.[39] During the time that both Stevenson-Hamilton and Fraser held the office of Special Justice of the Peace, prison labour was used by the Sabi and Singwitsi Reserves; however, after Fraser's retirement the Department of Justice refused to extend Stevenson-Hamilton's jurisdiction in this respect into the northern area.[40] Game reserve staff appear to have ignored this proscription and simply used trespassers in any part of the game reserves for purposes of labour without any formal sentence having been passed on them. When this illegal action came to the notice of the Native Affairs Department, it was stopped and all prisoners thenceforth had to be taken to Sabi Bridge to be detained there for a fortnight under conditions that provided for trial and imprisonment. A commentator of the time, sympathizing with the labour requirements of the game reserves, declared this to be mere 'idleness at the expense of the government . . . a foolish arrangement and very unpopular with the natives'.[41]

In 1924 the problem was partially solved to the satisfaction of the game reserves by the introduction of 'movable lock-ups', transportable prison cells which could be moved around the reserve wherever labour was needed.[42] This arrangement was ended in 1926 when an immigration agreement was concluded between Mozambique and South Africa which included an extradition treaty. Stevenson-Hamilton deplored this treaty, complaining that the reserve suffered in consequence from a labour shortage and that the steady stream of Mozambican trespassers had saved his reserve expenditure in the form of salaries of about £2 000 each year.[43] In the 1930s, some rangers regarded it as 'customary' to make trespassers work for fourteen days before allowing them to proceed. Stevenson-Hamilton was adamant that this was not the case and that prisoners must either be paid for their labour or not employed. The Deputy Commissioner of Police warned the Kruger National Park authorities in 1938 that the illegal deprivation of liberty was regarded very seriously by the government and that claims for damage could be laid against rangers for doing so.[44]

In popular accounts of the Kruger National Park history, the labour situation has generally been overlooked. This might be explained by the strength of the white romantic myth which has come to infuse nature conservation literature. One book, written by a scientist employed in the Kruger National Park, describes the early labour position as follows: 'There were eight rangers, each with a small number of black assistants to do the work; build roads, build huts, keep a vigilant eye on the never-ending bands of poachers, and patrol a wilderness area larger than the state of Israel.'[45] Such statements pander to the sentimental and obscure the labour of many thousands of prisoners upon which the national park effort has been secured.

Not all African labour was coercive and there were paid African officials as well. The first employees of the Sabi Game Reserve – apart from the Warden – were black.[46] As the formal organizational structure of the game reserve took shape, an important category of African worker was the 'native police' force, which in 1941 consisted of eight sergeants and about a hundred and twenty African rangers.[47] These men were generally recruited from the local resident community, being familiar with the terrain and its inhabitants. Their relationship with the game reserve was a complex one of co-operation and resistance. Available evidence suggests that the police usually collaborated with their white superiors – even to the extent of informing on their relatives.[48] But there were instances of overt resistance, most often in the form of poaching or dereliction of duty.[49] Although the records reflect interaction between the different squatter communities only tangentially, the 'police' may have exploited their positions by targeting unpopular individuals or groups. Collusion between white and African rangers also occurred, as in 1941 when poaching and dagga production by African police was not reported to the National Parks Board in Pretoria, since the white staff within the Kruger Park were reluctant to dismiss some of their most efficient trackers and protectors.[50]

Although the cult of the heroic individual typifies protectionist literature (the encounter between game ranger Harry Wolhuter and a lion being prominently depicted in popular accounts and in the Skukuza museum, for example) African employees who devoted themselves to wildlife conservation, or even gave their lives for it, having been killed by wild animals or by poachers, have not received the same degree of public acclaim. Stevenson-Hamilton privately expressed his admiration for the sense of duty demonstrated by African rangers given their poor pay and lack of incentives.[51] However, as was customary throughout colonial Africa at the time, 'police boys' were never promoted into the higher ranks of the white rangers.

Stevenson-Hamilton's own attitude to Africans was typical of an educated man of his time. While he deplored the exploitative actions of the Johannesburg capitalist community, he was patronizing and paternalistic towards Africans, believing that they were often well off under white rule. They were peasants still climbing the ladder of civilization. For him, too, they were 'primitive' creatures whose traditional way of life was as deserving of study and observation as the behavourial patterns of wild animal species. Stevenson-Hamilton went to considerable trouble to interview rural leaders in an attempt to elucidate African history and traditional customs. Although in *The Low Veld: Its Wildlife and its People* he commented adversely on the emerging segregationist land and labour policies of the Union, he, like other gamekeepers, was dependent on African domestic staff and 'police boys' who helped him to get to know the game reserves, and referred to them often in derogatory terms. While African 'police boys' were complimented for their courage and their dedication to duty, they were always subordinates, never equal partners, in the preservationist exercise.

Ownership of and access to land was a major point of confrontation between conservation authorities and Africans. After Union in 1910 the supposed 'worthlessness' of game-reserve land was reviewed. Additional areas were needed by the state for African and white agriculture, and for mining and industry. The Native Affairs Administration Bill had suggested the abolition of the Singwitsi Game Reserve and its use for African settlers, but the Transvaal Game Reserves Commission gave the idea short shrift, considering the Singwitsi unsuitable for any prolonged human habitation.[52]

The inhospitable landscape of the north thus remained a protected area. However, as a result of pressure from the Native Affairs Department in 1923, before the proclamation of the national park occurred, a large area was excised from the south of the Sabi Game Reserve (in the Acornhoek district) on its western boundary for an African 'reserve'.

The borders of the Kruger National Park remained substantially unaltered from 1926 until 1969 when a long-standing and acrimonious battle for land between the authorities and the Makuleke community in the north ended.[53] This Tsonga group, living at the confluence of the Levubu and Limpopo rivers, had in the nineteenth century had a large share in the ivory trade of the district and later subsisted on hunting, agriculture and fishing.[54] While scattered squatters were acceptable to game reserve officials, settled or expanding communities conflicted with protectionist aims, and in 1912 several Makuleke villages under Mhinga in the northern part of the Singwitsi were excised, thus reducing the game reserve area.[55]

But owing to the scarcity of rangers in the north, the Makuleke community – who had a 'location' on the northern bank of the Levubu River – in time spilled back into the game reserve zone. Officials regarded the whole area as a 'danger spot',[56] and in the early 1930s the proposal was put forward by the National Parks Board to include the tropical forest between the Levubu and the Limpopo rivers within the park boundaries. The plan was to evict the Makuleke and move them on to land further south which would be excised from the park for this purpose. Relocating the Makuleke was not, however, a simple matter because the Native Affairs Department took the side of the Makuleke and refused to give its permission.[57]

In order to circumvent the Native Affairs Department, the National Parks Board – determined to gain control of the Pafuri area – approached the provincial authorities. They had no objection to assisting the National Parks Board and, in 1933, issued a proclamation which declared the district to be the Pafuri Game Reserve. The province gave it to the National Parks Board to administer. The Makuleke were thus presented with a *fait accompli*. Makuleke's 'location' was surrounded by this reserve, although excluded from it.[58] A stalemate followed because the Native Affairs Department continued to oppose any translocation of the Makuleke community, particularly to the unsuitable piece of land which the National Parks Board was offering.[59] Indeed, so unfair did the situation appear to be, that even National Parks Board secretary Van Graan, pleaded with Board members: 'Is it wise to take this step in view of the reputation of the alleged suppression of native races? It is obvious that Pafuri is better agriculturally than the dry piece of grazing land we offer in exchange . . . frankly, I foresee in this gain of today, if we acquire the Pafuri, the future germ of destruction of the whole Park.'[60]

Van Graan was ignored and the impasse continued until 1952, when the Board returned the Pafuri Game Reserve to provincial control, explaining that the situation was unworkable.[61] In 1969, during the era of 'grand apartheid', the Makuleke found themselves without allies and they were relocated to the Ntlaveni area. At that date, the Pafuri Game Reserve was incorporated into the park.

Regarded as poachers and hounded from national park boundaries, Africans were never invited to enjoy the South African national parks as visitors. The value of the Kruger National Park for whites after 1926 was linked to sentimentality and nostalgia for a romantic and rural past which was engendered by urbanization and increased industrialization. For Africans, however, alienation from the natural environment and their experience of modernization was different and they did not share in the values which whites wished to perpetuate in their national park.

The new national park ideology in 1926 reinvigorated the exclusion of Africans and consolidated the process of co-opting wildlife conservation into the orbit of white culture. Within decades, the national park was being overtly exploited to exemplify and inculcate white South African culture,[62] including casting Africans homogeneously in the role of poachers and whites in the role of conservationists.

When the Kruger National Park was opened to tourists in the late 1920s, Stevenson-Hamilton would probably not have objected to African tourists. But under the National Parks Board of Trustees, the Warden did not have a free hand, and visitor access for Africans was on an unequal basis in terms of accommodation and recreational facilities.[63] The issue of African tourists was raised frequently at National Parks Board meetings. In 1932 Gustav Preller recorded his distress that Indians were using the same camp as whites, an incident which Stevenson-Hamilton dismissed with the tongue-in-cheek comment that he had thought that they were Portuguese.[64] Once when the Japanese chargé d'affaires was visiting, the Warden wrote, 'Pray God these fatheads do not treat him as "Asiatic"'.[65]

After the National Party election victory, the Board was addressed by J. G. Strijdom, Minister of Lands, on the issue of apartheid and he expressed his deep regret not only that different race groups shared camps, but that they even shared the roads. Strijdom presented a scheme for dismembering the national park and setting a portion of it aside for exclusive 'non-white' use.[66] There was, in fact, a tented camp for Africans, called Balule, which was established in 1932. However, the facilities were so rudimentary in comparison with Skukuza and the other white camps that it was described even in 1983 as having a 'spartan atmosphere' and none of the 'civilized, modern conditions so prevalent in most other camps. There is no shop, fuel station or reception office . . . .'[67] It was this kind of discriminatory action which was to deepen the wedge between white and African experiences within 'the wild animal elysium', the 'wonderland' of South Africa.[68]

As segregationist policies became more rigid, the National Parks Board determined to replace all African skilled labour with whites. Stevenson-Hamilton was appalled, not least because he considered the 'poor white' vehicle drivers to be 'awful'. Good 'natives' were far better he contended, although it 'would be heresy to say so'.

The increasing Afrikaner nationalization of wildlife conservation philosophy manifested itself as far as Africans were concerned in escalating attempts by the National Parks Board to belittle Africans. By focusing on Paul Kruger and emphasizing the Afrikaner role in establishing national parks, the Board directly encouraged the perception that national parks were manifestations of apartheid.[69] In publicity literature of the time, the National Parks administration presented Hendrik Verwoerd, apartheid's main agent, in the tradition of Paul Kruger, as involved in a twelve-year struggle for the establishment of the Augrabies National Park.[70] And while the Wild Life Society referred to African poachers as being hungry and uneducated people deserving of understanding,[71] the Board's attitude was stated clearly: 'poachers [are] undoubtedly the most bloodthirsty, cruellest and most ruthless of the earth's inhabitants', an opinion consistent with the Board's portrayal of Africans historically as 'cannibals' and 'bloodthirsty barbarians'.[72]

Thus, although Africans themselves played no direct part in shaping the conservation laws which were framed in the early twentieth-century Transvaal, white perceptions that Africans destroyed vast numbers of wildlife, that they trespassed in order to do so, that they killed in a cruel manner, that they spoilt the recreation of sportsmen and managed to evade wage labour by subsisting on wildlife, determined to a considerable extent the kind of protectionist ethos which emerged.

In addition, within state game reserves and national parks the African experience of nature conservation either meant removal or, as tenants on crown land, responsibility for providing labour or rent. Although the financial benefits of a national park are considerable in terms of eco-tourism and infrastructural development, the costs and benefits are not equally shared by all the parties involved, and benefits have largely bypassed impoverished neighbours.

During the twentieth century in South Africa the interface between culture and nature has been transformed for all human communities. In particular, cultural conflicts have been exacerbated by imbalances of power and public participation which have impinged directly on state efforts at nature conservation. In the African version of wildlife conservation history, the experience has been that game reserves are white inventions which elevate wildlife above humanity and which have served as instruments of dispossession and subjugation. No Africans became partners in the conservationist enterprise: either their presence was suffered as squatters or 'courageous and loyal native rangers', or they were cast in the role of 'evil, cruel poachers' who were able to stave off wage labour by living off the land. Whatever their status, however, Africans could not continue their traditional subsistence lifestyle in conserved areas, but nor were they fully co-opted into the system of Western conservation which was imposed on them.

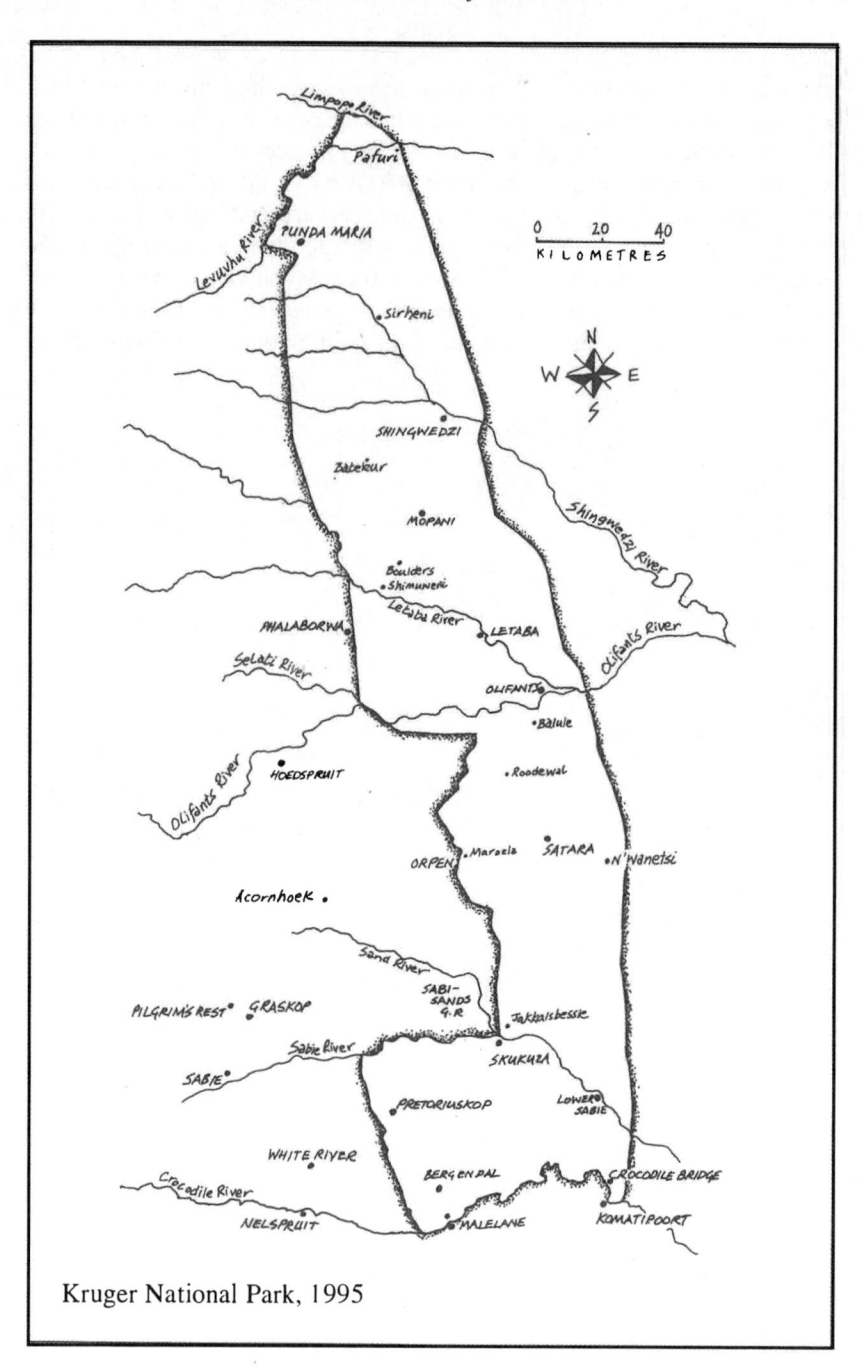

Kruger National Park, 1995

'Playing God'
Wilderness and Science

Nature conservation strategies, and the evolution of national parks in South Africa, have been influenced not only by the pragmatic political and socio-economic concerns which have been discussed, but also by intellectual and ethical changes in society. Protectionist philosophy has shifted in response to the advancement of science and to changes in public ideas about wildlife and nature. Since 1846, when the first steps to save wildlife were taken in the Transvaal, humans have come to think differently about wild animals and their attitudes and principles have developed considerably, playing their part in creating the ethos of the Kruger National Park. Ideas of Africa as an unconstrained and untameable Eden, in which the protection of individual species was paramount, belong to the past. Today the world is troubled about environmental degradation on a once-unknown scale, while harm from pollution and a fractured ozone layer are real dangers. The burgeoning numbers of wild animals in conserved areas in southern Africa often require culling, not saving. The number of protected species has increased enormously, and sportsmen protectionists at the turn of the century, who gave their attention only to antelope, would be astounded to learn that equal consideration is given, not only to 'vermin' such as wild dog and crocodile, but even to moths, butterflies, termites, bats and snakes. Trophic levels and energy flows are the buzzwords of modern ecologists. The manner in which this philosophical change has come about needs to be elucidated and related to the current scientific management of the Kruger National Park.

Developments in wildlife ethics over the last century can be traced through many strands. Pre-colonial hunting restrictions, either by way of taboos or by active protectionist restraints, have yet to be systematically investigated and their effects on conserving wildlife populations evaluated. In the Transvaal, the process of Westernizing wildlife began with the visits of traders, scientists and hunters in the 1820s and 1830s. It also coincided with an era of mass destruction. Cornwallis Harris and his sportsmen followers were influential butchers of the abundant wildlife of the Transvaal. The exploits of the Voortrekker settlers and their African allies were equally detrimental, though their motives for killing differed in that subsistence and commerce, rather than sport, were paramount.

When humans had slaughtered the Transvaal wildlife a change of attitude came about in the late nineteenth century. People came to condemn the huge sporting and commercial extermination which had taken place, but sanctioned hunting for natural history museums and the destruction of vermin species. Early in the twentieth century, a further change in Western attitudes to wildlife developed as the collecting and vermin destruction mania was replaced by the growing importance of field observations on live animals. In time, designations of vermin came to be re-evaluated in the conservation ethic and the interrelatedness of all elements of an ecosystem came to be recognized. In the specific context of the Kruger National Park, the 1930s and 1940s are important because in those decades a strong divergence in attitudes became apparent as a conflict erupted between old perspectives and the new. On the one hand, there were those who sought to retain the Kruger National Park as a wilderness experience, a place in which emotion was dominant and human intervention minimal. 'Keep it simple; keep it wild', was the motto of those who wanted to leave Nature to her own devices and who considered that the best way to learn about the natural world was simply by experiencing it. Opposing this point of view, a strong body of opinion emerged in the late 1930s, and strengthened after the Second World War, arguing that the landscape and wildlife of national parks should be scientifically managed and closely studied. This is the scientific intellectual ethic which prevails today. However, fresh ideas are once more in the ascendant, particularly the view that wildlife science has excluded the human dimension too completely. People must be brought back into the environmental equation and more of them allowed to enjoy the benefits of nature conservation. At the same time, in international circles there is also an increasing emphasis on 'wilderness', and it is possible that conditions in the Kruger National Park will revert to some degree from active management to encompass the promotion of wilderness. Ecological concerns are generating some of the most important modern philosophical debates, including economic and political proposals which might secure an environmentally healthy planet, and issues of animal rights. Attitudes to nature are always social constructs, tied to their time, and they illuminate much about the prevailing culture.

The abundance and diversity of the southern African faunal and floral kingdoms generated a vast literature almost from the outset of white occupation of the Cape. Naturalists and collectors such as John Barrow,

William Burchell, Anders Sparrman and Francois le Vaillant revelled in the natural environment they explored, naming its components, describing what they saw and exporting specimens to the museums of Europe. One of the first written records relating to the Transvaal was by a person in this intellectual mould, Dr Andrew Smith, Director of the South African Museum in Cape Town. Smith's report for the South African Literary and Scientific Institution on his investigation into the politics, geography and ethnography of the interior was objectively written and well illustrated, but it had no influence on the public because it was not published at the time.[1]

Not long after Smith's visit, however, William Cornwallis Harris visited the Transvaal and his emotional and exuberant hunting record caused a sensation. Quite different from the preceding natural history accounts, most of which were couched in rather dull language, Harris wrote in an exciting and lively style. His focus was different too, and he enthused over wildlife as objects of sport – killing for fun or entertainment – rather than as objects of study. The ritual of the hunt came to the fore in Harris's descriptions of the wildlife he saw. He claimed, for example, to worship at the altar of Diana, the chaste goddess of hunting, and the sexual imagery regarding the pursuit and subjugation of aesthetically pleasing animals is quite clear. However, the relationship between Harris and his prey was also one of combat. Sportsmen liked to link sport with war, and wild animals were the enemy against which a 'campaign' was mounted and with which 'hostilities' commenced each day.[2] The enemy, being 'noble' and 'brave', was a worthy one[3] and, as in the vanquishing of a human enemy, Harris's real joy came from demonstrating his superiority and in humiliating the foe.[4] The death of a beautiful creature for pure pleasure was the sportsman's objective, but for the animal victims of course, unaware of the ideals of nobility and courage which hunters attributed to them, their 'magnificent' deaths were simply a biological reality.[5] In Harris's work there is no inkling of reverence for the vanquished, no apology to the slain and little appreciation of their value as living beings. Pre-colonial societies, by contrast, usually had a somewhat different perspective on hunting. For the San, for example, wildlife which provided food also formed a social bond between band members. Moreover, veneration of certain species provided a spiritual dimension to community life which is apparent from the rock paintings executed by shamans in states of trance.[6] Harris's on the other hand was a particularly Western view of hunting.

The publicity which Harris's books generated for the wildlife of the Transvaal soon brought other sportsmen in his wake. In *Southern African Literature: An Introduction*, Stephen Gray refers to these people as 'raiders', for as he explains, although they were committed to engaging with and changing the land, they had no sense of belonging to it.[7] Unlike Africans or Boer settlers, they had no stake in the Transvaal, exploiting it only transitorily. The lack of any sense of responsibility, the sheer abundance of wildlife, and the absence of any ceremonial or other restrictions, made these hunting forays quite different from anything which could be experienced in Britain at that time. Part of the thrill of wildlife in the Transvaal was that such abundant bounty promoted the view that hunting ethics could be abandoned. H.H. Methuen shot what he called 'Namaqua partridges' as they drank, took ostrich eggs from under a sitting parent ostrich, killed a rhinoceros calf as it ran behind its mother, and deliberately set the veld ablaze. The excuse was, he wrote, 'the English sportsman will shrug his shoulders at such barbarism, but we were often constrained to shoot for food, and neglect conscientious qualms'.[8]

In addition to the delight in irresponsible slaughter there was also exhilaration and glamour.[9] Harris gloried in the wildness of the environment, insisting that the privations of southern African hunting were preferable to any luxury. The landscape was alluring because it was a 'savage loneliness' with adventure and 'freedom'[10] which was impossible to find in northern Europe. This was, to some degree, an aspect of Romanticism which held that 'nature "improved" was nature destroyed'[11] and that aesthetic beauty could be found only in wild nature. Hunter-visitors were therefore not frightened in any way by wilderness, but found it very attractive. The process of 'settling down' was abhorrent to many men of action, and a widely held opinion seems to have been that while drinking and gambling formed the major pursuits in Europe for a man in search of excitement, hunting wild animals in Africa could replace such undesirable occupations.[12]

The absence of almost any human intrusion was also an important element in the attraction which the wilderness of the Transvaal held for sportsmen. Solitude was a rare pleasure for urbanized Europeans and antisocial feelings were integral to the emotions of Romanticism.[13] In short, on a visit to Africa, the norms of civilized society were placed in abeyance. Africa was indeed 'a world apart . . . too alien to be encompassed within the rubrics of civilized understanding'.[14] These often-expressed emotions of pleasure in killing, excitement at being surrounded by an abundance of wild animals, enjoyment of solitude, and the desire to experience privation, would have bemused African and Boer hunters of the time whose attitudes were quite different. They killed wildlife in order to survive or to enrich themselves and their main purpose in doing so was to subdue and tame the landscape. For the Boer communities wildlife offered a means of subsistence, items of trade and, more often than not, represented a serious obstacle to modernization and agricultural development.

Although many of the visiting hunters proclaimed an interest in natural history, from their accounts it is clear that this was secondary to considerations of enjoyment. Collecting data or specimens had a low priority and whatever was discovered of zoological or taxonomic interest was a by-product of, rather than a motivation for, the killing. The hunter-publicist material has a class dimension, in that the reason for hunting was regarded as an indicator of social status.[15] Both market-hunters and sportsmen killed animals and engaged in the same physical hunting behaviour, but Boers and Africans found it hard to believe that some people were foolish enough to hunt wild animals solely for amusement and that the economic by-products of their hunting were so unimportant to them.[16]

Sportsmen had to denigrate other groups of hunters in order to prove that killing for pleasure, which was 'good', was the prerogative of the upper classes while market-hunting, which was 'evil', was for the lower class. Boers were arraigned for being primitive or backward, the traveller A.A. Anderson was one of many who considered that only people who believed that the earth was flat would kill animals for hides rather than for entertainment or the pot.[17] At the time there was a common belief that a staple diet of venison was unhealthy for 'civilized' people. Boers were vilified for living on game meat,[18] while many explorers in the interior were said to have died from 'the necessity for so many years of feeding on the tough and indigestible flesh of the elephant, rhinoceros, lion and other large game'.[19]

After the British annexation of the Transvaal in 1877, and with the later discoveries of gold, immigration from Europe soared. Some attitudes to wildlife evident in the Transvaal remained ingrained, but a change in the discourse can also be discerned and probably traced to two factors. The first of these was the marked diminution of wild animals in southern Africa, while the second was the increasingly overt expression of British imperialism in the Transvaal. This initiated a new attitude of possessiveness towards wildlife, because many of the British who came to the Transvaal in the later nineteenth century were 'stayers', rather than transients, and thus inclined to consider wildlife to be an imperial asset and thus 'theirs'. A writer of that time, for example, described what was left of the wildlife of Africa as 'a precious inheritance of the Empire to be most jealously safeguarded'.[20] This was so because it was so aesthetically pleasing and thus enhanced the value of the empire. A scene in which wild animals wandered freely about the countryside was reminiscent of paradise and that paradise was now being taken firmly under British control. For that reason, wildlife had to be protected. To writers at that time, it was unquestionable that wildlife had to be saved *from* market and subsistence hunters, the corollary of which was that it had to be saved *for* sportsmen – agents of imperialism.

The visible shortage and the growing appreciation of the beauty of wild animals made sheer pleasure in slaughter morally less respectable. However, fresh justifications for killing were found. Hunting for food or the market was seen not so much as bestial, but as evidence of laziness and a way of avoiding wage labour and labour meant imperial advancement. Vituperation against 'cruel' hunting methods gained ground to prevent the poor from hunting. The manner in which death occurred and the infliction of suffering were much debated. It has been suggested that growing compassion towards all animals at that time was part of a larger social question exacerbated by sentiments influenced by the industrial revolution and the exercise of social control. Ideas of showing kindness to animals thus buttressed the new political economy by declaring that those who killed 'cruelly' were not allowed to hunt.[21] These attitudes had not featured greatly during the life of the Transvaal Republic; on the contrary, hunters there or emanating from the Transvaal had a widespread reputation for ruthless hunting habits.[22]

Ideas of avoiding cruelty become quite evident when later naturalists and hunters were careful not to couch their reminiscences in bloodthirsty language. The turn of the century was the age of the 'penitent butchers', who, like many reformed characters, were vocal and persuasive in their attempts to prevent others from following in their former sinful ways. By the end of the nineteenth century there was no longer public admiration for the actions of people like Harris. Writers condemned 'unsporting' hunters who seemed proud of their wantonness,[23] praising those who were 'the most sparing and the least wasteful'.[24]

Disapproval of wanton killing allowed ideas of being a 'nature lover' rather than a sportsman to gain respectability. Ideals of manliness slowly began to encompass the view that protection and nurturing was as socially acceptable as killing. Henry Bryden was not ashamed to describe himself publicly as 'a true lover of nature'.[25] The notion of extinction was a rallying cry and Bryden was only one of many who considered the extinction of wild animal species to be a disgrace to mankind.[26] While not as outspoken as Bryden, other writers of the time, such as Selous,[27] also lamented the disappearance of wildlife.

Early hunting accounts had almost always included an implicit invitation to others to enjoy a similar hunting experience, but under the new ethos this outlook altered: the books of the late nineteenth century were conceived in the sure knowledge that the paradise of sport in southern Africa had vanished for ever. Romanticism turned from glorifying solitude, adventure and freedom and began to focus on sentimentalizing the past. Readers did not take up the work of Selous, for example, thinking that they could share the same experiences as the author, but they were fascinated by the delineations of a world which would never be recreated because the wild animals which had once filled it to capacity would never again do so.

In contrast to the United States at this time, where the influence of John Muir and other Transcendentalists was important for the course of nature protection, mysticism or pantheism did not feature to any extent in the protectionist ideology of the imperial government. The sole philosophical imperative was an aesthetic one, expressed by E.N. Buxton, the head of the Society for the Preservation of the Wild Fauna of the Empire, who considered wild animal species to be akin to works of art, the best of which should be considered to be as 'sacred from molestation as the bulls of Apis'.[28]

Although denigrating early hunter-explorers who had over-indulged for the sheer pleasure of slaughter,[29] writers at this time not only forgave, but indeed encouraged and supported, hunters who killed for 'scientific' reasons. As long as detailed records of destroyed animals were maintained, horn measurements for example, there was no moral restraint to the numbers killed. One author went as far as to state that as long as a lofty determination to learn, rather than pride, was the dominant emotion, a hunter could be excused almost any amount of carnage.[30] In this vein, Bryden forgave Selous for killing large numbers, because he did so 'only for the sake of procuring specimens' which he 'sent home . . . to the Natural History and other museums'.[31]

The other major pretext for hunting in this period was the slaughter of predators or vermin species which had not provided 'sport' for the hunters of the mid-nineteenth century and which had therefore not been given much attention in the literature. These increasingly became the object of hunting expeditions, and regarding species such as hyaena, birds of prey, reptiles, jackal and cheetah among others, as vicious and evil seemed to be enough to justify their extermination.[32] Vermin thus became a culturally acceptable target for human bloodthirstiness. There was an upsurge in 'vermin' killing once the great herds of elephant and antelope had disappeared and a new hierarchy developed as certain species came to be regarded as worthy opponents of man. Chief of these was the lion, the 'king of the beasts'. Lion-hunting was supposed to have demanded great bravery and strength and many hunter-writers included tales of exciting adventures with 'the great and terrible man-eating cat, the monarch of the African wilderness'[33] among their anecdotes. Entire books were devoted to descriptions of lion hunting,[34] and lively rivalry existed among hunters as to who had killed the greatest number.[35]

After the first decade of the twentieth century emphasis gradually shifted away from pure hunting adventures to accounts of protectionist endeavours within designated game reserves. Major writers of this time were thus gamekeepers or game wardens, people who took imperial possession one step further by actually living among the wild creatures and taking care of them for the first time. This new approach, which has been called 'the gamekeeper's chorus',[36] was refreshing to people such as William Hornaday, Director of the New York Zoological Park who was interested in the wildlife of Africa and who belonged to many learned societies. He wrote to Stevenson-Hamilton when *Animal Life* was published in 1912; 'I have grown *weary* of tales of slaughter and extermination, and your book of Preservation comes like a cold spring bursting forth in a sun-parched desert.'[37] Judging by the brisk sales of these books, the reading public enjoyed the change as well.

The output of wardens such as Stevenson-Hamilton, A. B. Percival of the Game Department of Kenya[38] and C.R.S. Pitman of Uganda,[39] was influential. Imparting knowledge was an explicit aim of these works, but there is also evidence of an attitude of arrogance. As one modern critic has expressed it, it is 'puzzling but true that gamekeepers are possessed by the conviction that they know all about the animals and that new information would be superfluous'.[40] For these authors were the men 'on the spot', proud to have learnt by personal encounter and long experience the habits of wild animals in their living state and in their own natural environment.[41] Personal observation was elevated to high status in terms of the acquisition of knowledge, while book-learning was decried.[42]

Although some of these gamekeepers, such as Stevenson-Hamilton, were more knowledgeable than others in natural history, none of them made systematic observations or compiled thorough checklists of species. Indeed, their role was primarily that of paramilitary administrator rather than resident naturalist. Lack of scientific training was not regarded as a disadvantage, partly because the biological sciences were museum- and taxonomy-orientated and not applied field sciences. But perhaps also, as many believe, the public actually preferred to hail the achievements of the brilliant amateur, rather than the considered, and perhaps more guarded, opinions of experts.[43] In his Foreword to Selous's *African Nature Notes and Reminiscences*, Roosevelt advocated that the views of 'closet naturalists' should be tested against competent field observers with long experience.[44]

The overtly propagandistic nature of the gamekeepers' output combined rationality with romance in an entirely new way. Fantasy still had its place, and descriptions of the magical world of the lone permanent white inhabitant of the game reserve were much enjoyed by readers. For life among the 'denizens of the wild' was romantic, even akin to living in paradise. The title of Stevenson-Hamilton's *South African Eden* is a case in

Stevenson-Hamilton at Tshokwane, 1913

Stevenson-Hamilton in his retirement

Early wildlife photo taken in the Kruger National Park by Paul Selby, *c.* 1928

Vermin culling: lion skulls at Sabi Bridge, 1924

Frederick Courteney Selous, the famous Victorian hunter

Early wildlife photo taken in the Kruger National Park by Paul Selby, *c.* 1928

An elephant carcase being loaded after a culling operation

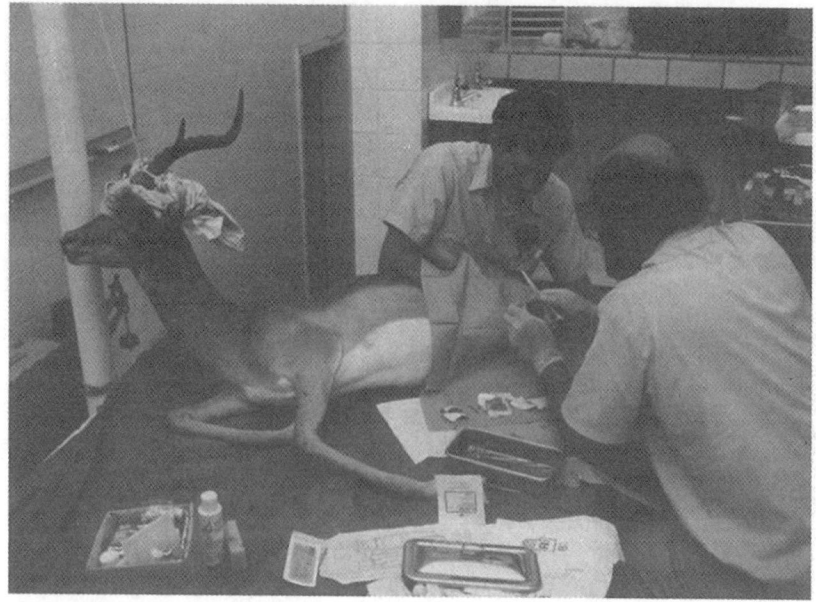

Scientific research conducted by the National Parks Board

point. Tales of everyday life in the outdoors, exploring, observing, camping, and dealing with poachers, enlivened throughout by the excitement of a dangerous lion or crocodile encounter, made these books extremely popular. Serious and useful observations of wildlife were indeed made and communicated to readers, while the notion of a courageous person enduring privations in taking care of his charges fed the market for romance.[45]

Anthropomorphism was a major means of imparting information, stemming no doubt from a belief that the more wild animals had in common with humanity, the more interest would be taken in their preservation. This was an anthropomorphism different from that of Harris, who had compared wildlife with noble, vanquished human maidens. Percival, for example, considered the footprints of rhinoceros and humans to be similar,[46] and Stevenson-Hamilton complimented wild mammals for having, and obeying, definite rules of social conduct.[47]

Preservationist propaganda and the educational format of these books, usually by way of species-by-species presentation, allowed gamekeepers to capture the moral high ground from imperialist sportsmen. Wildlife protection became an increasingly popular concept, but for the most part it remained an exclusive kind of protection, in that it concentrated on 'game' species. For this reason, all predators on antelope continued to be ruthlessly exterminated. Lion, especially, were singled out for conflicting with the preservationist goal by eating antelope. The sporting perspective endured to the extent that game preservation meant not only the extermination of lion, cheetah or wild dog, but also an absorption with population biology.[48] Herbivore numbers were presumed at this time to be directly controlled by predators, and the gamekeeper books are full of observations about the 'condition' of game, or of 'increasing' or 'decreasing' herds – although no reliable census methods had yet been devised.

Population dynamics was also assumed to be the 'Balance of Nature' with 'Mother Nature' in charge of the scales.[49] While deferring to 'Mother Nature' would appear to suggest that all species should be allowed their place on earth, this was not so. Many species were killed merely for having habits repulsive had they manifested themselves in human society. The wild dog, which, as one later writer has observed, should have been dear to any gamekeeper's heart, being so close in appearance to a domestic dog, is a good example.[50] Stevenson-Hamilton devoted an entire paper to the wild dog, having obtained his knowledge from his 'somewhat exceptional opportunities of observing this animal'. He gives a graphic description of their hunting methods, and concludes that 'the facial expression' of a wild dog prevents him from ever being a friend of man.[51] Pitman confessed to loathing crocodile, considering them 'an animated trap, something lower than the meanest of reptiles'.[52]

Human characteristics came to be applied to wild animals, and became a justification for doing away with certain species. In reality, a wild dog is not cruel to tear a living animal apart for food, for the dog is not experiencing either the enjoyment of power or the distress of his victim. In decrying certain behavioural or character traits as being unacceptable even in wild animals, gamekeepers were denouncing what they considered to be a moral evil. A belief in Darwinism can be increasingly identified; the survival of the fittest is the aspect of evolution which is most emphasized. Yet, in a manner which seems illogical, the gamekeepers saw no harm in benefiting the unfit by killing off the predators. However, whatever sentimentality was apparent in the literature of the first few decades of the twentieth century, it does not include any form of life other than large mammals. There is no 'land ethic', and grass is appreciated only in the context of providing grazing for antelope, and ticks are 'horrible creatures'.[53]

As the twentieth century progressed, and as more tourists became acquainted with the Kruger National Park, preservationism and the days of the solitary, courageous ranger seemed to run their course. For one thing, visitors loved sighting lion, in contrast to the game rangers who felt obliged to kill them. Indeed, as tourists today still attest, such a sighting is the highlight of the national park experience. Whether lion should be exterminated in the Kruger National Park became a major debate in National Parks Board circles in the mid-1930s. When the Kruger National Park was proclaimed in 1926, Stevenson-Hamilton had stopped all killing of lion. Not only did visitors love them, but antelope populations had increased to such an extent by that time that there was no need to control predator numbers. However, in the drought conditions of the 1930s the antelope herds thinned and National Parks Board members and many of the game rangers (not Stevenson-Hamilton, who felt that nature could take care of itself) wanted lion hunts to begin again. From the rangers' point of view, selling lion skins, skulls and fat brought in a small income and lion stories provided good tourist material.[54]

Game wardens and rangers have, themselves, impacted on how national park philosophy has developed. Their paramilitary origins as defenders of wildlife against humans has meant that a uniform has became an important component of their image. Until the late 1980s, any training in natural history was considered unnecessary for the tasks of policing, construction or the overseeing of African labour. In the Kruger National Park early game rangers came from the ranks of former hotel- and store-keepers, railway foremen and storemen and junior civil servants.[55] In common with other senior conservationists of his time, Stevenson-Hamilton actually preferred this kind of man to any naturalist. He believed that the desirable traits in a ranger were physical strength and activity, and reliability. Further recommendations were a knowledge of 'natives', bushcraft, horses, firearms and agriculture and, preferably, the absence of a wife. University degrees were unnecessary, he thought, even detrimental, because they led to specialization, whereas a ranger's knowledge ought to be broad and diverse. 'It is best that a man pick up his biological knowledge direct from the face of nature, unhampered by previous prejudices and preconceived notions.'[56] The public seemed to agree with Stevenson-Hamilton that rangers needed experience in the field and personal involvement. An article in the *Rand Daily Mail* in 1932 applauded 'cognoscenti' like game rangers, who could be informative on bizarre issues such as how many stomach grunts could follow a lion's full-throated roar. The answer was apparently twenty-two, the average being seventeen.[57]

The involvement of amateurs at all levels of national park management meant that many of the decisions taken in those years would now be considered environmentally inappropriate. The National Parks Board members presented particular problems to Stevenson-Hamilton. For example, in 1930, they wanted to introduce lechwe into the national park, despite there being no suitable habitat.[58] Preller enjoyed bird-watching and thought there were too few birds when he visited the Park. Without producing any evidence, he said that this was due to jackal destroying fledglings, and he thus persuaded his fellow Board members to instruct Stevenson-Hamilton to exterminate jackal throughout the national park.[59] Ludorf had a craving to see springbuck and blesbuck in the veld around Pretoriuskop, although there were no records of these species ever having been there[60] and, in 1939, Campbell, under the influence of the Kenyan game department of the time, advocated that grass and fruits from Kenya should be imported to provide additional feed for the wildlife of the Kruger Park.[61]

Throughout his long career as Warden, Stevenson-Hamilton insisted that no wildlife management intervention take place. Not only did he maintain that nature could take care of itself, but he also considered that the natural world had a integral component of 'wonder' which too much knowledge would dispel. He wrote, 'It pays best to trust to nature in all matters pertaining to wild life. In the course of many millions of years she has evolved a system which has continued to work . . . [Scientists have] . . . developed a feeling that man can by his own efforts improve upon nature . . . science with its classical approaches and verbose jargon . . . can be very dangerous.' He was even against having a wildlife museum at Skukuza.[62] This did not mean, however, that he thought that people ought not to learn about nature. On the contrary, it was merely that he believed that the veld itself should be the classroom. He stated in 1930 that one of the prime objects of any national park was to assist in finding answers to scientifically interesting questions which could be resolved only in the wilderness, and not in any artificial surroundings.[63]

Towards the end of the 1930s, Stevenson-Hamilton's long-held principle of leaving nature alone came under increasing pressure.[64] Far more threatening to his management philosophy than the naïve interference of Board members, was the growing interest of scientists in wildlife and their determination to be included in its administration. Stevenson-Hamilton hated scientists – 'our most dangerous enemies' he called them[65] – because he had encountered them as veterinarians or agronomists who had consistently attempted to sabotage his protectionist endeavours by arguing that wildlife was the reservoir of livestock diseases.[66] Scientists of this kind had advocated exterminating wildlife when nagana broke out, instructed Stevenson-Hamilton to spray poison against locusts, to kill all the livestock in the Kruger Park when foot-and-mouth disease appeared in 1939,[67] and to put a film of oil on the surface of all the rain pools and waterholes to suffocate mosquito larvae – with dire consequences for the animals which drank from them.[68]

Nonetheless, Stevenson-Hamilton tried to keep abreast of scientific developments, reading widely and sending specimens to herbaria for identification. He even used the word 'ecology' in 1940 but for him – perhaps inevitably – it was a simple term meaning 'the reactions of wild animals to their surroundings'.[69] But by then science itself had undergone transformations and the discipline of wildlife management was ready to take its place as the leading form of conservation.

By 1946, the year of his retirement as Warden of the Kruger National Park, many of Stevenson-Hamilton's views had become anachronistic in South African protectionist circles. He was elderly, an English-speaking Victorian imperialist brought up in a sporting environment, and out of touch with the growing power of the biological sciences. He also seems to have been unaware of how the Kruger National Park, which had in earlier days formed only a part of a vast area of lowveld wilderness, was more and more surrounded and isolated by development of all kinds.

The Wild Life Protection Society and its representative on the National Parks Board began to take serious account of the scientific arguments which were being advanced, even by members of the general public, and pleaded for scientific collaboration in the educational responsibility of the National Parks Board.[70] A Publicity Conference held at Pretoriuskop in 1939 demanded that better educational material and scientific opportunities should be offered by the Park and that zoological, botanical and geological surveys be conducted as a matter of course.[71]

With Stevenson-Hamilton's retirement, a clean sweep was made and the brilliant amateur, the 'man of action' was displaced almost at once by the professional scientist and administrator. Influential in this respect were Sandenbergh, the new Warden, and Dr R. Bigalke, Director of the National Zoological Gardens in Pretoria, the nominee of the Wild Life Society on the National Parks Board and a keen educationalist and author. Sandenbergh welcomed scientific intervention, and Bigalke was keen to co-operate having long held the opinion that the Warden of the Kruger Park ought to be a scientist.[72] When he was appointed to the National Parks Board in 1949, Bigalke was delighted, aware that only a short time previously his presence would not have been tolerated.[73]

Bigalke proved himself an energetic member of the Board, presenting at almost every meeting well-considered reports in connection with matters such as ridding the Kruger National Park of exotic vegetation, beginning serious educational endeavours, collecting African place-names and history, arranging the establishment of a scientific division and employing a resident scientist.[74]

This whirlwind activity of Bigalke's ceased when he resigned suddenly. The Hoek investigation which had uncovered irregularities within the National Parks Board administration had disillusioned Bigalke, a pure scientist who abhorred the political agendas and interpersonal squabbles which characterized the Board at that time. Bigalke's transient efforts at changing the direction of wildlife conservation in the Kruger National Park were, however, extremely successful, particularly as they facilitated the affirmative action programme which was initiated by the Nationalist government in the 1950s: the Kruger National Park became a haven for Afrikaans zoology graduates. In 1951 a professional biologist was appointed and basic ecological work began. Scientific record-keeping started, surveys of fauna and flora were executed, exotic vegetation was cleared and soon considerable stature became attached to those scientists who managed and studied wildlife. By 1957 the motto of the National Parks Board had become 'management by intervention'.[75]

The dominant wildlife literature is now scientific, the age of anecdotes and anthropomorphism almost ended. Wildlife management and ecology have replaced zoology and botany as the naturalist's discipline. Wildlife management was pioneered in the United States by Aldo Leopold in 1933, and in 1965 a degree in wildlife management was inaugurated in South Africa, significantly offered only at the Afrikaans-medium University of Pretoria.

The scientific output which has been generated in the Kruger National Park since the 1950s can be gauged by reference to the National Parks Board's journal *Koedoe*. Where earlier writing had romanticized and elevated man's subservience to 'Mother Nature', conquest has become the dominant ideological position. Sentimentality and emotion, including the element of wonder, has vanished entirely.

The loss of an emotional dimension finally ended the era of romance, and the solitary game warden has been superseded by teams of scientists and administrators working together in advancing national parks. But the natural world has become a 'team' as well, for it has come to be appreciated that all elements of the ecological landscape are interrelated. 'Game' has been replaced by 'wildlife' and ecological considerations have introduced new species into the literature, species which had been previously ignored on account of their lack of importance to sportsmen, or their small size. These forms of life have become as vital to the natural environment as any large and beautiful antelope, and molerats and woodlice have taken their rightful place alongside elephant or lion.[76]

Claims to total rationality, and conceit, are the hallmarks of scientific work and anthropomorphism has disappeared. Wildlife managers have come to believe that their approach is the only correct one, and the haphazard observations or sentimentality of earlier naturalists are referred to in disparaging terms.[77] However, the point has been made by a member of the Kenyan Parks Service, that it is as well to reflect that this somewhat arrogant attitude is really not rational at all, but closer to faith and religious belief than to the questioning approach which should be the principal characteristic of scientific endeavour.[78]

One of the most important developments of post-war scientific control of the Kruger National Park has centred around culling. While the national park authorities publicly advertise very seriously that wildlife within national parks is 'safe'[79] the creatures themselves could be forgiven for failing to realize that their circumstances have changed at all since Cornwallis Harris wrote his hunting accounts in 1836. Increased control and protection have allowed the numbers of many species, which were previously rare and whose existence was formerly carefully nurtured, to swell, straining the ability of the veld to feed them. In order to protect the total ecosystem, controlled killing of over-abundant species – including some which were the highlight of many a sportsman's career – was introduced and has come to be 'a smooth working routine' within the Kruger National Park.[80] The public, fed on a preservationist literary diet, initially required some persuasion that thinning wildlife numbers was desirable, but this has been successfully accomplished. Harris's pleasure in random bloodshed has therefore been replaced by sanitized and efficient killing by means of poisoned darts, often fired from helicopters circling over terrified herds. The clinical refinement of a painless death, before carcasses are brought to an abattoir in the Kruger National Park, has removed some of the 'wildness' from the wild creatures. It has brought them, in death at least, closer to their domestic counterparts for whom being consumed as tinned or dried meat, has had a far longer history. Practices such as radio-tagging and translocation are part of the same philosophy of scientific conquest, and yet, in many instances, these events are as traumatic and painful for the animals as being hunted for trophies. An American publication has characterised such actions as 'playing God'.[81]

Along with post-war ideas of the interrelationship between all forms of life, an 'island mentality' has, perhaps surprisingly, developed simultaneously. Contact with the physical landscape has been in the hands of professional managers and other people, whether visitors or neighbours on national park boundaries, have become increasingly isolated. Until walking trails were introduced recently, visitors were not permitted to leave their vehicles outside of specified camps to enjoy the wilderness, and the Kruger National Park was fenced to prevent unauthorized access by neighbours and any escape by wildlife. Contact with the wild has come to be confined more and more to scientists, and less and less accessible to the public, a possibility which Stevenson-Hamilton foresaw and deplored.[82]

Epilogue

The value of any historical analysis lies in its elucidation of how present situations have come into being. While history cannot be used to predict the future, it can throw light on the root causes of the current problems which face organizations. To some extent, it can also provide clues as to which avenues might best be followed in order to solve them.

There is no doubt that the twenty-first century will present enormous difficulties to the National Parks Board of South Africa – indeed to all the nature conservation structures in the country. Many of these derive from the history which has been examined in this work.

A major theme of this book has been the very close connection between nature conservation and national politics. The allocation of resources – to whom? in what proportion? – is an issue which has been at the heart of politics since wildlife was first used for hominid consumption. When a San hunter-gatherer economy dominated the sub-continent, the use of natural resources played a large role in shaping many aspects of society. It determined that communities would be nomadic, that labour would be divided between men and women (women gathered and men hunted), that the optimum group size would be influenced by the fragility or scarcity of those resources, and that no political or social hierarchy evolved because the bounty of nature was shared by all.

Once farmers began to intrude into southern Africa, society became more complex than any San group in its use of the natural environment. And, as has been shown, the question of who should share in the benefits which natural resources have to offer, became ever more enmeshed in the political economy. For this reason, while Afrikaner Nationalism and apartheid were the country's controlling political philosophies, whites alone were able to enjoy the full recreational benefits of the Kruger National Park. African employees within the Park were permanently subservient, while Africans outside it were penalized by being denied access to its natural resources.

The culture of the Park was, as has been shown, tied to white, Western ways.

During the period surveyed in this book, whites alone were voters and thus played a commanding role in how resources would be shared. In the future, however, the enfranchisement of all South Africans will alter this. The specifications of national parks may change, and these will certainly manifest themselves in a change in the management structure of the Kruger National Park. At present, the reins of power are still generally held by the old guard, but affirmative action is sure to come about, whether welcomed or not. And, as has been revealed in previous chapters, affirmative action has been successful before in transferring nature conservation from the hands of one group (imperialist sportsmen) into another (Afrikaner scientists and bureaucrats).

With changes in staff structure there will certainly be alterations in management style. Public participation and transparency are the watchwords of the post-apartheid government. In the past, the Kruger Park authorities co-operated with clandestine groups such as the discredited CCB; this ceased with the appointment of Dr G. A. Robinson, the Chief Executive Director of the National Parks Board. Dr Robinson is aware of the poor public image of the national parks, of entrance gates closing, for example, at lunch-time leaving visitors sitting in the sun for up to an hour before being allowed within, of meals served at times which suit the staff rather than visitors, and of civil servants who have prided themselves on generally being rude to tourists.[1] Steps have already been taken to try to improve these matters, and the composition of the new National Parks Board will provide more central government direction.

The history of the Kruger National Park, as described in this work, has also shed some light on the destructive tendency – from the point of view of nature conservation – of rivalries and contests between various governmental departments, each seeking the expansion of its own power. There were clashes, for example, between the provincial administrations and central government, which may well be perpetuated as the new provinces test their mettle and as strong regional governments emerge to challenge national structures. When, for instance, should a national, rather than a regional (or provincial), park be desirable? Should provincial conservation authorities be constituted as an integral part of the civil service, or as parastatal boards, along the same lines as the National Parks Board itself?

This leads on to the issue of what sort of physical environment should a national park comprise? There are, at present, areas, such as the small Mountain Zebra National Park and the Bontebok National Park, which hardly seem worthy of the national park designation, when an area like the

Drakensberg or the northern Zululand coast is under provincial control. Guidelines will have to be worked out by the relevant authorities and in this connection a perception that conservation is a world-wide issue, will be crucial. Some of South Africa's landscape may well deserve world conservation status and a tier of conserved land which is placed above that of a national park may come into existence.

Indeed, there may be more differentiation between the various kinds of conserved areas, perhaps principally to attract the eco-tourists upon whom rests so much hope for re-igniting the South African economy. The meaning and direction of national parks may change under this kind of pressure. Already there are exclusive private nature reserves, national and provincial parks, and other areas in which the division between private and public utility is less rigidly devised. 'Contract parks' have already been established in the Richtersveld, for example. There, traditional graziers continue to exercise their agricultural rights, but ally themselves to the principles of the national park while accepting payment for allowing communal land to be managed by conservation authorities.

Neighbouring communities which have been excluded from conservation endeavours will certainly play a larger role in the future, and already, cognisance is being taken of their needs and wants. In principle, the issues revolve around local groups deriving greater benefit from conserved areas by way of financial stake-holding in national parks and game reserves, usage of some natural resources and, ultimately, being part of the planning process which determines how regional economies will emerge.

The new emphasis on public participation will affect the scientific outlook of national parks, although it will take time for any change to become apparent. Although scientific investigation will certainly continue to be prominent in national park endeavours, it is probable – indeed desirable – that studies may take on a more human-directed and orientated approach, and that greater educational emphasis will be provided by way of literature and other material easily accessible to the general public. Local people will have to be attracted to conserved areas using different tactics from those directed at international visitors.

Any developments of this nature may well lead to the broadening of nature conservation philosophy in South Africa to include African cultural concerns. There are indications already that these may encompass the importance and the history of traditional conservation structures, African wildlife folklore and traditional medicine.

As the earlier chapters of this work have demonstrated, nothing is as certain as change. The values attached to national parks constantly mutate, as do attitudes towards nature itself and to its place in society and culture.

In the past, while nature conservation has divided Africans and whites, it has proved at other times to be a point of contact and conciliation between the various white groups in the country. In the new dispensation appreciation of the natural environment and the conservation of nature may engender a bond between all South Africans and become an aspect of political maturation of which everyone can be proud.

Notes

Prologue

1. The most recent and detailed of these is U. de V. Pienaar, *Neem uit die Verlede* (Pretoria, 1990).
2. See, for example, J. Stevenson-Hamilton, *South African Eden* (London, 1937 and later editions); H. Wolhuter, *Memories of a Game Ranger* (Johannesburg, 1948 and later editions); H. Kloppers, *Game Ranger* (Cape Town, n.d.); G. Adendorff, *Wild Company* (Cape Town, 1984).
3. See, for instance, R. Bigalke, *A Guide to Some Common Animals of the Kruger National Park* (Pretoria, 1939); G. L. Smuts, *Lion* (Johannesburg, 1982); A. C. Brown, ed., *A History of Scientific Endeavour in South Africa* (Cape Town, 1977); D. H. S. Davis, ed., *Ecological Studies in South Africa* (The Hague, 1964); and D. J. Potgieter, et al., *Animal Life in Southern Africa* (Cape Town, 1971).
4. These include R. J. Labuschagne, *60 Years Kruger Park* (Pretoria, 1958) and *The Kruger Park and Other National Parks* (Johannesburg, n.d.); C. S. Stokes, *Sanctuary* (Cape Town, 1941); L. E. O. Braack, *The Kruger National Park* (Cape Town, 1983); P. Meiring, *Behind the Scenes in Kruger Park* (Johannesburg, 1982); P. Meiring, *Kruger Park Saga* (n.p., 1976); K. Newman, *The Kruger National Park* (Johannesburg, n.d.); D. Paynter, *Kruger: Portrait of a National Park* (Cape Town, 1986); A. Bannister and R. Gordon, *The National Parks of South Africa* (Cape Town, n.d.).
5. The literature dealing with the heroes of conservation, particularly Paul Kruger and James Stevenson-Hamilton, includes Labuschagne, *The Kruger Park*; H. P. H. Behrens, '"Oom Paul's" Great Fight to Preserve Game', *African Wild Life* 1(1), 1946, pp. 12–22; 'Paul Kruger-Wildbeskermer: Aspek van President se Lewe wat Selfs sy Biograwe Vergeet', *Huisgenoot* 37(1542), 12 October 1951, pp. 6–7; and 'His Name is Skukuza', *African Wild Life* 1(2), 1947, pp. 46–66; D. Tattersall, *Skukuza* (Cape Town, 1972); H. P. H. Behrens, 'Hunter Turns Protector: The Story of Henry Wolhuter', *African Wild Life* 1(3), 1947, pp. 36–50.
6. See, for example, D. Anderson and R. Grove, eds, *Conservation in Africa: People, Policies and Practice* (Cambridge, 1987) and the *Journal of Southern African Studies*, Special Issue, 'The Politics of Conservation in Southern Africa' 15(2), January 1989.

A Wildlife Paradise

1. See, for example, G. B. Silberbauer, *Hunter and Habitat in the Central Kalahari Desert* (Cambridge, 1981), pp. 78, 120, 291–2.
2. J. D. Lewis-Williams, *The Rock Art of Southern Africa* (Cambridge, 1983).

3. J.M. Feely, 'Did Iron Age Man have a Role in the History of Zululand's Wilderness Landscapes?', *South African Journal of Science* 76 (1980), p.151; M.Hall, 'Shakan Pitfall Traps: Hunting Technique in the Zulu Kingdom', *Annals of the Natal Museum* 22(1), 1977; K. Shillington, *The Colonisation of the Southern Tswana, 1870–1900* (Johannesburg, 1985).
4. H.B. Thom, *The Journal of Jan van Riebeeck*, vol.1, 14/15 April 1654 (Cape Town, 1952), pp.229–30.
5. Proclamation 21 March 1822; R. Grove, 'Incipient Conservationism in the Cape Colony and the Emergence of Colonial Environmental Policies in South Africa, 1846–1890', paper presented to the Conference on Conservation in Africa, April 1985.
6. T.H. le Roux, ed., *Die Dagboek van Louis Trigardt* (Pretoria, 1964).
7. Minutes of the Volksraad of Andries Ohrigstad, Articles 3 and 5, 21 January 1846; *South African Archival Records: Transvaal [SAAR]* (Cape Town, n.d.), vol.1, p.29.
8. F.V. Engelenburg, *'n Onbekende Paul Kruger* (Pretoria, 1925), p.23. Engelenburg claimed that one of the first nationalistic actions performed by the young Paul Kruger was his killing of thirty to forty elephant; see p.30. D.W. Kruger, in *Paul Kruger* (Johannesburg, 1961), vol.1, also mentions that Kruger engaged in professional hunting; see p.23; P. Kruger, *The Memoirs of Paul Kruger* vol.1, (London, 1902), p.18.
9. The Schoemansdal hunting community has been analysed by R. Wagner in S. Marks and A. Atmore, eds, *Economy and Society in Pre-Industrial South Africa* (London, 1980), pp.313–49.
10. P. Huet, *Het Lot der Zwarten in Transvaal* (Utrecht, 1869), p.21.
11. TA [Transvaal Archives] SS72 R1374/65, Petition from H.A. Schell and 20 others, 28 December 1865; TA SS78 R732/66, Petition from J.A. Weeber and 9 others, 25 July 1866; Petitions from A.H. Potgieter and 33 others on 9 January 1866 and G.J. Snyman and 62 others on 15 January 1866: *SAAR*, vol.6, pp.101–2.
12. *Index der Staatscouranten over de Jaren 1857 tot en met 1870* (Pretoria, 1897) and *Index der Staatscouranten over de Jaren 1871 tot en met Julie 1881* (Pretoria, 1898).
13. *Staatscourant*, 20 October 1875, Notice 2093.
14. A. Aylward, *The Transvaal of Today* (Edinburgh, 1878), pp.236–7.
15. A.T. Cunynghame, *My Command in South Africa, 1874–1878* (London, 1879), p.281; H. Roche, *On Trek in the Transvaal* (London, 1878), p.272; A.A. Anderson, *Twenty-Five Years in a Waggon* (London, 1888), p.27.
16. Anderson, *Twenty-Five Years*, p.27.
17. For a detailed study of 'the hunt' in colonial Africa, see J.M. Mackenzie, *The Empire of Nature: Hunting, Conservation and British Imperialism* (Manchester, 1988).
18. Details of the debate can be found in the Minutes of the Volksraad, Article 109, 14 August 1884.
19. Meiring, *Kruger Park Saga*, p.49.
20. Stevenson-Hamilton, *South African Eden*, p.xvii.
21. For instance in H.H. Curson and J.M. Hugo, 'Preservation of Game in South Africa', *South African Journal of Science* 21, 1924; C.A. Yates, *The Kruger National Park* (London, 1935); and the Union of South Africa, *House of Assembly Debates*, 31 May 1926.
22. S-HA [Stevenson-Hamilton Archives, Fairholm, Lanarkshire], Diary entries 18 May 1935, 20 May 1935.
23. TA SS831 R3298/83, Circular CB37/83, 24 July 1883.
24. The replies are in TA SS882 R6074/83 and SS893 R333/84; TA SS893 R333/84, Waterberg Landdrost to State Secretary, 19 November 1883.
25. TA SS302 R3130/78, Letter to Administrator, 31 August 1878.
26. Minutes of the Volksraad, Article 527, 25 June 1891.
27. Minutes of the Volksraad, Articles 678, 679, 3 July 1894.
28. TA SS3739 R5467/93, E.P.A. Meintjes to State Secretary, 5 May 1893; TA Landdrost Barberton, vol.11, Register ontvangste jaglisensies, 1892–1900.
29. Minutes of the Volksraad, Article 372, 17 June 1893.

30. TA SS3739 R5467/93, E.P.A. Meintjes to State Secretary, 5 May 1893.
31. Minutes of the Volksraad, Article 668, 3 July 1894.
32. TA SS5048 R10803/95, Petition from Zwagershoek, 9 July 1898; Petition from Elandsriver, 1 June 1898; Petition from Kwaggashoek, 27 April 1898; SS6626 R10645/97, Petition to President and Executive Council, July 1897; SS6626 R10645/97; the entire file is devoted to this matter.
33. F.D. Smit, *Die Staatsopvattinge van Paul Kruger* (Pretoria, 1951), pp. 18–19.
34. TA SS1865 R2573/89, Wakkerstroom Landdrost to Private Secretary of the President, 13 March 1889.
35. TA UR9, Article 482, 31 July 1889.
36. Little is known about these areas and further investigation into the localities and dates of establishment is needed.
37. Minutes of the Volksraad, Article 1244, 2 August 1889.
38. The situation around Tongaland at this time is well analysed in N.G. Garson, 'The Swaziland Question and a Road to the Sea', *AYB*, 1957, II; D.W. Kruger, 'Die Weg na die See', *AYB*, 1938, I; Kruger, *Paul Kruger*, vol. 1 and M.C. van Zyl, 'Die Uitbreiding van Britse Gesag oor die Natalse Noordgrensgebiede, 1879–1897', *AYB*, 1966, I.
39. Balliol College MS 443, Journal of J.E.C. Bodley's visit to South Africa, 1887–1889, vol. 2, pp. 25–6.
40. TA SS2595 R15541/90, G.J. Louw to government, 6 November 1890.
41. TA SS1875 R3068/89, J.A. Erasmus to Superintendent of Native Affairs, 8 May 1889, 22 September 1890, 5 November 1890.
42. TA SSA176/177 R865/95, Lottering to government, 30 November 1893.
43. See Glynn's approach to the government in 'Another Mighty Hunter: An Interesting Crack with Mr H.T. Glynn', *South Africa*, 5 September 1896, p. 557; and in Glynn's autobiography, H.T. Glynn, *Game and Gold: Memories of over 50 Years in the Lydenburg District* (London, n.d.), p. 208. Streeter's letter is located in TA SS5733 R12183/96, Streeter to State Secretary, 24 September 1895; TA SSA176/177 R865/95, Erasmus to Executive Council, 28 February 1896; Van Oordt to State President, 24 May 1895.
44. Labuschagne, *Kruger Park*, p. 2.
45. Minutes of the Volksraad, Article 1125, 9 September 1895.
46. Minutes of the Volksraad, Articles 1229, 1230, 17 September 1895.
47. The game reserves were not officially accorded names at the time of their proclamation; the areas in question were merely geographically demarcated.
48. TA SS4975a R8745/95, 'Resume van minute R8745/95 re stichting van eene gouwernements wildtuin in het distrikt Lydenburg', 8 July 1898.
49. TA SS4975 R8748/95, Loveday to State Secretary, 21 February 1896.
50. Minutes of the Volksraad, Article 1723, 15 November 1897.
51. TA UR15, Article 1011, 29 December 1897.
52. TA SS4975 R8748/95; this file contains the original proclamation which was published in the *Staatscourant*, 960, 13 April 1898.
53. TA SS4975 R8748/95, Gunning to Superintendent of Education, 15 June 1898; Mining Commissioner, Barberton to State Secretary, 2 August 1898.
54. Minutes of the Volksraad, Article 1707, 14 November 1898; TA SS4975a R8748/95, A. Ashley to Director of the State Museum, 5 September 1898; G.J. Louw to State Secretary, 13 September 1898. An article also appeared in *The Gold Fields News and Barberton Herald* on 5 August 1898, complaining that no 'caretaker' had yet been employed.
55. TA UR16, Article 843, 9 September 1898.
56. TA SS4975a R8745/95, Mining Commissioner to State Secretary, 18 August 1899.
57. Pienaar, *Neem uit die Verlede*, pp. 395–8.
58. See *The Gold Fields News and Barberton Herald*, 5 August 1898.
59. TA SS4562/3 R872/95, Van der Walt to State Secretary, 14 January 1895. Van der Walt mentioned specifically that farmers Erasmus and Opperman had already established private game reserves in the vicinity.

60. TA UR16, Article 407, 13 April 1898. See also *Staatscourant*, 4 May 1898. The farms included in the reserve were Kweeklaagte, Turfloop, Brakplein, Uitkyk, Hamburg, Delftzyl, Kortom, Rusland, Turfvlakte, Turfbult, Kalkbult and Afzet.
61. TA UR16, Article 767, 18 August 1898.
62. TA SS4343 R7212/94, Petition from 110 citizens of Pretoria, [July] 1894. The signatories included Leo Weinthal, Calla Juta, Sammy Marks, J.W. Leonard and E.P.A. Meintjes; TA SS4569 R11888/94, Meintjes and Marais to State Secretary, 11 January 1895; TA UR12B, Article 63, 23 January 1895. Meintjes wrote to the government again in 1898 asking that the prohibition be extended for another three years, a request which was granted; see TA SS4569 R11888/94, Marais to State Secretary, 11 January 1898.
63. *Staatscourant* 817, 4 March 1896, Notice 55.
64. TA SS5098 R11653/98, Petition from Marico, 12 November 1895; UR16, Article 409, 13 April 1898; TA SS7693 R1698/99, Petition from Middelburg Landdrost, 31 January 1899; UR17, Article 152, 7 February 1899; TA SS7748 R3589/99, Potchefstroom gamekeepers to State Secretary, 6 March 1899; TA SS7791 R5151/99; UR101, Article 403, 18 April 1899.
65. TA SS5304 R3190/96.
66. TA SS2031 R8009/89, Van Oordt to State Secretary, 1 August 1895; A.E. Charter, 'Game Preservation in Zululand', *Southern African Museum Association Bulletin*, September 1943, pp. 69–70.

Imperialists and Sportsmen

1. This society is still in existence but has twice altered its name: in 1919 it became the Society for the Preservation of the Fauna of the Empire and in 1950, the Fauna Protection Society. In 1904 the society began publication of a journal which continues today under the name of *Oryx*.
2. For example, H.A. Bryden, *Kloof and Karroo in Cape Colony* (London, 1889); *Gun and Camera in Southern Africa* (London, 1893) and *Nature and Sport in South Africa* (London, 1897); F.C. Selous, *African Nature Notes and Reminiscences* (London, 1908) and *A Hunter's Wanderings in Africa* (London, 1881); F. Vaughan Kirby, *In Haunts of Wild Game* (Edinburgh, 1896); A. Chapman, *On Safari: Big Game Hunting in British East Africa* (London, 1908); T. Roosevelt, *African Game Trails* (London, 1910).
3. E.N. Buxton, *Two African Trips: With Notes and Suggestions on Big Game Preservation in Africa* (London, 1902), p. 116.
4. H.A. Bryden, 'The Extermination of Great Game in South Africa', *Fortnightly Review*, October 1894, p. 540.
5. C. Wittwer, 'The 1908 White House Governor's Conference' in C. Schoenfield, ed., *Interpreting Environmental Issues* (Madison, 1973).
6. PRO [Public Record Office, Kew] FO403/302 7322; FO2/818; Cd3189, *Correspondence Relating to the Preservation of Wild Animals in Africa, 1906*, pp. 86–91; FO368/108; FO367/355; FO403/55.
7. TA LAJ7 L489, Legal Adviser to Military Governor, 20 September 1900; MGP119 11930A/01.
8. JPL [Johannesburg Public Library] TLOA, vol. 1, Minutes of informal meeting, 9 December 1902.
9. JPL TLOA, vol. 1, Membership list at the end of 1905.
10. TA CS396 10370/03, TGPA to Colonial Secretary, 18 November 1903.
11. TA SNA305 NA11/06, Commissioner for Native Affairs to Secretary of Native Affairs, 11 January 1906; TAD405 G946/06, Assistant Colonial Secretary to TGPA, 23 January 1906.
12. TA SNA158 NA1702/03, Stewart to TGPA, 8 August 1904.
13. TA CS396 10370/03, TGPA to Colonial Secretary, 18 November 1903.
14. A.B. Percival, *A Game Ranger on Safari* (London, 1928), pp. 214–15.

Notes to pages 32–35 127

15. Bryden, *Gun and Camera*, p. 59.
16. J.M. Powell, *Environmental Management in Australia, 1788–1914* (Melbourne, 1976), p. 114; J.J. Green, 'Government and Wildlife Preservation, 1885–1922: The Emergence of a Protective Policy' (Ph.D. thesis, York University, Toronto, 1975), p. 30; T.P. Ofcanksy, 'A History of Game Preservation in British East Africa' (Ph.D. thesis, University of West Virginia, 1981), p. 15. A game reserve was established in the Knysna Forests to protect elephant: see Grove, 'Incipient Conservationism', p. 6. In addition, the existence of an elephant reserve in the Knysna area was mentioned in 1903 by E.N. Buxton, 'The Preservation of Big Game in Africa', *Journal of the Society of Arts* 2(634), 15 May 1903, p. 569. It seems that game protection was sufficiently well established by the turn of the century for it to have been regarded as a suitable site for a 'National Park for Cape Colony' in 1905; see Cd3189, p. 255, Minutes of proceedings at a deputation from the Society for the Preservation of the Fauna of the Empire to the Right Honourable Alfred Lyttelton, 2 February 1905. In the early years of the century, the Cape Colony acquired two other game reserves – in 1903 the Namaqualand Game Reserve and in 1908 the Gordonia-Kuruman Game Reserve; see Curson and Hugo, 'Preservation of Game in South Africa', p. 411.
17. Bryden, 'Extermination of Great Game', p. 551; J.A. Nicolls and W. Eglington, *The Sportsman in South Africa* (London, 1892), p. 11; Cd3189, pp. 46–7, Under-Secretary for Agriculture, Cape Colony to Secretary to the Prime Minister, 15 April 1898.
18. TA SNA15 NA295/02, Lagden's notes, 21 January 1902; SNA40 NA1303/02, Barberton Resident Magistrate to Commissioner for Native Affairs, 12 July 1902; *The Star*, 27 October 1902; TA CS115 8288/02, Gardyne to Colonial Secretary, 27 July 1902; TA CS37 5066/01, Casement to Duncan, 14 September 1901.
19. TA CS2 211/01, Chapman's proposals, December 1900. In 1928 when the Kruger National Park had been successfully founded in substantially the same area as Chapman had suggested in 1900, Chapman claimed the creation of that park as his personal accomplishment; see A. Chapman, *Retrospect: Reminiscences of a Hunter-Naturalist in Three Continents* (London, 1928), pp. 210–14. It is, however, noteworthy that in 1908, before the successful proclamation of the national park, Chapman does not mention in his book *On Safari*, his role in the reserve's establishment; p. 5.
20. TA CS5 464/01, Gunning to Military Governor, 20 February 1901.
21. Re-establishment was effected by Notice 312 of 12 July 1902, and the boundaries were given in Notice 322 of 15 July 1902. After the 1902 Game Ordinance was passed, formal re-proclamation took place by way of Proclamations 11 and 12 of 20 November 1902.
22. TA CS4 460/01, Glynn to Foreign Office, 16 October 1900.
23. TA CS10 1032/01, Casement to Controller of the Treasury, 18 February 1901, 27 March 1901, 2 April 1901.
24. TA CS24 3082/02, Commissioner of Mines to Casement, 2 July 1901.
25. TA CS24 3082/02, Francis to Casement, 13 May 1901; Casement to Francis, 4 July 1901; Casement to Duncan, 18 May 1901.
26. TA CS30 3972/02, Casement to Duncan, 3 August 1901; Francis to Casement, 26 July 1901.
27. TA CS31 4159/02, Casement to Controller of the Treasury, 30 August 1901.
28. TA CS31 4159/01, Casement to Controller of the Treasury, 30 August 1901.
29. Executive Council Resolution 399, 25 September 1901; TA BN5/1/1, McInerney to Davidson, 11 December 1901, 2 January 1902.
30. TA BN5/1/1, McInerney to Assistant Secretary, 2 January 1901.
31. TA CS43 5820/01, Undated note on file cover; CS66 1176/02, McInerney to Assistant Secretary, 3 February 1902.
32. TA CS66 1295/02, Resident Magistrate, Barberton to Colonial Secretary, 7 February 1902, an application from G.G. Elphick; CS74 2348/02, application from A.H. Glynn; CS83 3653/02, application from H. Jackson; CS97 5748/02, Colonial Secretary to Secretary for Native Affairs, 8 July 1902, application from W.G. Treadwell.
33. TA CS2 211/01, Chapman's proposals, p. 2.

34. TA SNA157 NA1702/303, Stevenson-Hamilton to Lagden, 11 June 1902; Lagden to Davidson 16 June 1902. The government had initially favoured Major A. St H. Gibbons, the leader of a recent expedition to Barotseland, but Gibbons would not take up the position. However, Stevenson-Hamilton had been a fellow-member of Gibbons's expedition.
35. See J. P. R. Wallis, ed., *The Barotseland Journals of James Stevenson-Hamilton, 1898–1899* (London, 1953).
36. S-HA, Diary entries 3, 4, 5, 9, 11, 12, 22, 29 June 1902.
37. Executive Council Resolution 258, 2 July 1902. Stevenson-Hamilton was originally seconded by his regiment for two years and after the expiry of that period he resigned his commission to remain in the reserve; see TA LtG2 6/5; KNP [Kruger National Park Archives, Skukuza] Opsieners Jaarverslae 1, Lagden to Stevenson-Hamilton, 21 June 1902; S-HA, Folder 'Hamilton of Fairholm', Lagden to W. Parker, 5 February 1929.
38. TA SNA157 NA1702/03, Rimington to Lagden, 9 June 1902.
39. *The Lowveld: Its Wildlife and its People* (London, 1934).
40. TA CS448 2479/04, Stevenson-Hamilton to Secretary for Native Affairs, 7 April 1904.
41. CA [Cape Archives] A848, Stratford Caldecott Collection, 4(6), Stevenson-Hamilton to Caldecott, 26 February 1929.
42. KNP Photograph albums.
43. 'Aantekeningen omtrent de Wild-reserve aan de Sabi', *Het Transvaalsche Landbouw Journaal* 4, 1906, pp. 636–50; 'Notes on the Sabi Game Reserve', *Transvaal Agricultural Journal* 5(20), 1907, pp. 603–17.
44. 'Game Preservation in the Eastern Transvaal', *The Field*, 14 March 1903.
45. 'Game Preservation in the Transvaal', *Blackwood's Magazine*, March 1906, pp. 407–11.
46. 'Observations on Migratory Birds at Komatipoort', *Journal of the South African Ornithologists' Union* 5, April 1909, pp. 19–22.
47. Stevenson-Hamilton contributed articles to this journal for many years; see for example, 'Game Preservation in the Transvaal', *Journal of the Society for the Preservation of the Wild Fauna of the Empire* 2, 1905, pp. 20–45.
48. S-HA, Diary entries 25, 26, 30 May 1910, 7 June 1910.
49. TA CS334 6821/03, Lagden to Colonial Secretary, 2 September 1903.
50. J. Stevenson-Hamilton, *Animal Life in Africa* (London, 1912), pp. 20, 27.
51. TA SNA52 NA1904/02, Stevenson-Hamilton to Lagden, 4 September 1902.
52. TA SNA178 NA2536/03, Report on northern and western extension of Sabi Game Reserve, 13 October 1903.
53. Cent. LDE26 44, Memorandum by Stevenson-Hamilton, 29 October 1902; Memorandum of the Department of Native Affairs, 6 April 1903.
54. TA SNA188 NA3112/03, TLOA Report for year ending 31 October 1903.
55. S-HA, Diary entry 28 October 1902.
56. JPL TLOA, vol. 1, Report for year ending 31 October 1904.
57. Executive Council Resolution 676, 17 August 1903.
58. TA SNA98 NA266/03, Ledeboer to Resident Magistrate, Pietersburg, 19 December 1902; CS285 4031/05, Secretary for Native Affairs to Assistant Colonial Secretary, 2 April 1903, Secretary for Native Affairs to Assistant Colonial Secretary, 22 April 1903.
59. Executive Council Resolution 365, 4/5 May 1903.
60. TA SNA178 NA2536/03, Report on Singwitsi Game Reserve, 13 October 1903.
61. S-HA, Diary entries 14, 23 July 1902.
62. TA SNA52 NA1904/02, Stevenson-Hamilton to Lagden, 4 September 1902.
63. S-HA, Diary entries, 3 March 1903; 5, 9 April 1903, and relating to A. A. Fraser 1 July 1905.
64. TA SNA15 295/02, Secretary of the Transvaal Administration to Secretary for Native Affairs, 18 June 1900.
65. TA SNA225 NA1477/04, Estimates for 1904–1905.
66. S-HA, Diary entry 25 June 1903.
67. TA AGT66 A1403/05.
68. TA TPS9 3086, Stevenson-Hamilton to Gorges, 10 October 1906.

69. A SNA40 NA13033/02, Stevenson-Hamilton to Hogge, 1 August 1902; MM19 CM3091/03, Secretary of Mines to Lawley, 1 October 1903; LtG65 73/6; Executive Committee Resolution 1303, 23 November 1904.
70. Annual Report of the Government Game Reserves 1905-1906 in *Transvaal Administration Reports, 1905-1906*.
71. TA CS338 6992/03, Assistant Colonial Secretary to Secretary Law Department, 21 October 1903.
72. TA LD463 AG2805/03, Statement by Jarvis, [undated].
73. S-HA, Diary entries 4, 11 January 1904.
74. S-HA, Diary entries 2, 31 October 1904; 3 November 1902.
75. S-HA, Diary entries 17 January 1903, 6, 9, 15 April 1903, 24 June 1903, 2 October 1904; TA SNA300 NA3647/05, Lagden to Colonial Secretary, 30 November 1905.
76. S-HA, Diary entries 26 February 1903, 8, 22 June 1905.
77. S-HA, Diary entry 22 June 1905.
78. TA SNA158 NA1702/03, Lagden to Fraser, 3 April 1905.
79. *Transvaal Leader*, 15 January 1905.
80. S-HA, Diary entry 13 December 1902.
81. Stevenson-Hamilton, *Animal Life*, p.27.
82. TA SNA52 NA1904/02, Stevenson-Hamilton to Lagden, 4 September 1902.
83. TA SNA50 NA1751/02, Stevenson-Hamilton to McInerney, 18 August 1902; Native Commissioner, Lydenburg to Secretary for Native Affairs, 18 November 1902; KNP Stevenson-Hamilton Documents in Trust, Report by ranger Gray, 1-7 October 1902; Report by ranger Gray, 5-12 November 1902.
84. TA SNA169 NA2063/03, Report on the Sabi Game Reserve for the year ending August 1903.
85. TA SNA321 1321/06, F. Steinaecker to Secretary for Native Affairs, 4 April 1906.
86. TA SNA178 NA2536/03, Report on Singwitsi Game Reserve, 13 October 1903. This was also the opinion of the Sub Native Commissioner at Sibasa: see TA SNA343 3384/06, C. N. Manning to Native Commissioner Soutpansberg, 4 October 1906.
87. S-HA, Diary entry 16 September 1903.
88. TA SNA193 NA177/04, Stevenson-Hamilton to Secretary for Native Affairs, 5 January 1904.
89. TA SNA392 NA4321/07, Native Commissioner Northern Division to Secretary for Native Affairs, 7 April 1908; Stevenson-Hamilton to Assistant Colonial Secretary, 24 April 1908.
90. Annual Report of the Government Game Reserves 1903-1904, in *Transvaal Administration Reports, 1904*.
91. KNP Stevenson-Hamilton Documents in Trust, List of cases (Natives), 1903, 1, 4 February 1903; 28 February 1903; 18, 27 March 1903.
92. TA CS334 6821/03, Lagden to Colonial Secretary, 2 September 1903.
93. TA SNA169 NA2063/03, Report on the Sabi Game Reserve for the year ending August 1903.
94. TA TPS8 3075, Annual Report of the Government Game Reserves, 1908-1909.
95. *Debates of the Legislative Assembly*, A. Woolls-Sampson, cols 1425-6, 24 July 1907.
96. TA TPS8 3075, Annual Report of the Government Game Reserves, 1908-1909.

Creating a National Park

1. Stevenson-Hamilton, *South African Eden*, p.223.
2. This is stressed in R. Nash, *Wilderness and the American Mind* (New Haven, 1982) and A. Runte, *National Parks: The American Experience* (Lincoln, Nebraska, 1979).
3. Powell, *Environmental Management in Australia*, p.53.
4. TA TPS11 TA3087, vol.1, TGPA to Secretary to the Administrator, 21 July 1910.

5. TA TPS11 TA3087, vols 1, 2 and 3.
6. TA TPS5 TA3018, Report of the Transvaal Game Protection Association for the year ended 30 September 1912; TA TPS5 TA3037, Reports of the Piet Retief Magistrate, 27 January 1914 and 15 June 1916, Marx to Magistrate, Piet Retief, 10 June 1920.
7. TA TPS5 TA3037, Native Commissioner, Piet Retief to Provincial Secretary, 27 January 1921; Marx to Magistrate, Piet Retief, 10 June 1920.
8. 'News from the Bushbuckridge District', *Transvaal Police Magazine*, 15 January 1911.
9. TA TPS8 TA3075, Gorges to Stevenson-Hamilton, 3 June 1909.
10. *Votes and Proceedings of the Provincial Council*, 14 and 15 June 1911.
11. Stevenson-Hamilton, *South African Eden*, pp. 134–35; *Report of the Game Reserves Commission*, TP5-18, (Pretoria, 1918), p.6.
12. TA TPS7 TA3054, Stevenson-Hamilton to Provincial Secretary, 12 February 1913; Provincial Secretary to Secretary for Lands, 11 June 1913.
13. Cent. [Central Archives, Pretoria] LDE288 3081, vol.2, Secretary for Lands to Provincial Secretary, 10 August 1916.
14. TA TPB513 TA1232, Minute of the Acting Under-Secretary for Mines, [undated].
15. TA TPS8 2/3072, Report of the Acting Inspector of Mines Pretoria, 11 November 1911.
16. TA TPS8 TA2/3072, Provincial Secretary to Stevenson-Hamilton, 7 November 1912.
17. JPL TLOA Sub-Committee Minute Book, Minutes of 13 February 1913 and 17 October 1916.
18. JPL TLOA Sub-Committee Minute Book, Minutes of 26 September 1916.
19. Cent. LDE288 3081, vol.2, Stevenson-Hamilton to Rissik, 25 August 1913. The private farms, on the boundary of the Kruger National Park, which were excised from the game reserve area were at first utilized by owners as hunting lodges. In the 1950s many joined the Sabi-Sand Wildtuin, a private game reserve enterprise. More recently, some – such as Londolozi, MalaMala and Sabi-Sabi, have become luxurious and lucrative tourist venues.
20. WLS [Wildlife Society Archives] TGPA Minutes 1902–1920, Annual General Meeting, 7 November 1911.
21. WLS TGPA Minutes 1902–1920, Annual General Meeting, 14 January 1913.
22. WLS TGPA Minutes 1902–1920, Minutes of 7 December 1910.
23. TA TPS7 TA3054, TGPA Minutes of Annual General Meeting, 7 November 1911.
24. TA TPS7 3054, Stevenson-Hamilton to Provincial Secretary, 26 November 1911, Provincial Secretary to TGPA, 23 February 1912.
25. Proclamation 48 of 1914 made provision for the area between the Groot Letaba and Olifants Rivers to be added to the Sabi Game Reserve, but the land was later transferred from the Sabi to the Singwitsi Game Reserve.
26. TA TPS7 TA3054, Secretary for Lands to Provincial Secretary, 4 February 1913.
27. TA TPS7 TA3054, Secretary for Lands to Provincial Secretary, 4 December 1913.
28. TA TPS8 TA3075, Annual Reports of the Sabi and Singwitsi Game Reserves for 1912, 1913, 1914, 1915 and 1916.
29. J. Stevenson-Hamilton, 'The Transvaal Game Sanctuary', *Journal of the African Society* 25(99), 1926, p.214.
30. See, for example, Stevenson-Hamilton, 'The Relation between Game and Tsetse-Flies', pp. 113–18; J. Stevenson-Hamilton, 'Tsetse Fly and the Rinderpest Epidemic of 1896', *South African Journal of Science* 53(8), 1957, pp. 216–18.
31. J. Hackel and E.J. Carruthers, 'Swaziland's Twentieth Century Wildlife Preservation Efforts: The Present as a Continuation of the Past', *Environmental History Review* 17(3), Fall 1993, pp.61–84; S. Brooks, 'Playing the Game: The Struggle for Wildlife Protection in Zululand, 1910–1930', (M.A. dissertation, Queen's University, 1990); A. de V. Minnaar, 'Nagana, Big-game Drives and the Zululand Game Reserves (1890s–1950s)', *Contree* 25, 1989, pp. 12–21.
32. Wits [University of the Witwatersrand, Manuscript Collection] A1403/1, F.C. Selous Papers, Stevenson-Hamilton to Selous, 12 September 1911.
33. W.C. Everhart, *The National Park Service* (Boulder, Colorado, 1983), p.5.

34. Curson and Hugo, 'Preservation of Game', p.412; *House of Assembly Debates*, col.4372, 31 May 1926.
35. *Debates of the Legislative Assembly*, cols 1425–6, 24 July 1907.
36. Stevenson-Hamilton, *South African Eden*, pp.123–4; J. Stevenson-Hamilton, *The Kruger National Park* (Pretoria, 1928), p.3. This was repeated by Labuschagne, in *The Kruger Park*, p.14.
37. TA TPS7 TA3054, Stevenson-Hamilton to Provincial Secretary, 12 February 1913.
38. Cent. LDE288 3081, vol.2, Stevenson-Hamilton to Rissik, 25 August 1913.
39. TA TPS5 TA3018, Report of the Transvaal Game Protection Association for the year ended 30 September 1912; WLS TGPA Minutes 1902–1920, Annual General Meeting, 14 January 1913.
40. JPL TLOA Sub-Committee Minutes, Minutes of 13 February 1913 and 13 May 1913; TA TPS7 TA3054, Extracts from Annual Report of the Transvaal Land Owners' Association, 1913.
41. *Votes and Proceedings of the Provincial Council*, 26 June 1913 to 25 September 1913.
42. TA TPS5 TA3018, Annual Report of the TGPA for 1914 and 1915.
43. *Votes and Proceedings of the Provincial Council*, 17 March 1916.
44. Cent. LDE26 44/1, Smuts to Minister of Lands, 29 May 1914.
45. TA TPS7 TA3054, Smuts to Rissik, 26 May 1914.
46. They were S.H. Coetzee, T.J. Kleinenberg (who was replaced by J.F. Ludorf), A. Grant, C. Wade, F.A.W. Lucas and H. de Waal.
47. TA TPS8 TA3072, Acting Provincial Secretary to Acting Warden, 16 July 1917.
48. Transvaal Province, *Report of the Game Reserves Commission* TP5–18 (Pretoria, 1918), pp.9–10.
49. Stevenson-Hamilton, *South African Eden*, pp.155–64; S-HA, Diary entry 25 March 1920; TA TPB1309 TA10841, Warden to Provincial Secretary, 12 August 1920; KNP K42 KNP28/2, Fraser to Provincial Secretary, 3 November 1919, Provincial Secretary to Fraser, 27 December 1919. Fraser might have been attempting deliberately to sabotage Stevenson-Hamilton's administrative efforts. Some years later, Stevenson-Hamilton discovered correspondence of Fraser's which showed that Fraser had despised his superior, although he had always appeared to be polite and friendly; see S-HA, Diary entry 25 January 1925.
50. TA TPS8 TA3075, Stevenson-Hamilton to Provincial Secretary, 3 May 1920.
51. J. Stevenson-Hamilton, 'Empire Fauna in 1922', *Journal of the Society for the Preservation of the Fauna of the Empire*, Part II, July 1922, p.38.
52. Curson and Hugo, 'Preservation of Game', pp.405, 414–16.
53. WLS TGPA Minutes 1902–1920, Minutes of 15 January 1919.
54. TA TPS7 TA3054, vol.3, Memorandum of Provincial Secretary, 23 September 1920.
55. TA TPS7 TA3054, vol.3, Approval of memorandum by Executive Committee, 21 December 1920; Notes on Departmental Conference, 25 February 1921; Cent. LDE537 7748/1, vol.1, Report on the conference of 25 February 1921, 4 March 1921.
56. TA TPS7 TA3054, vol.3, Notes on Departmental Conference, 25 February 1921.
57. Ibid.; Cent. LDE537 7748/1, vol.1, Minute of Department of Lands, 11 October 1921.
58. Cent. LDE537 7748/1, vol.1, Private Secretary of the Minister of Lands to Sommerville, 22 February 1922.
59. Cent. LDE537 7748/1, vol.1, Secretary to the Prime Minister to Secretary for Lands, 6 November 1922.
60. Details of this inspection can be found in the diary of surveyor Schoch; Wits A839, H.E. Schoch Papers, Db3.
61. TA TPS7 TA3054, vol.3, Annual Report of the Transvaal Land Owners' Association for the year ended 28 February 1923; Cent. LDE537 7748/1, vol.1, Memorandum of the Department of Lands, 19 December 1922.
62. By Proclamation 71 of 5 December 1923 the combined area was called 'The Transvaal Game Reserve' and referred to as a 'proposed national park'.
63. WLS H.B. Papenfus file, Stevenson-Hamilton to Grobler, 5 October 1925.
64. S-HA, Diary entries 12 February 1925, 2 March 1925, 9 December 1925.
65. D. O'Meara, *Volkskapitalisme: Class, Capital and Ideology in the Development of Afrikaner Nationalism, 1934–1948* (Johannesburg, 1983), p.34.

66. Details of these land exchanges can be found in Cent. LDE563–570.
67. R. G. Morrell, 'Rural Transformations in the Transvaal: The Middelburg District, 1919 to 1930' (M.A. thesis, University of the Witwatersrand, 1983), pp.238–9.
68. *Rand Daily Mail*, 15, 17 May 1922.
69. TA TPS7 TA3054, vol. 3, Secretary for Lands to Provincial Secretary, 28 September 1923.
70. T. Gutsche, *The History and Social Significance of Motion Pictures in South Africa, 1895–1940* (Cape Town, 1972), pp. 313–18.
71. I. Hofmeyr, 'Popularizing History: The Case of Gustav Preller', *Journal of African History* 29(3), 1988, pp. 521–35.
72. D. Reitz, *No Outspan* (London, 1943), p.69.
73. D. Reitz, *Commando* (London, 1929), p.126.
74. *House of Assembly Debates*, cols 4366–7, 31 May 1926.
75. CA A848, Stratford Caldecott Collection, 2(6), S. Caldecott to W. A. Caldecott, 4 February 1926; *House of Assembly Debates*, col. 4369, 31 May 1926.
76. CA A848, Stratford Caldecott Collection, 2(4), Caldecott to Stevenson–Hamilton, 6 March 1926.
77. TA A878, J.J.S. Smit Collection, vol.15, Grobler to Smit, 19 January 1926.
78. WLS H.B. Papenfus file, Stevenson-Hamilton to Papenfus, 29 December 1925.
79. CA A848, Stratford Caldecott Collection, 2(4), Stevenson-Hamilton to Caldecott, 3 April 1926, the emphasis is in the original.
80. Stevenson-Hamilton had sought support from the National Monuments Commission in March 1925; see KNP K5 KNP5, vol.2, Stevenson–Hamilton to Secretary Monuments Commission, 15 March 1925; see also CA A848, Stratford Caldecott Collection, 2(6), S. Caldecott to W.A. Caldecott, 4 February 1926.
81. CA A848, Stratford Caldecott Collection, 1(1), W.A. Caldecott to S. Caldecott, 17 January 1926; W. A. Caldecott to S. Caldecott, 14 February 1926. Sir Lionel and Lady Phillips were vehemently opposed to the name, and Stevenson-Hamilton feared that Lady Phillips had 'ruined things' with Grobler by her objection; see Stratford Caldecott Collection, 2(4), Caldecott to Stevenson-Hamilton, 24 March 1926; S-HA, Diary entry 2 April 1926.
82. CA A848, Stratford Caldecott Collection, 2(6), S. Caldecott to W. A. Caldecott, 4 February 1926.
83. *The Senate of South Africa: Debates*, col. 1079, 3 June 1926.
84. CA A848, Stratford Caldecott Collection, 2(6), S. Caldecott to W. A. Caldecott, 4 February 1926.
85. CA A848, Stratford Caldecott Collection, 2(4), Stevenson-Hamilton to Caldecott, 19 January 1926.
86. S-HA, Diary entry 6 August 1925.
87. S. Caldecott, 'Create a National Park!', *South African Nation* 2(85), 21 November 1925.
88. *Cape Argus*, 11 June 1926.
89. *Rand Daily Mail*, 21 November 1925.
90. CA A848, Stratford Caldecott Collection, 2(4), Stevenson-Hamilton to Caldecott, 23 March 1926.
91. *Cape Argus*, 11 January 1926, letter from S. Caldecott.
92. *Cape Argus*, 23 February 1926, letter from Charles Astley Maberly. See also, A. K. Haagner, 'The Conservation of Wild Life in South Africa', *South African Journal of Industries*, December 1925, pp.766–7.
93. KNP K27, Caldecott to Stevenson-Hamilton, 1 July 1926; H. R. Carey, 'Saving the Animal Life of Africa: A New Method and a Last Chance', *Journal of Mammalogy* 7(2), 1926, p. 77.
94. CA A848, Stratford Caldecott Collection, 2(4), Stevenson-Hamilton to Caldecott, 9 January 1926; S-HA, Diary entry 22 March, 1926.
95. Perusal of almost any South African daily newspaper of the time will bear out this comment, as will many issues of *The Farmer's Weekly* and *Die Huisgenoot* in 1926.
96. CA A848, Stratford Caldecott Collection, 2(8), Baden Powell to Caldecott, 30 September 1927; 2(4), Caldecott to Stevenson-Hamilton, 21 May 1926; 2(5), 4(1), 4(2).
97. CA A848, Stratford Caldecott Collection, 4(1).

Notes to pages 63–72

98. *House of Assembly Debates*, cols. 4367 and 4376–7, 31 May 1926.
99. J. Stevenson-Hamilton, 'The Great Game of South Africa', *South African Railways and Harbours Magazine*, December 1927, pp. 20–32.
100. WLS H. B. Papenfus file, Selby to Papenfus, 4 March 1926.
101. Haagner, 'Conservation of Wild Life', pp. 766–7.
102. Ibid., pp. 763–5.
103. Cent. CEN691 E7717, Fuller to Stevenson-Hamilton, 16 April 1926.
104. WLS H. B. Papenfus file, Stevenson-Hamilton to Papenfus, 10 March 1926, 22 July 1926.
105. *House of Assembly Debates*, cols 4366–81, 31 May 1926; *The Senate of South Africa: Debates*, cols 1077–11, 3 June 1926.
106. *House of Assembly Debates*, col. 4367, 31 May 1926.
107. *House of Assembly Debates*, cols 4371–2, 31 May 1926.
108. CA A848, Stratford Caldecott Collection, 2(4), Caldecott to Stevenson-Hamilton, 22 June 1926.
109. S-HA, Diary entry 28 July 1920 and 8 January 1926.
110. K. Thomas, *Man and the Natural World: Changing Attitudes in England, 1500–1800* (London, 1983), p. 301.
111. A. Graham, *The Gardeners of Eden* (London, 1973), p. 196; *House of Assembly Debates*, col. 4371, 31 May 1926.
112. WLS H.B. Papenfus file, Stevenson-Hamilton to Papenfus, 13 February 1926; Cent. LDE537 7748/1, vol. 1, Stevenson-Hamilton to Reitz, 12 April 1922, Stevenson-Hamilton to Sommerville, 12 April 1922.

Politics and the Park

1. National Parks Act, No. 56, 1926; *Senate Debates*, cols 1081, 1083, 3 June 1926; *House of Assembly Debates*, col. 4369, 31 May 1926.
2. S-HA, Diary entry 3 September 1926.
3. *Dictionary of South African Biography*, vol. 3, p. 762.
4. CA A848, Stratford Caldecott Collection, 2(4), Stevenson-Hamilton to Caldecott, 15 June 1926.
5. CA A848, Stratford Caldecott Collection, 2(4), Stevenson-Hamilton to Caldecott, 5 February 1929.
6. London, 1912.
7. CA A848, Stratford Caldecott Collection, 2(4), Stevenson-Hamilton to Caldecott, 5 February 1929.
8. S-HA, Stevenson-Hamilton to National Parks Board, 19 January 1927.
9. S-HA, National Parks Board to Stevenson-Hamilton, 14 March 1927.
10. Hoek Report, 'Verslag oor 'n ondersoek van die bestuur van die verskeie nasionale parke en die Nasionale Parkeraad se administrasie', 1 September 1952, p. 13.
11. S-HA, Diary entry 17 June 1927.
12. NPB [National Parks Board] Minutes 16 September 1926; S-HA, Diary entry 3 February 1928.
13. S-HA, Diary entries, 15 May 1939, 16 November 1944, 28 September 1933, 12 October 1934, 27 April 1942.
14. S-HA, Diary entry 13 November 1942.
15. NPB Minutes 9 December 1932.
16. S-HA, Pirow to Stevenson-Hamilton, 30 October 1941.
17. KNP Stevenson-Hamilton documents in trust, Reitz to Stevenson-Hamilton, 10 October 1941.
18. S-HA, Diary entries 15 November 1944, 3 April 1945, 21 June 1946.
19. S-HA, Diary entry 3 August 1926.
20. S-HA, Diary entry 4 May 1937.
21. S-HA, Diary entry 18 July 1945; NPB Minutes 13 November 1950.

22. S-HA, Diary entries 21 and 26 March 1933.
23. S-HA, Diary entry 16 November 1944.
24. S-HA, Diary entry 5 April 1903.
25. S-HA, Diary entry 30 March 1940.
26. S-HA, Diary entry 14 June 1926.
27. S-HA, Diary entry 20 March 1937.
28. S-HA, Diary entries 1939 *passim.*
29. S-HA, Diary entry 30 April 1946.
30. KNP Files K11 KNP2, 4 October 1944; 14 November 1994; 20 November 1945; 22 November 1945; KNP K30, report March 1946.
31. S-HA, Diary entry 20 June 1945.
32. S-HA, Diary entry 1 May 1946.
33. KNP K11, Stevenson-Hamilton to National Parks Board, 3 February 1927.
34. CA A848, Stratford Caldecott Collection, 3(11), Mrs Wolhuter to Caldecott, 5 September 1926.
35. KNP Annual Report of the National Parks Board, 1929 and 1930; S-HA, Diary entry 7 July 1929.
36. CA A848, Stratford Caldecott Collection, 2(4), Caldecott to Stevenson-Hamilton, 22 June 1926.
37. S-HA, Diary entry 15 July 1929.
38. S-HA, Diary entry 30 October 1937.
39. S-HA, Diary entry 8 January 1933.
40. Cape Town, n.d.
41. KNP K11, M.E. Wood, 'A visit to the Kruger National Park, 1935'.
42. KNP T.C. Sinclair, 'Recollections of a visit to the Kruger National Park in 1932.'
43. KNP K33, KNP16/5/6/2/3.
44. S-HA, Diary entry 19 June 1930.
45. KNP NPB Meetings 12 May 1931; 8 July 1931.
46. *The Star* 5, 7, 11, 17, 21, 25 August 1937; KNP Veldwagters Dagboek, Bowling to National Parks Board, January 1946.
47. Stevenson-Hamilton, *South African Eden, passim.*
48. KNP National Parks Board meeting 28 January 1939; Annual Report of the National Parks Board 1938.
49. KNP K30 KNP30, 'General report on the Kruger National Park', [1946].
50. Annual Report of the National Parks Board, 1940.
51. KNP, S. Joubert, 'Masterplan for the Kruger National Park', p. 1.
52. H. Rompel, 'Wildtuin op die Kruispad', *Huisgenoot*, 1390, 12 November 1948.
53. KNP Joubert, 'Masterplan', p. 2.
54. *The Star*, 13 September 1993.
55. TA A787, Preller Collection, vol. 161, p. 202.
56. See E. Hobsbawm and T. Ranger, eds, *The Invention of Tradition* (Cambridge, 1983); Maclean, C.R. *Charles Rawden Maclean: The Natal Papers of 'John Ross'* edited by S. Gray (Durban, 1992); Thompson, *Political Mythology of Apartheid*; A. Grundlingh and H. Sapire, 'From Feverish Festival to Repetitive Ritual? The Changing Fortunes of Great Trek Mythology in an Industrializing South Africa, 1938–1988, *South African Historical Journal* 21 (1989), pp. 19–38, all of which deal with myth construction and effect.
57. Labuschagne, *The Kruger Park*, pp. 111–12.
58. Minutes of the Volksraad, Article 671, 3 July 1894.
59. M. Juta, *The Pace of the Ox: A Life of Paul Kruger* (Cape Town, 1975), pp. 210–12. The same wording is used by J. Fisher in his *Paul Kruger: His Life and Times* (London, 1974), pp. 233–4.
60. Behrens, '"Oom Paul's" Great Fight'; 'His Name is Skukuza'; 'Hunter Turns Protector: The Story of Henry Wolhuter'.
61. Behrens, 'Paul Kruger – Wildbeskermer'.

Notes to pages 83–87 135

62. For example, in publicity material prepared by professional authors, and reminiscences and field guides by game rangers or Parks Board employees which contain prefaces, forewords or other indications of approval from senior members of the Board.
63. Labuschagne, *Kruger National Park*, pp. 26, 28.
64. J. Carruthers, 'The Dongola Wild Life Sanctuary: "Psychological Blunder, Economic Folly and Political Monstrosity" or "More Valuable than Rubies and Gold"?', *Kleio* 24, 1992, pp. 82–100. This sanctuary is not mentioned in any popular record, although it was debated in parliament over a five-year period and was responsible for the longest Select Committee Report on record.
65. NPB, Minutes 12 February 1951.
66. Smuts's conservation efforts include his founding of the Rustenburg Game Reserve in 1909 and his close personal interest in establishing the Kruger National Park; see Carruthers, 'Game Protection', chapters 6, 7 and 8. His lack of interest in such projects is alleged by A. Cattrick in *Spoor of Blood* (Cape Town, 1959), p. 155 and by Meiring in *Kruger Park Saga*, p. 18.
67. Labuschagne, *60 Years*, p. 104. This book was published in 1958, thus commemorating the Sabi Game Reserve's proclamation rather than that of the national park.
68. Meiring, *Kruger Park Saga*, p. 25; Meiring, *Behind the Scenes*, p. 47.
69. Stevenson-Hamilton was in Pietermaritzburg with his regiment, the Inniskilling Dragoons, in 1890 – thus making Meiring's assertion 'plausible' – an essential element in a successful myth.
70. Labuschagne, *60 Years*; p. 32, Labuschagne, *Kruger National Park*, pp. 14–16; Behrens, 'His Name is Skukuza'. Tattersall's *Skukuza* is also full of invented anecdotes but is principally a paraphrase in Afrikaans of *South African Eden*.
71. S-HA, National Parks Board to Stevenson-Hamilton, 13 June 1947; Secretary of Lands to Stevenson-Hamilton, 16 September 1948.
72. S-HA, B.A. Key to Stevenson-Hamilton, 12 December 1948.
73. Personal communication, Chief Director, Kruger National Park, 24 August 1987; Pienaar, *Neem uit die Verlede*, pp. 395–8.
74. O'Meara, *Volkskapitalisme*. The Broederbond connections between the Board and its employees have yet to be researched. Certainly at least E.A.N. Le Riche, of the Kalahari Gemsbok National Park, has been recorded as a member; I. Wilkins and H. Strydom, *The Super-Afrikaners: Inside the Afrikaner Broederbond* (Johannesburg, 1979), p. A146.
75. S-HA, Diary entry 1 July 1954.
76. *Rand Daily Mail*, 27 October 1952, 1 November 1952.
77. S-HA, Diary entry 16 February 1952.
78. S-HA, Diary entry 8 January 1934.
79. NPB, Minutes 20 October 1952.
80. Labuschagne, *60 Years*, p. 71.
81. Annual Report of the Sabi Game Reserve 1903, p. 48; H.H. Methuen, *Life in the Wilderness or Wanderings in South Africa* (London, 1846); Bryden, 'The Extermination of Great Game in South Africa'; J.A. Nicolls and W. Eglington, *The Sportsman in South Africa* (London, 1892); Ofcansky, 'History of Game Preservation in British East Africa'.
82. A.M. Brynard, 'Die Nasionale Parke van die Republiek van Suid-Afrika – Die Verlede en Die Hede', *Koedoe* 1977, Supplement on the Proceedings of a Symposium on the State of Nature Conservation in Southern Africa, p. 24.
83. NPB, Minutes 11 March and 23 September 1968.
84. Hobsbawm and Ranger, *Invention of Tradition*, pp. 1, 9.
85. Labuschagne, *60 Years*, Foreword by Board Director Rocco Knobel; Labuschagne, *Kruger National Park*, Foreword by Prime Minister B.J. Vorster.
86. *Koedoe*, 1977 supplement, p. 9.
87. A view shared by the Board, see Labuschagne, *60 Years*, p. 72.
88. M. Wilson and L.M. Thompson, eds, *The Oxford History of South Africa* (Oxford, 1969–1975), vol. 2, p. 373.

89. Stevenson-Hamilton, *The Low Veld*, dedication; *South African Eden*, chapter 11.
90. Meiring, *Kruger Park Saga*, p. 17.
91. Labuschagne, *60 Years*, pp. 26–27, pp. 63–64.
92. See for example, Stevenson-Hamilton, *South African Eden*, pp. 210–12.
93. In Brown, *A History of Scientific Endeavour*, see Dr Douglas Hey, 'The History and Status of Nature Conservation in South Africa', pp. 132–63.
94. Thompson, *Political Mythology*, pp. 2, 12.

The 'Other Side of the Fence'

1. E. Koch, D. Cooper and H. Coetzee, *Water, Waste and Wildlife: The Politics of Ecology in South Africa* (London, 1990), p. 15. See also J. Cock and E. Koch, *Going Green: People, Politics and the Environment in South Africa* (Cape Town, 1991).
2. SABC Radio statement by the African National Congress, 9 March 1993; *Business Day*, 5 March 1993; and *The Star*, 9 March 1993; This has happened in Zimbabwe according to T. Ranger, 'Whose Heritage? The Case of the Matobo National Park', *Journal of Southern African Studies* 15(2), January 1989, pp. 217–49.
3. Ranger, 'Whose Heritage?', p. 227.
4. Harris, *Portraits of the Game*, p. 159; *Wild Sports*, pp. 159, 264.
5. TA A68, F. da Costa Leal Accession, p. 78.
6. Thomas, *Man and the Natural World*, p. 27.
7. TA SS1875 R3068/89, Erasmus to Superintendent of Natives, 22 September 1890. For a recent appraisal of Erasmus's career see P. Delius, 'Abel Erasmus: Power and Profit in the Eastern Transvaal' in P. Delius and W. Beinart eds, *Putting a Plough to the Ground: Accumulation and Dispossession in Rural South Africa, 1850 to 1930* (Johannesburg, 1986).
8. TA SS302 R3130/78, Letter to Administrator, 31 August 1878; Minutes of the Volksraad, Article 674, 3 July 1894.
9. TA CS396 10370/03, TGPA to Colonial Secretary, 18 November 1903; J. Stevenson-Hamilton, 'Game Preservation in the Transvaal', *Blackwood's Magazine*, March 1906, p. 409.
10. TA CS396 10370/03, TGPA to Colonial Secretary, 18 November 1903; TA SNA305 NA11/6, Commissioner for Native Affairs to Secretary of Native Affairs, 11 January 1906; TAD405 G946/06, Assistant Colonial Secretary to TGPA, 23 January 1906. See also TA SNA305 11/06, Assistant Colonial Secretary to Secretary of Native Affairs, 30 December 1905.
11. TA CS396 10370/03, TGPA to Colonial Secretary, 18 November 1903.
12. TA SNA305 NA11/6, Commissioner for Native Affairs to Secretary of Native Affairs, 11 January 1906; TAD405 G946/06, Assistant Colonial Secretary to TGPA, 23 January 1906. See also TA SNA305 11/06, Assistant Colonial Secretary to Secretary of Native Affairs, 30 December 1905.
13. TA SNA321 1321/06, F. Steinacker to Secretary of Native Affairs, 4 April 1906; Cent. NTS 7612 9/329, Chief Native Commissioner to Secretary of Native Affairs, 11 November 1946. TA SNA169 NA2063/03, Report on the Sabi Game Reserve for the year ending August 1903; TA SNA52 NA1904/02, Stevenson-Hamilton to Lagden, 4 September 1902; KNP Stevenson-Hamilton Documents in Trust, Reports by ranger Gray, 1–7 October 1902 and 5–12 November 1902; TA SNA169 NA2063/03, Report on the Sabi Game Reserve for the year ending August 1903; TA SNA50 NA1751/02, Stevenson-Hamilton to McInerney, 18 August 1902; Native Commissioner Lydenburg to Secretary of Native Affairs, 18 November 1902.
14. Braack, *Kruger National Park*, p. 12.
15. Stevenson-Hamilton, *Animal Life*, p. 27; KNP Annual Report of the National Parks Board, 1928, p. 4; 1932, p. 5.
16. S-HA, Diary entry 23 April 1904; Cent. LDE26 44/2, Under-Secretary to Inspector of Lands, 23 May 1905.

Notes to pages 92–97

17. In 1926 the 'respectable sum' of £444 was raised; KNP Annual Report of the Kruger National Park, 1928, p. 6.
18. KNP Opsienersjaarverslae, vol.2, Annual Report of the Warden, Kruger National Park, 1930.
19. TA TPS8 Annual Report of the Sabi and Singwitsi Game Reserves for 1920, p.3.
20. KNP Rangers' Diaries, Section 4, June 1936, pp.1–2.
21. TA TPS8 TA3075, Annual Report of the Sabi and Singwitsi Game Reserves for 1912.
22. TA TPB784 TA3006, Stevenson-Hamilton to Secretary to the Administrator, 13 March 1911.
23. TA TPS8 TA3075, Annual Report of the Sabi and Singwitsi Game Reserves for 1913.
24. TA TPS8 TA3075, Annual Report of the Sabi and Singwitsi Game Reserves for 1918.
25. TA TPS8 TA3075, Annual Report of the Sabi and Singwitsi Game Reserves for 1913.
26. TA TPS8 TA3075, Annual Report of the Sabi and Singwitsi Game Reserves for 1912.
27. TA TPS8 TA3075, Annual Report of the Sabi and Singwitsi Game Reserves for 1915.
28. WLS H.B. Papenfus file, Stevenson-Hamilton to Papenfus, 13 February 1926; Cent. LDE537 7748/1, vol. 1, Stevenson-Hamilton to Reitz, 12 April 1922, Stevenson-Hamilton to Sommerville, 12 April 1922.
29. Curson and Hugo, 'Preservation of Game', p. 401.
30. TA LD784 TA3006, Note to Colonial Secretary, 15 February 1909; KNP Stevenson-Hamilton Documents in Trust, List of cases (Natives), 1903, 1 February 1903; March 1903; 18 March 1903; 27 March 1903; KNP Rangers' Diaries January 1936, Section 3.
31. TA LD784 TA3006, Note to Colonial Secretary, 15 February 1909; KNP Stevenson-Hamilton Documents in Trust, List of cases (Natives), 1903, 1 February 1903; March 1903; 18 March 1903; 27 March 1903; KNP Rangers' Diaries January 1936, Section 3.
32. KNP Rangers' Diaries, Section 3, March 1936; Section 4, January 1938.
33. J. Berger, 'Wildlife Extension – A Participatory Approach to Conservation: A Case Study Among the Maasai People of Kenya' (Ph.D. thesis, University of California, Berkeley, 1989); p. 27.
34. TA TPS8 TA3075, Annual Reports of the Sabi and Singwitsi Game Reserves for 1912, 1913, 1914, 1916 and 1918.
35. KNP, H. Mockford, 'History of the Witwatersrand Native Labour Association in the Kruger National Park'.
36. TA TPB784 TA3006, Stevenson-Hamilton to Secretary to the Administrator, 15 February 1911.
37. Wits A839, H.E. Schoch Papers, Db3, 30 July 1923.
38. TA TPB1309 TA10841.
39. Cent. JUS385 3/651/23, Barberton Magistrate to Secretary for Justice, 21 October 1923.
40. Cent. JUS294 3/710/20, Secretary for Justice to Provincial Secretary, 24 September 1920.
41. Wits A839, H.E. Schoch Papers, Db3, 30 July 1923.
42. KNP K42 KNP28/2, Warden to Commissioner, 5 June 1924, Commissioner to Warden, 24 June 1924.
43. KNP Opsienersjaarverslae, vol. 2, Annual Report of the Warden, Kruger National Park, 1929.
44. KNP K42 28/1 Warden to Rowland Jones, 13 August 1938; Warden to Tomlinson, 13 September 1938; Deputy Commissioner to Warden, 16 September 1938.
45. Braack, *Kruger National Park*, p. 16.
46. S-HA, Diary entry 23 July 1902.
47. KNP Rangers' Diaries, 1940.
48. KNP Annual Report of the Sabi and Singwitsi Game Reserves for 1911, p. 3.
49. S. Trapido, 'Poachers, Proletarians and Gentry in the early 20th Century Transvaal', paper presented to the African Studies Institute, University of the Witwatersrand, March 1984, p. 20.
50. KNP Rangers' Diaries, Section 2, 1941, p. 1.
51. KNP K15 KNP3, Warden to all Rangers, 30 October 1937; KNP Annual Report of the National Parks Board, 1928, p.2; KNP Annual Report of the National Parks Board, 1931, p.2; KNP Annual Report of the National Parks Board, 1935, p. 4; S-HA, Diary entry 30 January 1946; KNP Newspaper cutting book I, 1945.

52. *Report of the Game Reserves Commission*, p.9; TA TPS8 TA3072, Acting Provincial Secretary to Acting Warden, 16 July 1917.
53. A recent popular source infers that without taking away territory from the Tsonga, there would have been no Kruger National Park; see Koch, *et al, Water, Waste and Wildlife*, p. 17.
54. For details of the history of the Makuleke and their removal from the Pafuri area see P. Harries, 'A Forgotten Corner of the Transvaal: Reconstructing the History of a Re-located Community through Oral Testimony and Song' in B. Bozzoli, ed., *Class, Community and Conflict* (Johannesburg, 1987).
55. KNP Annual Report of the Sabi Game Reserve, 1905, item B57; TA TPS8 TA3072, Acting Secretary for Native Affairs to Provincial Secretary, 1 April 1912; TA TPS8 TA3075, Annual Report of the Sabi and Singwitsi Game Reserves for 1913; TPS8 TA3072, Acting Secretary for Native Affairs to Assistant Colonial Secretary, 16 May 1908.
56. KNP Annual Report of the National Parks Board, 1932, p.5.
57. Cent. NTS 2527 147/293 I, 1910–1911; NTS 3589 853/308, 1930–1939; NTS 7612 8/329, 1922; KNP Minutes of the National Parks Board of Trustees, 1933; S-HA, Diary entry, 30 July 1933.
58. S-HA, Diary entry, 20 May 1933; TA SNA 392 4321/07; Cent. NTS 76/6 17/329, Assistant Native Commissioner Sibasa to Native Commissioner Louis Trichardt, 24 July 1933.
59. KNP Minutes of the National Parks Board, 19 March 1933; 3 May 1938; 11 May 1938; K1/7-9-10, Warden to Secretary National Parks Board, 30 October 1948.
60. 'Verslag oor 'n ondersoek van die bestuur van die verskeie nasionale parke en die Nasionale Parkeraad se administrasie', September 1952, p.136 (Hoek Report); KNP K7/6 K7/7, Van Graan to Chairman and members of the National Parks Board, 31 March 1950.
61. KNP Joubert, 'Masterplan' pp.136–7.
62. A good example of this can be found in R. Knobel, 'The Economic and Cultural Values of South African National Parks', in I. Player, ed., *Voices of the Wilderness* (Johannesburg, 1979).
63. KNP Joubert, 'Masterplan', p.96.
64. KNP Minutes of the National Parks Board, 4 April 1934, item 24.
65. S-HA, Diary entry 8 January 1933, 2 September 1937.
66. KNP Minutes of the National Parks Board, 19 September 1949, item 3.
67. Braack, *Kruger National Park*, p.162.
68. *The Graphic*, 25 June 1928; Prance, *Wonderland*.
69. Koch, *et al, Water Waste and Wildlife*, p.15 and Cock and Koch, *Going Green*.
70. *Koedoe*, 1977 Supplement, p.36.
71. *African Wild Life* 4(1), 1948.
72. Labuschagne, *60 Years*, pp.53 and 78.

'Playing God'

1. W. F. Lye, ed., *Andrew Smith's Journal of his Expedition into the Interior of South Africa, 1834–1836* (Cape Town, 1975), p.255.
2. Harris, *Portraits of the Game*, pp.83, 89, 117. See also Gray, *Southern African Literature*, p.98.
3. For example, see Harris, *Portraits of the Game*, pp.31, 74, 94, 121.
4. Harris, *Wild Sports*, p.197.
5. R. A. Caras, *Death as a Way of Life* (Boston, 1970), p.112.
6. On this subject, see for example, Lewis-Williams, *The Rock Art of Southern Africa*.
7. Gray, *Southern African Literature*, p.97.
8. Methuen, *Life in the Wilderness*, pp.107–8.
9. D. D. Lyell, ed., *African Adventure: Letters from Famous Big-game Hunters* (London, 1935), p.194.
10. Harris, *Portraits of the Game*, pp.62, 89.

11. Thomas, *Man and the Natural World*, p. 266.
12. P. Gillmore, *The Hunter's Arcadia* (London, 1886), p. vi.
13. Thomas, *Man and the Natural World*, p. 268.
14. D. Hammond and A. Jablow, *The Africa That Never Was: Four Centuries of British Writing about Africa* (New York, 1970), p. 124.
15. Y.F. Tuan, *Topophilia: A Study in Environmental Perception, Attitudes and Values* (Englewood Cliffs, New Jersey, 1974), p. 63.
16. Anderson, *Twenty-Five Years*, p. 27.
17. Cunynghame, *My Command in South Africa*, p. 281; Roche, *On Trek in the Transvaal*, p. 272; Anderson, *Twenty-Five Years*, p. 27.
18. Aylward, *The Transvaal of Today*, p. 239.
19. T. Baines, *The Gold Regions of South Eastern Africa* (London, 1877), p. xv.
20. Buxton, *Two African Trips*, p. 116.
21. Thomas, *Man and the Natural World*, p. 187.
22. Ofcansky, 'History of Game Preservation in British East Africa', p. 25.
23. Buxton, *Two African Trips*, p. 116.
24. Bryden, *Nature and Sport*, p. 299.
25. Bryden, *Nature and Sport*, p. viii.
26. Bryden, *Kloof and Karroo*, p. 402.
27. Selous's most popular books were *African Nature Notes and Reminiscences* (London, 1908) and *A Hunter's Wanderings in Africa* (London, 1881).
28. Buxton, *Two African Trips*, pp. 116, 119.
29. H.A. Bryden, 'The Extermination of Great Game in South Africa', *Fortnightly Review*, October, 1894, p. 540.
30. Chapman, *Memories of Fourscore Years*, p. 546.
31. Bryden, 'Extermination of Great Game', p. 546.
32. Bryden, *Gun and Camera*, p. 59.
33. Selous, *African Nature Notes*, vol. 1, p. 44.
34. See, for example, J.H. Patterson, *The Man-Eaters of Tsavo and Other East African Adventures* (London, 1907).
35. Lyell, *African Adventure*, chapter 3.
36. Graham, *Gardeners of Eden*, p. 83.
37. S-HA, Hornaday to Stevenson-Hamilton, 22 August 1912.
38. A.B. Percival, *A Game Ranger on Safari* (London, 1928); *A Game Ranger's Note-book* (London, 1924).
39. C.R.S. Pitman, *A Game Warden Takes Stock* (London, 1942) and *A Game Warden Among his Charges* (London, 1931).
40. Graham, *Gardeners of Eden*, p. 78.
41. Percival, *Game Ranger*, p. vi; Stevenson-Hamilton, *Animal Life*, p. x; 'Wild Life Ecology in Africa', *Associated Scientific and Technical Societies of South Africa*, 1941–1942, p. 102.
42. Graham, *Gardeners of Eden*, p. 88; Stevenson-Hamilton, for example, admits to never having seen an adult ant-lion, *Low Veld*, p. 147; Percival did not know, or care to know, the scientific name of the Blue Monkey, *Game Ranger*, p. 98.
43. Mackenzie, *Imperialism and the Natural World*, p. 187.
44. Selous, *African Nature Notes*, p. xiii.
45. Stevenson-Hamilton, *South African Eden*, p. 90.
46. Percival, *Game Ranger*, p. 48.
47. Stevenson-Hamilton, *Low Veld*, p. 88.
48. J. Stevenson-Hamilton, 'The Health of Wild Animals', *Journal of the South African Veterinary and Medical Association* 10(2), 1939, pp. 56–64.
49. Stevenson-Hamilton, *South African Eden*, p. 57; 'Wild Life Ecology', p. 98, 100; *Wild Life*, introduction.
50. Graham, *Gardeners of Eden*, p. 178.
51. J. Stevenson-Hamilton, 'Game Preservation in the Transvaal', *Society for the Protection of the Wild Fauna of the Empire*, 2, 1905, pp. 23, 42.

52. Pitman, *Game Warden among his Charges*, p.111.
53. Stevenson-Hamilton, *Low Veld*, pp.104, 149.
54. WLS H.B. Papenfus file, National Parks Board meeting 16 August 1937; KNP K1/11(II) KNP5/6, Warden to all rangers, 22 June 1937.
55. WLS H.B. Papenfus file, National Parks Board meeting, 16 August 1937.
56. KNP K11, Stevenson-Hamilton to Secretary NPB, 4 October 1944.
57. *Rand Daily Mail*, 30 August 1932.
58. Annual Report of the National Parks Board, 1931.
59. National Parks Board meeting, 21–22 June 1932.
60. National Parks Board meeting, 15 August 1936.
61. KNP K1/11(I) K29, W.A. Campbell to Secretary NPB, 27 February 1939.
62. KNP K47 K47/2, Secretary NPB to Warden, 5 April 1939. KNP K30 KNP30, Stevenson-Hamilton, 'General Report on the Kruger National Park' [March 1946].
63. Annual Report of the Kruger National Park, 1930.
64. See for example, R. Bigalke, 'Our National Parks; Past and Future', *South African Journal of Science*, 40, November 1943, pp.248–53; R. Bigalke, *National Parks and their Functions, with Special Reference to South Africa*, Pamphlet No.10, South African Biological Society (Pretoria, 1939).
65. S-HA, Diary entry 7 July 1933.
66. Stevenson-Hamilton, *South African Eden*, pp.210–12.
67. Stevenson-Hamilton, *South African Eden*, pp.292–8.
68. KNP K46 KNP34, Warden to Secretary NPB, 8 March 1945.
69. Stevenson-Hamilton, 'Wild Life Ecology', p.95.
70. WLS Report of the Society for the Year Ended 31 December 1943.
71. National Parks Board meeting, 8 November 1939, 6/7 November 1946; WLS Annual General Meeting, 21 September 1939.
72. KNP Stevenson-Hamilton Documents in Trust, A.J.A. Roux to Blaine, 6 November 1946; Minutes of the National Parks Board, 6/7 November 1946.
73. Minutes of the National Parks Board, 19 September 1949.
74. See for example, Minutes of the National Parks Board, 12 January 1950; 24 January 1950; 13 November 1950.
75. Annual Report of the Warden of the Kruger National Park 1957.
76. G. de Graaff, *Koedoe* 22, 1979, pp.89–107; R.F. Lawrence, *Koedoe* 20, 1977, pp.175–8.
77. Bigalke, 'Science and the Conservation of Wild Life', p.169.
78. I. Parker, 'Conservation Realism and the Future', paper presented to the Symposium on the Management of Large Mammals in African Conservation Areas, April 1982.
79. National Parks Board spokesman in a radio interview, 5 April 1993.
80. V. de Vos, 'The Practice of Culling in the Kruger National Park', paper presented to the Symposium on the Management of Large Mammals in African Conservation Areas, April 1982.
81. A. Chase, *Playing God in Yellowstone: The Destruction of America's First National Park* (San Diego, 1987).
82. Stevenson-Hamilton, *South African Eden*, p.255.

Epilogue

1. Bridgeland, F., 'Here's to you Doctor Robinson', *Living*, September 1993, pp.40 and 42.

Bibliography

OFFICIAL MANUSCRIPTS

SOUTH AFRICA

Transvaal Archives, Pretoria

South African Republic
Eerste Volksraad (EVR) – Minutes 1882 to 1899
Landdrost, Barberton (T32/44/163) – Correspondence files 1892 to 1900
Kommandant-Generaal (KG) – Correspondence files 1893 to 1900
Onderwys Departement (OD) – Correspondence files 1897 to 1898
Staatsprokureur (SP) – Correspondence files 1890 to 1899
Staatssekretaris (SS) – Incoming correspondence 1857 to 1899
Uitvoerende Raad (UR) – Minutes 1860 to 1899

Transvaal Colony
Auditor-General (AGT) – Correspondence files 1900 to 1910
Barberton Resident Magistrate (BN) – Correspondence files 1901 to 1902
Clerk of the Executive Council (EC) – Volume 32, 1903
Colonial Secretary (CS) – Correspondence files 1900 to 1906
Colonial Treasurer (CT) – Correspondence files 1903 to 1908
Director of Customs (DCU) – Correspondence files 1907
Executive Council of the Transvaal (ECO) – Files 1908 to 1910
Governor of the Transvaal and Orange River Colony (GOV) – Correspondence files 1901 to 1910
Legal Assistant to the Military Governor (LAJ) – Correspondence files 1900
Lieutenant Governor (LtG) – File series 73/1–23, 1902 to 1906; Correspondence files, volumes 2, 89, 124, 1903 to 1905
Military Governor Pretoria (MGP) – Correspondence files 1900

Prime Minister (PM) – Correspondence files 1907 to 1909
Private Secretary to the Governor of the Transvaal and Orange River Colony
    (GOV) – Correspondence files 1902, 1906, 1907, 1908, 1909
Secretary for Mines (MM) – Correspondence files 1903 to 1909
Secretary for Native Affairs (SNA) – Correspondence files 1902 to 1910
Transvaal Law Department (LD) – Correspondence files 1902 to 1910

Transvaal Province

Transvaal Agricultural Department (TAD) – Correspondence files 1900 to 1919
Transvaal Department of Local Government (TPB) – Correspondence files 1904 to 1930
Transvaal Provincial Secretary (TPS) – Correspondence files 1905 to 1920

Central Archives, Pretoria

Department of Justice (JUS) – Correspondence files 1910 to 1930
Department of Lands (LDE) – Correspondence files 1902 to 1930
Department of Mines and Industries (MNW) – Correspondence, volume 691
Entomology Department (CEN) – Correspondence, volume 80
Native Affairs Department (NTS) – Correspondence files 1910 to 1943
Prime Minister (PM) – Correspondence files 1910 to 1930

Kruger National Park, Skukuza and Pretoria

Diaries of Rangers: 1923 to 1942
Files: K1–K52
Minutes and Annual Reports: National Parks Board of Trustees – 1926 to 1992
Opsienersjaarverslae: Assorted Early Correspondence and Annual Reports

BRITAIN

Public Record Office, Kew, London

Cabinet Papers CAB 58/86–94: International Conferences 1933 and 1938
Colonial Office CO 291/14: Transvaal, Miscellaneous Original Correspondence
Foreign Office FO 367: Africa, Miscellaneous General Correspondence
FO 2/181: General Correspondence, Africa Sessional Papers ZHC1: 3495, 7753

UNITED STATES OF AMERICA

National Archives of the United States of America, Washington

Record Group 79: Selected Documents Relating to Parks in South Africa, 1924 to 1946

PRIVATE MANUSCRIPTS

SOUTH AFRICA

Cape Archives, Cape Town

A848: Stratford Caldecott Collection

Johannesburg Public Library

333.3(06)(682): Transvaal Land Owners' Association

Kruger National Park, Skukuza

Newspaper Cuttings
Photograph Albums
Stevenson-Hamilton Documents in Trust
Miscellaneous unpublished manuscripts

Transvaal Archives, Pretoria

A17: J.F. Churchill Accession
A68: F. da Costa Leal Accession
W179: H.T. Glynn Accession
A248: J. Albasini Collection
A249: G.R. von Wielligh Accession
A878: J.S. Smit Collection, vol. 15
A1570: Sekukuniland; J.F.D. Winter Accession
J.C. Smuts Archive: Private Papers

University of the Witwatersrand, Johannesburg, Manuscript Collection

A58: Johannesburg Field Naturalists Club Records
A210: T. Ayres Papers
A839: H.E. Schoch Papers
A1375: F.J. Newnham Papers
A1403/1: F.C. Selous Papers

Wildlife Society of Southern Africa, Pietermaritzburg
(now Johannesburg)
Minutes: Transvaal Game Protection Association 1902–1920
Minutes: Wildlife Society Council 1926–1945
Minutes: Annual General Meetings 1927–1961
Minutes: Western Districts Game Protection Association 1886–1915
Letters: Western Districts Game Protection Association 1886–1905
General Correspondence: 1926–1928
Correspondence: Transvaal Game Protection Association 1925
H.B. Papenfus File: Correspondence 1925–1937

BRITAIN

Rhodes House Library, Oxford
MSS Afr.s. 398: Cowie Papers
MSS Afr.r. 143–148: Hobley Papers
MSS Afr.r. 93: Patterson Papers

Stevenson-Hamilton Archives, Fairholm, Larkhall, Lanarkshire
Assorted MSS: James Stevenson-Hamilton
Folder: Hamilton of Fairholm
Diaries: 1879 to 1957

PRINTED OFFICIAL AND SEMI-OFFICIAL SOURCES

SOUTH AFRICA

Transvaal

Bigalke, R.C. *Nature conservation in the Transvaal.* Bulletin No. 2. Pretoria: Transvaal Provincial Administration, Nature Conservation Branch, 1968.
Goldman, P.L.A. *Beredeneerde Inventarissen van de Oudste Argief-Groepender Zuid-Afrikaanse Republiek.* Pretoria: Government Printer, 1927.
Index der Staatscouranten over de Jaren 1857 tot en met 1870. Pretoria: Government Printer, 1897.
Index der Staatscouranten over de Jaren 1871 tot en met Julie 1881. Pretoria: Government Printer, 1898.

Krynauw, D. W., and H. S. Pretorius. *Transvaalse Argiefstukke: Staatsekretaris Inkomende Stukke*, 1850–1852. Pretoria: Government Printer, 1949.
Pretorius, H. S., and D.W. Kruger. *Voortrekker-Argiefstukke*, 1829–1849. Pretoria: Government Printer, 1937.
South African Archival Records: Transvaal. 6 vols. Cape Town: Government Printer, [1949–1956].
South African Republic, *Staatscourant*, 1870–1899.
Transvaal Administration Reports, 1902 to 1909.
Transvaal Colony, *Annual Reports of the Transvaal Museum*, 1905 to 1908.
Transvaal Colony, *Government Gazette*, 1900 to 1910.
Transvaal Colony, *Debates of the Legislative Assembly*, 1907 to 1909.
Transvaal Colony, *Debates of the Legislative Council*, 1903 to 1906.
Transvaal Colony, *Debates of the Legislative Council*, 1907 to 1910.
Transvaal Colony, *Minutes of the Executive Council*, 1901 to 1906.
Transvaal Colony, *Minutes of the Legislative Council*, 1902 to 1906.
Transvaal Colony, *Minutes and Proceedings of the Legislative Council of the Transvaal*, 1907 to 1910.
Transvaal Colony, *Votes and Proceedings of the Legislative Assembly*, 1907 to 1910.
Transvaal Province, *Official Gazette*, 1910 to 1930.
Transvaal Province, *Votes and Proceedings of the Provincial Council*, 1910–1930.
Transvaal Province, *Report of the Game Reserves Commission*, TP5–18. Pretoria: Government Printer, 1918.
Transvaal Province, *Report of the Game Preservation Commission*, TP6–46. Pretoria: Government Printer, 1946.

Union of South Africa

Acocks, J. P. H. *Veld Types of South Africa*. 2 ed. Memoirs of the Botanical Survey of South Africa No. 40. Pretoria: Botanical Research Institute, 1975.
Fuller, C. *Tsetse in the Transvaal and Surrounding Territories: An Historical Review*. Entomology Memoir No. 1. Pretoria: Department of Agriculture, 1923.
Union of South Africa, *Government Gazette*, 1910 to 1930.
Union of South Africa, *House of Assembly Debates*, 1926.
Union of South Africa, *The Senate of South Africa: Debates*, 1926.
Union of South Africa, *Majority Report of the Eastern Transvaal Natives Land Committee, 1918*, UG 31–18. Cape Town: Government Printer, 1918.

BRITAIN

Foreign Office Confidential Print, FO 403

7322 *Correspondence relating to the preservation of wild animals in Africa 1896–1900* Parts I and II (1901)

8384 *Further correspondence respecting the preservation of wild game in Africa 1902–1904* (1904)

8991 *Further correspondence respecting the preservation of wild game in Africa 1905* (1905)

Parliamentary Papers published by Command of the Government

C310 *Reports from Her Majesty's representatives abroad on the laws and regulations relative to the protection of game and to trespass* (1871)

C401 *Reports from Her Majesty's representatives abroad on the laws and regulations relative to the protection of game and to trespass* (1871)

C351 *Laws in force in the colonies as to trespass and also as to the preservation of game* (1871)

Cd3189 *Correspondence relating to the preservation of wild animals in Africa* (1906)

Cd4472 *Further correspondence relating to the preservation of wild animals in Africa* (1909)

Cd5136 *Further correspondence relating to the preservation of wild animals in Africa* (1910)

Cd5775 *Further correspondence relating to the preservation of wild animals in Africa* (1911)

Cd6671 *Further correspondence relating to the preservation of wild animals in Africa* (1913)

Cmd4453 *Agreement respecting the protection of the fauna and flora of Africa* (1933)

Cmd5280 *International Convention for the protection of the fauna and flora of Africa* (1936)

NEWSPAPERS

Burger
Cape Argus
Cape Times
Daily News
Goldfields News and Barberton Herald
Johannesburg Times

Natal Witness
Natal Mercury
Pretoria News
Rand Daily Mail
Star
Sunday Times
Transvaal Advertiser
Transvaal Leader
Transvaal Messenger
Volksstem

PUBLISHED SOURCES TO 1930

Anderson, A.A. *Twenty-Five Years in a Waggon.* London: Chapman and Hall, 1888. Repr. Cape Town: Struik, 1974.

Atcherley, R.J. *A Trip to Boerland.* London: Richard Bentley and Son, 1879.

Aylward, A. *The Transvaal of Today.* Edinburgh: Blackwood, 1878.

Baines, T. *Journal of Residence in Africa, 1842–1853.* 2 vols. Cape Town: Van Riebeeck Society, vol.1, 1961, vol.2, 1964.

Baldwin, W.C. *African Hunting and Adventure from Natal to the Zambezi, including Lake Ngami, the Kalahari Desert etc., 1852–1860.* 2 ed. London: Richard Bentley, 1863.

Balfour, A.B. *Twelve Hundred Miles in a Waggon.* London: Edward Arnold, 1896.

Blackwoods (Edinburgh) Magazine. 'The Boers at Home: Jottings from the Transvaal', vol.130, no.794, December 1881, pp.753–70.

Bryden, H.A. 'The Extermination of Great Game in South Africa', *Fortnightly Review*, October 1894, pp.538–51.

—— *Gun and Camera in Southern Africa.* London: Edward Stanford, 1893.

—— *Kloof and Karroo in Cape Colony.* London: Longmans Green, 1889.

—— *Nature and Sport in South Africa.* London: Chapman and Hall, 1897.

Buxton, E.N. 'The Preservation of Big Game in Africa', *Journal of the Society of Arts*, vol.2, no.634, 15 May 1903, pp.566–78.

—— *Two African Trips; With Notes and Suggestions on Big Game Preservation in Africa.* London: Edward Stanford, 1902.

Caldecott, S. 'Create a National Park!', *South African Nation*, vol.2, no.85, 21 November 1925, pp.7–8.

—— 'Sabi Bushman Paintings', *South African Nation*, vol.3, no.113, 5 June 1926, p.17.

Caldwell, K. 'The Commercialisation of Game', *Journal of the Society for the Preservation of the Fauna of the Empire*, part 7, 1927, pp. 83–90.
—— 'Game Preservation: Its Aims and Objects', *Journal of the Society for the Preservation of the Fauna of the Empire*, part 4, 1924, pp. 45–56.
Carey, H.R. 'Saving the Animal Life of Africa: A New Method and a Last Chance', *Journal of Mammalogy*, vol. 7, no. 2, 1926, pp. 73–85.
Chapman, A. *Memories of Fourscore Years Less Two, 1851–1929*. London: Gurney and Jackson, 1930.
—— *On Safari: Big Game Hunting in British East Africa*. London: Edward Arnold, 1908.
—— *Retrospect: Reminiscences of a Hunter-Naturalist in Three Continents*. London: Gurney and Jackson, 1928.
Cumming, R.G. *Five Years' Adventures in the Far Interior of South Africa, with Notices of the Native Tribes and Savage Animals*. 8 ed. London: John Murray, 1911.
—— *A Hunter's Life in South Africa*. 2 vols. London: John Murray, 1850. Repr. Bulawayo: Books of Zimbabwe, 1980.
Cunynghame, A.T. *My Command in South Africa, 1874–1878*. London: Macmillan, 1879.
Curson, H.H., and J.M. Hugo. 'Preservation of Game in South Africa', *South African Journal of Science*, vol. 21, 1924, pp. 400–24.
Engelenburg, F.V. *'n Onbekende Paul Kruger*. Pretoria: Volksstem, 1925.
Finaughty, W. *The Recollections of William Finaughty: Elephant Hunter, 1864–1875*. Philadelphia: J.B. Lippincott, 1916. Repr. Bulawayo: Books of Rhodesia, 1973.
FitzPatrick, J.P. *Jock of the Bushveld*. London: Longmans Green, 1907.
—— *South African Memories*. London: Cassell and Co., 1932.
Forssman, O.W.A., comp. *A Guide for Agriculturalists and Capitalists, Speculators, Miners, etc., Wishing to Invest Money Profitably in the Transvaal Republic, South Africa*. Cape Town, William Foster & Co., 1874. Repr. Pretoria: State Library, 1984.
Fynney, F.B. 'The Geographical and Economic Features of the Transvaal, the New British Dependency in South Africa', *Proceedings of the Royal Geographical Society*, vol. 22, 14 January 1878, pp. 114–25.
Gassiott, H.S. 'Notes from a Journal kept during a Hunting Tour in South Africa', *Journal of the Royal Geographical Society*, vol. 22, 1852, pp. 137–40.
Gillett, F. ' Game Reserves', *Journal of the Society for the Preservation of the Wild Fauna of the Empire*, vol. 4, 1908, pp. 42–45.
Gillmore, P. *The Hunter's Arcadia*. London: Chapman and Hall, 1886.
Glynn, H.T. *Game and Gold: Memories of over 50 Years in the Lydenburg District, Transvaal*. London: Dolman Printing, n.d.

Haagner, A. K. 'The Conservation of Wild Life in South Africa', *South African Journal of Industries*, December 1925, pp. 761–75.
—— 'Game and Bird Protection in South Africa: A Short Comparison with some other Countries', *South African Journal of Science*, vol. 12, 1915, pp. 519–29.
Harris, W. C. *Portraits of the Game and Wild Animals of Southern Africa.* London: n.p., 1840. Repr. Cape Town: Sable Publishers, 1986.
—— *The Wild Sports of Southern Africa.* London: Henry G. Bohn, 1852. Repr. Cape Town: Struik, 1963.
Hewitt, C. G. *The Conservation of the Wildlife of Canada.* New York: Charles Scribner's Sons, 1921.
Hingston, R. W. G. 'The Only Way of Saving African Fauna', *The Illustrated London News*, 13 December 1930, p. 1062.
Hofmeyr, S. *Twintig Jaren in Zoutpansberg.* Cape Town: J. H. Rose, 1890.
Hornaday, W. T., and A. K. Haagner. *The Vanishing Game of Southern Africa.* New York: Permanent Wildlife Protection Fund, Bulletin No. 10, September 1922.
Huet, P. *Het Lot der Zwarten in Transvaal.* Utrecht: Van Peursem, 1869.
Jeppe, C. *The Kaleidoscopic Transvaal.* London: Chapman and Hall, 1906.
Kruger, P. *The Memoirs of Paul Kruger.* 2 vols. London: T. Fisher Unwin, 1902.
Le Roux, T. H. *Die Dagboek van Louis Trigardt.* Pretoria: J. H. van Schaik, 1964.
Leyland, J. *Adventures in the Far Interior of South Africa.* London: Routledge, 1866.
Lye, W. F., ed. *Andrew Smith's Journal of his Expedition into the Interior of South Africa, 1834–1836.* Cape Town: Balkema, 1975.
Lyell, D. D., ed. *African Adventure: Letters from Famous Big-game Hunters.* London: John Murray, 1935.
Methuen, H. H. *Life in the Wilderness or Wanderings in South Africa.* London: Richard Bentley, 1846.
Millais, J. G. *A Breath from the Veldt.* London: Henry Sotheran, 1895.
'Minutes of Proceedings at a Deputation from the Society for the Preservation of the Wild Fauna of the Empire to the Right Hon. Alfred Lyttelton (His Majesty's Secretary for the Colonies)', *Journal of the Society for the Preservation of the Wild Fauna of the Empire*, vol. 1, 1905, pp. 9–18.
'Minutes of Proceedings at a Deputation from the Society for the Preservation of the Wild Fauna of the Empire to the Rt. Hon. The Earl of Elgin, His Majesty's Secretary of State for the Colonies', *Journal of the Society for the Preservation of the Wild Fauna of the Empire*, vol. 2, 1906, pp. 20–32.

Minutes of Proceedings at a Deputation from the Society for the Preservation of the Wild Fauna of the Empire received by the Right Hon. The Earl of Crewe K.G. (Principal Secretary of State for the Colonies), at the Colonial Office', *Journal of the Society for the Preservation of the Wild Fauna of the Empire*, vol.5, 1909, pp.11–27.

Muir, J. *Our National Parks*. New York: Houghton Mifflin & Co., 1901. 2 ed. Madison, Wisconsin: University of Wisconsin Press, 1981.

Nicolls, J.A., and W. Eglington. *The Sportsman in South Africa*. London: British and Colonial Publications, 1892.

Patterson, J.H. *The Man-Eaters of Tsavo and other East African Adventures*. London: Macmillan, 1907.

Pease, A. 'Game and Game Reserves in the Transvaal', *Journal of the Society for the Preservation of the Wild Fauna of the Empire*, vol.4, 1908, pp.29–34.

Percival, A.B. *A Game Ranger on Safari*. London: Nisbet and Co., 1928.

Praagh, L.V., ed. *The Transvaal and its Mines*. London: Praagh & Lloyd, [1906].

Preller, G.S. *Piet Retief*. Cape Town: Nasionale Pers, 1930.

Preller, G.S., ed. *Dagboek van Louis Trichardt, 1836–1838*. 2 ed. Cape Town: Nasionale Pers, 1938.

Reitz, D. *Commando*. London: Faber and Faber, 1929.

Roche, H. *On Trek in the Transvaal*. London: Sampson Low, 1878.

Roosevelt, T. *African Game Trails*. London: John Murray, 1910.

Sandeman, E.F. *Eight Months in an Ox-Waggon*. London: Griffith and Farran, 1880. Repr. Johannesburg: Africana Book Society, 1975.

Sanderson, J. *Memoranda of a Trading Trip into the Orange River (Sovereignty) Free State and the Country of the Transvaal Boers*. Originally published in the *Journal of the Royal Geographical Society*, vol.30, 1860, pp.233–55. Repr. Pretoria: State Library, 1981.

Saturday Review, 'The Dying Fauna of an Empire', *Journal of the Society for the Preservation of the Wild Fauna of the Empire*, vol.3, 1907, pp.75–79.

Selous, F.C. *African Nature Notes and Reminiscences*. London: Macmillan, 1908. Repr. Salisbury: Pioneer Head, 1969.

—— *A Hunter's Wanderings in Africa*. London: Richard Bentley, 1881. Repr. Bulawayo: Books of Zimbabwe, 1981.

Selous, P. *Travel and Big Game*. London: Bellairs, 1897.

Silver and Co's Handbook to the Transvaal, British South Africa. London: S.W. Silver and Co., 1878.

South Africa, 'Another Mighty Hunter: An Interesting Crack with Mr H.T. Glynn', 5 September 1896, p.557.

Stevenson-Hamilton, J. 'Aantekeningen Omtrent de Wild-Reserve aan de Sabi', *Het Transvaalsche Landbouw Journaal*, vol. 4, 1906, pp. 636–50.
—— *Animal Life in Africa*. London: Heinemann, 1912.
—— 'The Coloration of the African Hunting Dog', *Proceedings of the Zoological Society of London*, no. 27, 1914, pp. 403–5.
—— 'Empire Fauna in 1922', *Journal of the Society for the Preservation of the Fauna of the Empire*, part 2, 1922, pp. 38–43.
—— 'Game Preservation in the Eastern Transvaal', *The Field*, 14 March 1903.
—— 'Game Preservation in the Transvaal', *Blackwood's Magazine*, March 1906, pp. 407–11.
—— 'Game Preservation in the Transvaal', *Journal of the Society for the Preservation of the Wild Fauna of the Empire*, vol. 2, 1905, pp. 20–45.
—— 'The Great Game of South Africa', *South African Railways and Harbours Magazine*, December 1927, pp. 2023–32.
—— *The Kruger National Park*. Pretoria: Government Printer, 1928.
—— 'The Kruger National Park', *The Illustrated London News*, 8 October 1927.
—— 'The Management of a National Park in Africa', *Journal of the Society for the Preservation of the Fauna of the Empire*, part 10, 1930, pp. 13–20.
—— 'Notes on a Journey through Portuguese East Africa from Ibo to Lake Nyasa, *Geographical Journal*, November 1909, pp. 514–29.
—— 'Notes on the Sabi Game Reserve, Part I', *Transvaal Agricultural Journal*, vol. 5, no. 19, 1907, pp. 603–17.
—— 'Notes on the Sabi Game Reserve, Part II', *Transvaal Agricultural Journal*, vol. 5, no. 20, 1907, pp. 866–71.
—— 'Observations on Migratory Birds at Komatipoort', *Journal of the South African Ornithologists Union*, vol. 5, April 1909, pp. 19–22.
—— 'Opposition to Game Reserves', *Journal of the Society for the Preservation of the Wild Fauna of the Empire*, vol. 3, 1907, pp. 53–60.
—— 'The Preservation of the African Elephant', *Journal of the Society for the Preservation of the Fauna of the Empire*, part 1, 1921, pp. 34–42.
—— 'The Relation between Game and Tsetse Flies', *Bulletin of Entomological Research*, vol. 2, 1911, pp. 113–18.
—— 'The Transvaal Game Reserve', *Journal of the Society for the Preservation of the Fauna of the Empire*, part 4, 1924, pp. 35–44.
—— 'The Transvaal Game Sanctuary', *Journal of the African Society*, vol. 25, no. 99, 1926, pp. 211–28.
Stuart, J. *De Hollandsche Afrikanen en hunne Republiek in Zuid-Afrika*. Amsterdam: G. W. Tielkemeijer, 1854.

Thom, H.B., ed. *Journal of Jan van Riebeeck.* 3 vols. Cape Town: Van Riebeeck Society, 1952–1958.
Transvaal Agricultural Journal, vol.6, no.23, 1908, pp.496–97, correspondence from J. Stevenson-Hamilton.
Het Transvaalsche Landbouw Journaal, vol.1, no.2, 1904, p.155, 'Editor's Notes'.
Van Oordt, G.A. *Striving and Hoping to the Bitter End: The Life of Herman Frederik van Oordt, 1862–1907.* Cape Town: G.A. van Oordt, 1980.
Vaughan-Kirby, F. 'Game and Game Preservation in Zululand', *South African Journal of Science,* vol.13, 1916, pp.375–96.
—— *In Haunts of Wild Game.* Edinburgh: Blackwoods, 1896.
Von Wielligh, G.R. *Langs de Lebombo.* Pretoria: Van Schaik, 1925.
Wallis, J.P.R., ed. *The Barotseland Journals of James Stevenson-Hamilton, 1898–1899.* London: Chatto and Windus, 1953.
Warren, C. *On the Veldt in the Seventies.* London: Ibister, 1902.

SELECTED MODERN WORKS

Adendorff, G. *Wild Company.* Cape Town: Books of Africa, 1984.
African Wild Life, Review Issue, vol.38, no.2, 1984.
Allin, C.W. *The Politics of Wilderness Preservation.* Westport, Connecticut: Greenwood Press, 1982.
Anderson, D. 'Depression, Dust Bowl, Demography and Drought: The Colonial State and Soil Conservation in East Africa during the 1930s', *African Affairs,* vol.83, no.332, 1984, pp.321–43.
Anderson D., and R. Grove, eds. *Conservation in Africa: People, Policies and Practice.* Cambridge: Cambridge University Press, 1987.
Ashby, E. *Reconciling Man with the Environment.* London: Oxford University Press, 1977.
Attfield, R. *The Ethics of Environmental Concern.* Oxford: Blackwell, 1983.
Bailey, J.A. et al., eds. *Readings in Wildlife Conservation.* Washington: The Wildlife Society, 1974.
Bannister, A., and R. Gordon. *The National Parks of South Africa.* Cape Town: Struik, n.d.
Barbour, I.G., ed. *Earth Might be Fair: Reflections on Ethics, Religion and Ecology.* Englewood Cliffs, New Jersey: Prentice-Hall, 1972.
—— ed. *Western Man and Environmental Ethics.* Reading, Massachusetts: Addison-Wesley, 1973.

Bates, M. *Man in Nature*. Englewood Cliffs, New Jersey: Prentice-Hall, 1964.

Behrens, H.P.H. 'His Name is Skukuza', *African Wild Life*, vol. 1, no. 2, 1947, pp. 46–66.

—— 'Hunter turns Protector: The Story of Henry Wolhuter', *African Wild Life*, vol. 1, no. 3, 1947, pp. 36–50.

—— '"Oom Paul's" Great Fight to Preserve Game', *African Wild Life*, vol. 1, no. 1, 1946, pp. 12–22.

—— 'Paul Kruger – Wildbeskermer: Aspek van President se Lewe wat Selfs sy Biograwe Vergeet', *Huisgenoot*, vol. 37, series 1542, 12 October 1951, pp. 6–7.

Beinart, W. 'Empire, Hunting and Ecological Change in Southern and Central Africa', *Past and Present*, no. 128, August 1990, pp. 162–86.

Beinart, W. et al., eds. *Putting a Plough to the Ground: Accumulation and Dispossession in Rural South Africa, 1850–1930*. Johannesburg: Ravan Press, 1986.

Benson, J. 'Duty and the Beast', *Philosophy*, vol. 53, 1978, pp. 529–49.

Bigalke, R.C.H. *A Guide to Some Common Animals of the Kruger National Park*. Pretoria: Van Schaik, 1939.

—— *National Parks and their Functions, with Special Reference to South Africa*. Pamphlet no. 10. Pretoria: South African Biological Society, 1939.

—— 'Our National Parks: Past and Future', *South African Journal of Science*, vol. 40, 1943, pp. 248–53.

—— 'Science and Nature Conservation in the Transvaal', *Fauna and Flora*, no. 27, 1976, pp. 13–15.

—— 'South Africa's First Game Reserve', *Fauna and Flora*, no. 17, 1966, pp. 13–18.

—— *The National Zoological Gardens of South Africa*. Johannesburg: C.N.A., 1954.

Bozzoli, B., ed. *Class, Community and Conflict*. Johannesburg: Ravan Press, 1987.

—— ed. *Town and Countryside in the Transvaal*. Johannesburg: Ravan Press, 1983.

Braack, L.E.O. *The Kruger National Park*. Cape Town: Struik, 1983.

Bridgeland, F. 'Here's to you Doctor Robinson', *Living*, September 1993, pp. 40–44.

Brooks, P. *The Pursuit of Wilderness*. Boston, Massachusetts: Houghton Mifflin Co., 1971.

Brown, A.C., ed. *A History of Scientific Endeavour in South Africa*. Cape Town: The Royal Society, 1977.

Bryden, H. A. *Wildlife in South Africa.* London: Harrap, 1936.
Bundy, C. *The Rise and Fall of the South African Peasantry.* London: Heinemann, 1979.
Burr, S. I. 'Towards Legal Rights for Animals', *Environmental Affairs*, vol. 4, no. 4, Spring 1975, pp. 205–54.
Burton, I., and R. W. Kates, eds. *Readings in Resource Conservation and Management.* Chicago: University of Chicago Press, 1965.
Carruthers, E. J. 'Creating a National Park, 1910 to 1926', *Journal of Southern African Studies*, vol. 15, no. 2, 1989, pp. 188–216.
—— 'Dissecting the Myth: Paul Kruger and the Kruger National Park', *Journal of Southern African Studies*, vol. 20, no. 2, June 1994, pp. 263–83.
—— 'Game Protectionism in the Transvaal, 1900 to 1910', *South African Historical Journal*, no. 28, 1988, pp. 33–56.
—— 'The Dongola Wild Life Sanctuary: "Psychological Blunder, Economic Folly and Political Monstrosity", or "More Valuable than Rubies and Gold"?, *Kleio*, no. 24, 1992, pp. 82–100.
—— '"Police Boys" and Poachers: Africans, Wildlife Protection and National Parks, the Transvaal 1902 to 1950', *Kleio*, vol. 36, no. 2, 1993, pp. 11–22.
—— 'The Pongola Game Reserve: An Eco-Political Study', *Koedoe*, no. 28, 1985, pp. 1–16.
—— 'Towards an Environmental History of South Africa: Some Perspectives', *South African Historical Journal*, no. 23, December 1990, pp. 184–95.
Carson, G. *Men, Beasts and Gods: A History of Cruelty and Kindness to Animals.* New York: Charles Scribner's Sons, 1972.
Cartmill, M. *A View to a Death in the Morning: Hunting and Nature through History.* Cambridge, Mass.: Harvard University Press, 1993.
Cattrick, A. *Spoor of Blood.* Cape Town: Timmins, 1959.
Charter, A. E. 'Game Preservation in Zululand', *Southern African Museums Association Bulletin*, September 1943, pp. 69–76.
Christopher, A. J. 'Environmental Perception in Southern Africa', *South African Geographical Journal*, vol. 55, no. 1, 1973, pp. 14–22.
Clark, S. R. L. 'The Rights of Wild Things', *Inquiry*, vol. 22, 1979, pp. 171–88.
Clepper, H., ed. *Origins of American Conservation.* New York: John Wiley and Sons, 1966.
Coates, P. 'Chances with Wolves: Renaturing Western History', *Journal of American Studies*, vol. 28, no. 2, 1994, pp. 241–54.
Cock, J., and E. Koch, eds. *Going Green: People, Politics and the Environment in South Africa.* Cape Town: Oxford University Press, 1991.

Cubbin, A.E. 'An Outline of Game Legislation in Natal, 1866–1912 (i.e. until the Promulgation of the Mkhuze Game Reserve)', *Journal of Natal and Zulu History*, vol. 14, 1992, pp. 37–47.

Darnovsky, M. 'Stories Less Told: Histories of US Environmentalism', *Socialist Review*, vol. 22, no. 4, 1992, pp. 11–57.

Dasmann, R.F. *Environmental Conservation*. 4 ed. New York: John Wiley, 1976.

Davis, D.H.S. ed., *Ecological Studies in South Africa*. The Hague: Junk, 1964.

Denevan, W.M., and S.O. Brooks. 'The Myth of Primeval Wilderness', *The World & I*, vol. 7, no. 10, October 1992, pp. 265–69.

Devall, W.B. 'Conservation: An Upper-Middle Class Social Movement: A Replication', *Journal of Leisure Research*, vol. 2, no. 2, 1970, pp. 123–26.

Dicke, B.H. 'The Tsetse Fly's Influence on South African History', *South African Journal of Science*, vol. 9, 1932, pp. 792–96.

Dictionary of South African Biography. 5 vols to date. Pretoria: H.S.R.C., 1968–1987.

Dodds, G.B. 'The Historiography of American Conservation: Past and Prospects', *Pacific Northwest Quarterly*, vol. 56, April 1965, pp. 75–81.

Dubos, R. *The Wooing of Earth*. London: Athlone Press, 1980.

Duminy, A., and B. Guest. *Interfering in Politics: A Biography of Sir Percy Fitzpatrick*. Johannesburg: Lowry Publishers, 1987.

Dunlap, T.R. 'Values for Varmints: Predator Control and Environmental Ideas, 1920–1939', *Pacific Historical Review*, vol. 53, no. 1, 1984, pp. 141–61.

—— 'Wildlife, Science and the National Parks, 1920–1940', *Pacific Historical Review*, vol. 59, 1990, pp. 187–202.

Ellis, S. 'Of Elephants and Men: Politics and Nature Conservation in South Africa', *Journal of Southern African Studies*, vol. 20, no. 1, March 1994, pp. 53–69.

Fitter, R., and P Scott. *The Penitent Butchers: The Fauna Preservation Society, 1903–1978*. London: Fauna Preservation Society, 1978.

Ford, J. *The Role of Trypanosomiasis in African Ecology: A Study of the Tsetse Fly Problem*. Oxford: Clarendon Press, 1971.

Francis, L.P., and R. Norman. 'Some Animals are more Equal than Others', *Philosophy*, vol. 53, 1978, pp. 507–27.

Freemuth, John C. *Islands Under Siege: National Parks and the Politics of External Threats*. Lawrence: University Press of Kansas, 1991.

Fuggle R.F., and M.A. Rabie, eds. *Environmental Concerns in South Africa: Technical and Legal Perspectives*. Cape Town: Juta, 1983.

Fuller, C. *Louis Trichardt's Trek across the Drakensberg.* Cape Town: Van Riebeeck Society, 1932.
Garson, N.G. 'The Swaziland Question and a Road to the Sea', *Archives Year Book for South African History*, 1957, II.
Glacken, C.J. *Traces on the Rhodian Shore.* Berkeley: University of California Press, 1967.
Graham, A. *The Gardeners of Eden.* London: Allen and Unwin, 1973.
Graham, F. *Man's Dominion: The Story of Conservation in America.* New York: M. Evans and Co., 1971.
Gray, S. *Southern African Literature: An Introduction.* Cape Town: David Philip, 1979.
Gunn, A.S. 'Why Should we Care about Rare Species?', *Environmental Ethics*, vol.2, Spring 1980, pp.17-37.
Hackel, J.D., and E.J. Carruthers. 'Swaziland's Twentieth Century Wildlife Preservation Efforts: The Present as a Continuation of the Past', *Environmental History Review*, vol.17, no.3, Fall 1993, pp.61-84.
Hague, H. 'Eden Ravished: The Land, Pioneer Attitudes and Conservation', *American West*, vol.14, no.3, 1977, pp.30-33 and pp.65-69.
Hahn, S. 'Hunting, Fishing and Foraging: Common Rights and Class Relations in the Postbellum South', *Radical History Review*, no.26, 1982, pp.37-64.
Hall, M. 'Shakan Pitfall Traps: Hunting Technique in the Zulu Kingdom', *Annals of the Natal Museum*, vol.22, no.1, 1977, pp.1-12.
Hammond, D., and A. Jablow. *The Africa That Never Was: Four Centuries of British Writing about Africa.* New York: Twayne, 1970.
Hammond, J.L. 'Wilderness and Heritage Values', *Environmental Ethics*, vol.7, Summer 1985, pp.165-70.
Hampton, H.D. 'Opposition to National Parks', *Journal of Forest History*, vol.25, no.1, 1981, pp.37-45.
Hay, D. et al. *Albion's Fatal Tree: Crime and Society in Eighteenth Century England.* London: Allen Lane, 1975.
Hays, S.P. *Conservation and the Gospel of Efficiency: The Progressive Conservation Movement, 1890-1920.* New York: Atheneum, 1980.
Heberlein, T.A. 'The Land Ethic Realized: Some Social Psychological Explanations for Changing Environmental Attitudes', *Journal of Social Issues*, vol.28, no.4, 1972, pp.79-87.
Hill, K.A. 'Zimbabwe's Wildlife Conservation Regime: Rural Farmers and the State', *Human Ecology*, vol.19, no.1, 1991, pp.19-34.
Hobley, C.W. 'The Conservation of Wildlife', *Journal of the Society for the Preservation of the Fauna of the Empire*, Section I, in part 32, 1937, pp.38-43; Section II, in part 33, 1938, pp.39-49.

Hobley, C. W. 'The London Convention of 1900', *Journal of the Society for the Preservation of the Fauna of the Empire*, part 20, 1933, pp. 33–49.

Hobsbawm, E., and T. Ranger, eds. *The Invention of Tradition*. Cambridge: Cambridge University Press, 1983.

Hofmeyr, I. 'Popularising History: The Case of Gustav Preller', *Journal of African History*, vol. 29, no. 3, 1988, pp. 521–35.

Huntley, B., R. Siegfried, and C. Sunter. *South African Environments into the 21st Century*. Cape Town: Human & Rousseau Tafelberg, 1989.

Huth, H. *Nature and the American: Three Centuries of Changing Attitudes*. Lincoln, Nebraska: University of Nebraska Press, 1972.

'International Congress for the Protection of Nature', *Journal of the Society for the Preservation of the Fauna of the Empire*, part 15, 1931, pp. 43–52.

Ittelson, W. H. et al. *An Introduction to Environmental Psychology*. New York: Holt, Rinehart and Winston, 1974.

Jarrett, H., ed. *Perspectives on Conservation*. Baltimore: Johns Hopkins Press, 1958.

Jones, D. J. V. *Crime, Protest, Community and Police in Nineteenth Century Britain*. London: Routledge and Kegan Paul, 1982.

—— 'The Poacher: A Study in Victorian Crime and Protest', *Historical Journal*, vol. 22, no. 4, 1979, pp. 825–60.

Juta, M. *The Pace of the Ox*. London: Constable, 1937.

Keegan, T. J. *Rural Transformations in Industrializing South Africa: The Southern Highveld to 1914*. Johannesburg: Ravan Press, 1986.

Klein, D. R. 'The Ethics of Hunting and the Anti-hunting Movement', in *Transactions of the 38th American Wildlife and Natural Resources Conference, 1973*. Washington: Wildlife Management Institute, 1973.

Kloppers, H. *Game Ranger*. Cape Town: Juta, n.d.

Koch, E., D. Cooper, and H. Coetzee. *Water, Waste and Wildlife: The Politics of Ecology in South Africa*. London: Penguin, 1990.

Kruger, D. W. 'Die Weg na die See', *Archives Year Book for South African History*, 1938, I.

—— *Paul Kruger*. 2 vols. Johannesburg: Afrikaanse Pers, 1961–1963.

Labuschagne, R. J. *The Kruger Park and Other National Parks*. Johannesburg: Da Gama, n.d.

—— comp. *60 Years Kruger Park*. Pretoria: National Parks Board of Trustees, 1958.

Le Duc, T. 'The Historiography of Conservation', *Journal of Forest History*, vol. 9, no. 3, 1965, pp. 23–28.

Leopold, A. *A Sand County Almanac*. New York: Oxford University Press, 1966.

Lewis-Williams, J.D. *The Rock Art of Southern Africa*. Cambridge: Cambridge University Press, 1983.

Livingston, J.A. *The Fallacy of Wildlife Conservation*. Toronto: McLelland and Stewart, 1982.

Lowenthal, D. 'Nature and the American Creed of Virtue', *Landscape*, vol.9, no.2, Winter 1959–1960, pp.24–25.

Mackenzie, J.M. *The Empire of Nature: Hunting, Conservation and British Imperialism*. Manchester: Manchester University Press, 1988.

—— ed. *Imperialism and the Natural World*. Manchester: Manchester University Press, 1990.

McCloskey, H.J. 'Moral Rights and Animals', *Inquiry*, vol.22, 1979, pp.23–54.

McEwen, A., and M. McEwen. *National Parks: Conservation or Cosmetics?* London: Allen and Unwin, 1982.

Marks, S., and A. Atmore, eds. *Economy and Society in Pre-industrial South Africa*. London: Longman, 1980.

Marks, S., and R. Rathbone, eds. *Industrialization and Social Change in South Africa*. New York: Longman, 1983.

Marks, S., and S. Trapido, eds. *The Politics of Race, Class and Nationalism in Twentieth Century South Africa*. London: Longman, 1987.

Meiring, P. *Behind the Scenes in Kruger Park*. Johannesburg: Perskor, 1982.

—— *Kruger Park Saga*. N.p.: R.M.P., 1976.

Miller, H.B., and W.H. Williams. *Ethics and Animals*. Clifton, New Jersey: Humana Press, 1983.

Minnaar, A. de V. 'Nagana, Big-game Drives and the Zululand Game Reserves (1890s–1950s)', *Contree*, 25, 1989, pp.12–21.

Mitchell, F. 'The Economic Value of Wildlife Viewing as a Form of Land Use', *East African Agricultural Journal*, Special Issue, June 1968, pp.98–103.

Mitchell, L.C. *Witness to a Vanishing America: The Nineteenth Century Response*. Princeton, New Jersey: Princeton University Press, 1981.

Mitchell, P.C. 'Zoos and National Parks', *Journal of the Society for the Preservation of the Fauna of the Empire*, part 15, 1931, pp.21–42.

Munsche, P.B. *Gentlemen and Poachers: The English Game Laws, 1671–1831*. Cambridge: Cambridge University Press, 1981.

Naess, A. 'The Shallow and the Deep, Long-range Ecology Movements: A Summary', *Inquiry*, vol.16, 1973, pp.95–100.

Nash, R. *The American Environment: Readings in the History of Conservation*. 2 ed. Reading, Massachusetts: Addison-Wesley, 1976.

Nash, R. 'American Environmental History: A New Teaching Frontier', *Pacific Historical Review*, vol. 41, no. 3, 1972, pp. 362–72.
—— 'The American Invention of National Parks', *American Quarterly*, vol. 23, no. 3, 1970, pp. 726–35.
—— 'The American Wilderness in Historical Perspective', *Journal of Forest History*, vol. 6, no. 4, 1963, pp. 2–13.
—— 'The Exporting and Importing of Nature: Nature Appreciation as a Commodity, 1850–1980', *Perspectives in American History*, vol. 12, 1979, pp. 519–60.
—— *The Rights of Nature: A History of Environmental Ethics*. Madison, Wisc.: University of Wisconsin, 1989.
—— 'The Value of Wilderness', *Environmental Review*, vol. 3, 1977, pp. 14–25.
—— *Wilderness and the American Mind*. 3 ed. New Haven, Connecticut: Yale University Press, 1982.
Newman, K. *Kruger National Park*. Johannesburg: Centaur, n.d.
Nuyen, A. T. 'An Anthropocentric Ethics towards Animals and Nature', *Journal of Value Inquiry*, vol. 15, no. 3, 1981, pp. 215–23.
O'Meara, D. *Volkskapitalisme: Class, Capital and Ideology in the Development of Afrikaner Nationalism, 1934–1948*. Johannesburg: Ravan, 1983.
Opie, J. 'Environmental History: Pitfalls and Opportunities', *Environmental Review*, vol. 7, no. 1, Spring 1983, pp. 8–16.
Owen-Smith, R. N. *The Management of Large Mammals in African Conservation Areas*. Pretoria: H.A.U.M., 1983.
Park, C. *History of the Conservation Movement in Britain*. Chertsey, Surrey: Conservation Trust, 1976.
Partridge, E., ed. *Responsibilities to Future Generations: Environmental Ethics*. New York: Prometheus Books, 1981.
Passmore, J. *Man's Responsibility for Nature*. 2 ed. London: Duckworth, 1980.
Paynter, D. *Kruger: Portrait of a National Park*. Cape Town: Struik, 1986.
Peterson, G. L. 'Evaluating the Quality of the Wilderness Environment: Congruence between Perception and Aspiration', *Environment and Behavior*, vol. 6, no. 2, 1974, pp. 169–93.
Pienaar, U. de V. *Neem uit die Verlede*. Pretoria: National Parks Board, 1990.
Pitman, C. R. S. *A Game Warden among his Charges*. London: Nisbet and Co., 1931.
—— *A Game Warden Takes Stock*. London: Nisbet and Co., 1942.
Potgieter, F. J. 'Die Vestiging van die Blanke in Transvaal (1837–1886) Met Spesiale Verwysing na die Verhouding tussen die Mens en die Omgewing', *Archives Year Book for South African History*, 1958, II.

Powell, J.M. *Environmental Management in Australia, 1788–1914*. Melbourne: Oxford University Press, 1976.
Power, T.M. *The Economic Value of the Quality of Life*. Boulder, Colorado: Westview Press, 1980.
Prance, E.L. *Three Weeks in Wonderland: The Kruger National Park*. Cape Town: Juta, n.d.
Preston, G.R., R.F. Fuggle, and W.R. Siegfried. 'Business Leaders' and Professional Ecologists' Perceptions of Mutual Attitudes to Conservation and Development in South Africa', *South African Geographical Journal*, vol. 76, no. 2, 1994, pp. 49–58.
Pringle, J.A. *The Conservationists and the Killers*. Cape Town: T.V. Bulpin, 1982.
Punt, W.H.J. *The First Europeans in the Kruger National Park*. Pretoria: National Parks Board of Trustees, 1975.
Pursell, C.W. ed. *From Conservation to Ecology: The Development of Environmental Concern*. New York: Thomas Y. Crowell, 1973.
Rabie, A. *South African Environmental Legislation*. Pretoria: University of South Africa, 1976.
Rakestraw, L. 'Conservation Historiography: An Assessment', *Pacific Historical Review*, vol. 41, no. 3, 1972, pp. 271–88.
Ranger, T. 'Whose Heritage? The Case of the Matobo National Park', *Journal of Southern African Studies*, vol. 15, no. 2., January 1989, pp. 217–49.
Reiger, J.F. *American Sportsmen and the Origins of Conservation*. New York: Winchester Press, 1975.
Redclift, M. *Development and the Environmental Crisis*. London: Methuen, 1984.
Regan, T. *The Case for Animal Rights*. London: Routledge and Kegan Paul, 1983.
Richardson, E. *The Politics of Conservation: Crusades and Controversies, 1897–1913*. Berkeley: University of California Press, 1962.
Robertson, V.L. 'Early Attempts to Protect Wild Life', *African Wild Life*, vol. 1, no. 2, 1947, pp. 21–23.
Rodman, J. 'Animal Justice: The Counter-revolution in Natural Right and Law', *Inquiry*, vol. 22, 1979, pp. 3–22.
—— 'The Liberation of Nature', *Inquiry*, vol. 20, 1977, pp. 83–145.
Runte, A. *National Parks: The American Experience*. Lincoln, Nebraska: University of Nebraska Press, 1979.
—— 'Worthless Lands: Our National Parks', *American West*, vol. 10, May 1973, pp. 5–11.
Rylatt, R.K. 'Conservation in Zimbabwe as seen by Europeans', *Zambezia*, vol. 17, no. 2, 1990, pp. 161–74.

Bibliography

Sax, J. *Mountains without Handrails.* Ann Arbor, Michigan: University of Michigan Press, 1980.

Sellars, R.W. 'National Parks: Worthless Lands or Competing Land Values', *Journal of Forest History*, vol. 27, no. 3, pp. 130, 135, 142 and 144.

Sheail, J. *Nature in Trust: The History of Nature Conservation in Britain.* Glasgow: Blackie, 1976.

Shelford, V.E. 'Conservation versus Preservation', *Science*, New Series, no. 77, 2 June 1933.

Shillington, K. *The Colonisation of the Southern Tswana, 1870–1900.* Johannesburg: Ravan Press, 1985.

Silberbauer, G.B. *Hunter and Habitat in the Central Kalahari Desert.* Cambridge: Cambridge University Press, 1981.

Singer, P. *Animal Liberation.* Wellingborough, Northamptonshire: Thorsons, 1983.

Smit, F.P. *Die Staatsopvattinge van Paul Kruger.* Pretoria: Van Schaik, 1951.

Smithers, R.H.N. *The Mammals of the Southern African Subregion.* Pretoria: University of Pretoria, 1983.

Smuts, G.L. *Lion.* Johannesburg: Macmillan, 1982.

Speight, A-M. *Game Reserves and Game Protection in Africa.* Cape Town: University of Cape Town Libraries, 1972.

Steinhart, E.I. 'Hunters, Poachers and Gamekeepers: Towards a Social History of Hunting in Colonial Kenya', *Journal of African History*, 30, 1989, pp. 247–64.

Stevenson-Hamilton, H. 'Preserving Wildlife in South Africa', *Optima*, vol. 2, no. 5, 1962, pp. 121–28.

Stevenson-Hamilton, J. 'Address at Rotary Club Luncheon, Pretoria, 17 November 1938', *Journal of the Society for the Preservation of the Fauna of the Empire*, part 36, 1939, pp. 18–24.

—— 'A Game Warden Reflects', *Journal of the Society for the Preservation of the Fauna of the Empire*, part 54, 1946, pp. 17–21.

—— 'A Great National Park', *The Field*, 6 May 1933.

—— 'The Kruger National Park', *S.P.C.A.*, 1942, pp. 5–9.

—— *The Low-Veld: Its Wild Life and its People.* 2 ed. London: Cassell and Co, 1934.

—— *South African Eden.* London: Cassell and Co., 1937.

—— 'The True Approach to Wild Life Preservation', *African Wild Life*, vol. 1, no. 2, 1947, pp. 9–11.

—— 'Tsetse Fly and the Rinderpest Epidemic of 1896', *South African Journal of Science*, vol. 53, no. 8, 1957, pp. 216–18.

Stevenson-Hamilton, J. 'Wild Life Ecology in Africa', in *Associated Scientific and Technical Societies of South Africa: Annual Proceedings, 1941–1942*, pp. 95–106.
—— *Wild Life in South Africa*. London: Cassell and Co., 1947.
Stokes, C. S. *Sanctuary*. 2 ed. Cape Town: Maskew Miller, 1953.
Stone, C. D. *Should Trees have Standing? Towards Legal Rights for Natural Objects*. Los Altos, California: William Kaufmann Inc., 1974.
Strong, D. H. 'The Rise of American Esthetic Conservation: Muir, Mather and Udall', *National Parks Magazine*, vol. 44, February 1970, pp. 5–9.
Strong, D. H., and E. S. Rosenfield. 'Ethics or Expediency: An Environmental Question', *Environmental Affairs*, vol. 5, no. 2, 1976, pp. 255–70.
Struben, F. E. B. 'A History of the Kruger National Park', *African Wild Life*, vol. 7, no. 3, 1953, pp. 209–28.
Swain, D. C. *Federal Conservation Policy, 1921–1933*. Berkeley: University of California Press, 1963.
Tattersall, D. *Skukuza*. Cape Town: Tafelberg, 1972.
Teague, R. D., and E. Decker, eds. *Wildlife Conservation: Principles and Practices*. Washington: The Wildlife Society, 1979.
Thomas, K. *Man and the Natural World: Changing Attitudes in England, 1500–1800*. London: Allen Lane, 1983.
Thompson, L. M. *The Political Mythology of Apartheid*. New Haven: Yale University Press, 1985.
Thomson, R. *On Wildlife 'Conservation'*. New York: United Publishers, 1986.
Tober, J. A. *Who Owns the Wildlife? The Political Economy of Conservation in Nineteenth Century America*. Westport, Connecticut: Greenwood Press, 1981.
Trench, C. C. *The Poacher and the Squire: A History of Poaching and Game Preservation in England*. London: Longmans, 1967.
Turner, J. *Reckoning with the Beast: Animals, Pain and Humanity in the Victorian Mind*. Baltimore: Johns Hopkins Press, 1980.
Van Coller, L. *Die Nasionale Krugerwildtuin: 'n Bibliografie*. Stellenbosch: University of Stellenbosch, 1969.
Van der Merwe, C. G., and M. A. Rabie. 'Eiendom van Wilde Diere', *Tydskrif vir Hedendaagse Romeinse Hollandse Reg*, vol. 37, no. 1, 1974, pp. 38–48.
Van der Merwe, N. J. 'The Position of Nature Conservation in South Africa', *Koedoe*, no. 5, 1962, pp. 1–127.
Van Jaarsveld, F. A. 'Gustav Preller: Sy Historiese Bewussyn en Geskiedsbeskouing', *Historia*, vol. 35, no. 2, 1990.
Van Onselen, C. 'Reactions to Rinderpest in Southern Africa, 1896–1897', *Journal of African History*, vol. 13, no. 3, 1972, pp. 473–88.

Van Rooyen, T. S. 'Die Verhouding tussen die Boere, Engelse en Naturelle in die Geskiedenis van die Oos-Transvaal tot 1882', *Archives Year Book for South African History*, 1951, I.

Van Zyl, M. C. 'Die Uitbreiding van Britse Gesag oor die Natalse Noordgrensgebiede, 1879–1897', *Archives Year Book for South African History*, 1966, I.

Wagner, R. 'Zoutpansberg; Some Notes on the Dynamics of a Hunting Frontier', in *Collected Seminar Papers on the Societies of Southern Africa in the 19th and 20th Centuries*, vol. 6. London: Institute of Commonwealth Studies, University of London, 1975.

West, P. C., and R. Brechin, eds. *Resident Peoples and National Parks: Social Dilemmas and Strategies in International Conservation*. Tucson: University of Arizona Press, 1991.

White, L. 'The Historical Roots of our Ecologic Crisis', *Science*, vol. 155, 10 March 1967, pp. 1203–7.

White, R. 'American Environmental History: The Development of a New Historical Field', *Pacific Historical Review*, vol. 54, no. 3, 1985, pp. 297–335.

Wilson, J. W. H. 'Game Reserves in Southern Africa', *Ostrich*, vol. 11, no. 2, 1941, pp. 108–11.

Wilson, M., and L. Thompson, eds. *The Oxford History of South Africa*. 2 vols. Oxford: Clarendon Press, 1969–1975.

Wolhuter, H. *Memories of a Game Ranger*. 12 ed. Johannesburg: Wild Life Protection and Conservation Society of South Africa, 1976.

Worster, D. E. *Nature's Economy: The Roots of Ecology*. San Francisco: Sierra Club Books, 1977.

—— *The Wealth of Nature: Environmental History and the Ecological Imagination*. New York: Oxford University Press, 1993.

Yates, C. A. *The Kruger National Park*. London: Allen and Unwin, 1935.

Zurhorst, C. *The Conservation Fraud*. New York: Cowles Book Co., 1970.

UNPUBLISHED THESES AND PAPERS

Brooks, S.J. 'Playing the Game: The Struggle for Wildlife Protection in Zululand, 1910–1930'. (M.A. dissertation, Queen's University, Ontario, 1990).

Capone, D. L. 'Wildlife, Man and Competition for Land in Kenya: A Geographical Analysis'. (Ph.D. thesis, Michigan State University, 1972).

Carruthers, E.J. 'Diverging Environments'. (Presented to the African Studies Association Conference, Boston, December 1993).

Carruthers, E. J. 'Game Protection in the Transvaal, 1846 to 1926'. (Ph.D. thesis, University of Cape Town, 1988).
Green, J.J. 'Government and Wildlife Preservation, 1885–1922: The Emergence of a Protective Policy'. (Ph.D. thesis, York University, Toronto, 1975).
Grove, R. 'Incipient Conservationism in the Cape Colony and the Emergence of Colonial Environmental Policies in South Africa, 1846–1890'. (Presented at the Conference on Conservation in Africa, 1884–1984, African Studies Centre, University of Cambridge, April 1985).
Kelly, N. 'In Wildest Africa: The Preservation of Game in Kenya, 1895–1933'. (Ph.D. thesis, Simon Fraser University, 1979).
Morrell, R.G. 'Rural Transformations in the Transvaal: The Middelburg District, 1919–1930'. (M.A. thesis, University of the Witwatersrand, 1983).
Ofcansky, T.P. 'A History of Game Preservation in British East Africa, 1895–1963'. (Ph.D. thesis, West Virginia University, 1981).
Peck, J.E. 'From Royal Game to Popular Heritage: Wildlife Policy and Resource Tenure under Colonial and Independent Rule in Zimbabwe'. (Presented at the African Studies Association Conference, Boston, December, 1993).
Pullan, R.A. 'Game Policies and Public Opinion in Southern Africa, 1884–1984'. (Presented at the Conference on Conservation in Africa, 1884–1984, African Studies Centre, University of Cambridge, April 1985).
Rich, P. 'Landscape, Social Darwinism and the Cultural Roots of South African Racial Ideology'. (Presented to the Southern African Studies Seminar, University of Natal, Pietermaritzburg, August 1983).
Trapido, S. 'Poachers, Proletarians and Gentry in the Early 20th Century Transvaal'. (Presented to the African Studies Institute, University of the Witwatersrand, March 1984).
Ward, G.B. 'Bloodbrothers in the Wilderness: The Sport Hunter and the Buckskin Hunter in the Preservation of the American Wilderness Experience'. (Ph.D. thesis, University of Austin, Texas, 1980).

Index

Administrator of the Transvaal 49, 54, 57
Africans. *See also* Poaching
   attitude to nature protection 2, 28, 43–5, 65, 68, 89, 97
   collaboration with whites 9, 10, 12, 90, 104
   control of 92, 94
   as convict labour 95–6
   evicted from Pafuri Game Reserve 98–9
   as game rangers/police 38, 49, 75, 92, 96
   hunting 7, 16, 31, 90, 91, 93, 103–8
   labour 31, 38, 42–3, 58, 91, 92, 96
   land needs 97–8
   nature protection strategies of 7, 31, 91
   resistance by 11, 12, 13, 93
   Stevenson-Hamilton's views on 97
   as tourists 99–100
   white opinion of 65, 90–2, 97
Afrikaner nationalism 59, 63, 69, 79, 80, 81, 100, 118
Agriculture 17, 28, 37, 41, 51, 53, 55, 98, 106, 113
Anderson, A.A. 106
Animal Life in Africa 36, 70, 110
Antelope 109, 111, 112, 116
Anthropomorphism 111–2, 116
Apartheid 68, 87, 89, 99
Atmore, R. 38
Augrabies National Park 100

Bailey, Sir Abe 69
Balance of nature 111
Balule rest camp 99
Barberton 24, 26, 33, 36, 69
Barrow, J. 104
Bats 77, 103
Behrens, H.P.H. 83

Bester, P. 26
Bigalke, R. 115
Blesbuck 113
Blue antelope 8, 63
Bontebok 8
Bontebok National Park 120
Bourke, E.F. 52
Brebner, W.J.C. 68
Broederbond 85
Bryden, H.A. 29, 108, 109
Buffalo 44
Burchell, W. 105
Bushveld Carbiniers 38
Butterflies 103
Buxton, E.N. 29, 109

Caldecott, S. 61, 62, 63, 64, 75
Campbell, W.A. 69, 113
Cape Argus 62
Casement, T. 33, 35, 39
Chapman, A. 32, 35
Charter, A.E. 69
Cheetah 32, 109, 111
Cholmondeley, H. 71
Coetzee, S.H. 54
Colonial Secretary 30, 32, 41, 48
Commercial hunting. *See* Hunting, commercial
Commissions of Inquiry 23, 54, 55, 56, 58, 74, 86, 97, 115
Conservation, concept of. *See also* Preservation 14, 18, 19, 30, 56
Crocodile 7, 32, 103, 111
Crocodile River 23, 24, 26, 32, 38, 93
Culling 116–17

Darwin, Charles 9
Darwinism 112

Index

De Beer, J. 21, 27
De Laporte, C. 39, 57
De Villiers, J.A.J. 61
Delagoa Bay 10
Department of Agriculture 40
Department of Customs 95
Department of Justice 95
Department of Lands 41, 51, 52, 58
Department of Mines 51, 58
Disease. *See also* names of specific diseases 22, 23, 41, 63, 114
Dongola Wild Life Sanctuary 84
Drakensberg Park 53
Drought 18, 52, 93, 112
Duiker 44
Duke, T. 39

Ecology 103, 104, 114–16
Eland 44, 63
Elephant 8, 44, 63, 107, 109, 116
Entomology 64
Environmental history 2, 3
Erasmus, J.A. 24, 25, 91
Evolution 112

Field-cornets 26
Firearms 8, 12, 13, 43, 44, 90, 93, 113
First World War 30, 52, 54, 55, 56, 57, 60, 93
Fish 14, 92, 98
Foot-and-mouth disease 114
Francis, H.F. 33, 35
Fraser, A.A. 38, 57, 93, 95

Game rangers 38, 39, 43, 44, 72–3, 75, 94, 96–7, 112
Game Reserves. *See also* Africans; names of individual reserves and parks
 boundaries 21, 23, 32–3
 in Cape Colony 8, 32
 establishment of 19–21, 24–7
 legislation 23–8
 pre-colonial 7
 private 13, 27, 37
 provincial 68
 state 8, 18, 19, 21, 22, 26–7, 28
Gamekeepers 13, 17
Giraffe 40, 44
Glynn, A. 33
Glynn, H.T. 24, 25
Gordonia-Kuruman 57
Gray, S. 105
Gray, E.G. 33, 38

Great Britain 8, 11, 14, 22–3, 30, 48, 105–7
Grobler, P.G.W. 59, 60, 63, 83
Groenkloof 27, 32
Gunning, J.W.B. 26, 33, 69

Haagner, A.K. 69
Harris, W.C. 9, 90, 103, 105, 106, 108, 116–17
Hartog, G. 55
Healy, T. 39
Hertzog, J.B.M. 60, 61, 69, 83
Hippopotamus 8, 44
Hluhluwe Game Reserve 28
Hockly, R.A. 69
Hoek Commission of Inquiry 74, 86, 115
Holtzhauzen, I.C. 26
Hornaday, W. 110
Horse-sickness 23, 52
Huisgenoot 83
Hume, D. 9
Hunting. *See also* Nature Protection
 African 7, 16, 31, 90, 91, 93, 103–8
 commercial 2, 7, 8, 9, 10, 14, 21, 29, 31, 32, 52, 104–8
 licences 16, 17
 restrictions on 12, 13, 16, 17
 sport 9, 10, 13, 14, 16, 18, 24, 31, 32, 33, 37, 41, 45, 52, 91, 103–6
Hyaena 32, 109

Impala 44
Imperialism 107–8, 114
Iron Age 7, 10
Ivory 9, 12, 30, 98

Jackal 32, 109, 113
'Jagtkaffers' 12
Jameson Raid 25, 82
Jarvis, F.W. 40
'John' 38
Juta, M. 82–3

Kenyan Parks Service 110, 113, 116
Khoikhoi 90
Kleinenberg, T.J. 54
Koedoe 116
Komatipoort 24, 26
Kosi Bay 22
Krogh, J.C. 19
Kruger Gate 87
Kruger 'millions' 40

Index

Kruger, Paul 3, 15, 17, 21, 22, 24, 25, 60, 61, 64, 80–8, 100
Kruger National Park. See also Sabi Game Reserve; Singwitsi Game Reserve
  affirmative action in 86, 120
  African resistance to 96–100
  and Afrikaner culture 80–8
  apartheid and 86–7
  area of 1, 32–3, 58
  Broederbond influence on 85
  control of Africans in 92
  culling in 103–10
  early development of 74–8
  in English-Afrikaner reconciliation 48
  establishment of 7, 47–8, 53–4
  eviction of Africans from 92
  financial affairs of 63, 77
  future of 118–21
  game rangers in 72
  governmental ties with 81, 83, 84
  history of 2, 3, 4, 15
  Hoek Commission of Inquiry into 74
  labour 92–7. See also under Africans
  naming of 60–1
  National Parks Board's inteference in 67–74
  Pafuri Game Reserve acquired 98–9
  philosophy of 62, 80, 103–4
  poaching in 93–4. See also Poaching
  relationships with Africans 84–5
  republican links of 87
  rest camps in 75–9
  romanticization of 62, 65, 96
  scientists in 63, 87–8, 103–4, 105, 107, 110–17
  symbolism of 1, 2, 67
  tourists to 65, 74–80, 99–100, 117
  wardens. See Stevenson-Hamilton, James; Sandenbergh, J.A.
  warden-Board relations 67–74
  as wilderness 104, 114
  wildlife management in 88, 103, 104, 113–14
Kruger Park Saga 15
Kudu 44
KwaZulu-Natal 9

Labour 31, 38, 39, 42–4, 58, 72–3, 75, 91, 92, 94, 96–7, 112
Labuschagne, R.J. 81, 87–8
Lagden, Sir Godfrey 30, 35, 37, 41
Landowners 13, 16, 17, 18, 31, 37, 48, 51, 55, 57, 58, 59, 91

Le Vaillant, F. 105
Lechwe 113
Ledeboer, L.H. 38
Leopard 32
Leopold, Aldo 115
Letaba rest camp 75
Letaba River 38, 52, 77, 93
Levubu River 38, 98
Leyds, W.J. 25, 26
Limpopo River 33, 84, 98
Lion 7, 32, 42, 64–5, 77, 95, 107, 111, 112, 116
Locusts 114
Lombard, D.P. 21
London Conference (1900) 29–30
Lottering, G.P.J. 24, 25
Louw, G.J. 24, 25, 26
Loveday, R.K. 24, 25, 26, 61, 82, 83
Lowveld 21, 23, 24, 33, 38, 41, 53, 63, 114
Ludorf, J.F. 84, 113
Lydenburg 11, 12, 13, 16, 24, 25, 52, 54

Makuba 44
Makuleke 98–9
Malaria 10, 23, 37, 44, 52, 75, 77, 114
Marico 27
Meiring, P. 15
Methuen, H.H. 106
Mhinga 44, 98
Middelburg 27
Milner, Alfred 61
Mining 40, 51, 95, 107
Minister of Lands 59, 68, 83, 99
Molerats 116
Moths 103
Mountain Zebra National Park 120
Mozambique 21, 33, 38, 93, 95, 96
Mpisane, Chief 44
Muir, J. 29, 109

Nagana 41, 53, 64, 114
Namaqua partridge 106
Namaqualand 57
Natal game reserves 53
National Monuments Commission 61
National Parks. See also Africans; Kruger National Park; Nature protection; Sabi Game Reserve
  future of 118–22
  new forms of 119–21
  objectives of 56

philosophy of 19, 46, 103–4, 112–13, 118–22
National Parks Act (1926) 46, 67, 68
National Parks Board 67–78, 80–8, 99–100, 112, 113, 114, 115, 118
National Party 59–60, 68, 69, 70, 87, 99
Nationalism 5
Native Affairs Administration Bill 55, 97
Native Affairs Department 23, 30, 36, 39, 41, 43, 58, 95, 98
Native Commissioner 24, 26, 40, 91
Natives' Land Act (1913) 55, 65
Natural history 110–11
Naturalists 104–5
Nature protection. *See also* Africans, nature protection; Kruger National Park
  definition of 5
  history of 2, 3
  international 2, 9, 32, 48
  legislation for 8, 12, 14, 10, 30–1
  morality of 12, 46, 80
  nationalism in 48, 61, 62, 65
  philosophy of 7–8, 28–30, 32, 36–7, 42–6, 52, 56–68, 87–9, 103–10, 113–14
  public opinion on 2, 13, 14–15, 16, 21, 46, 62
  reasons for 4, 5
  science 32, 103–4, 105, 107, 110–17
  status after 1918 57
  wildlife management in 103, 104, 113–14
Nondwaai 49

Ohrigstad 11, 12, 24
Olifants River 33, 52, 92
Ostrich 39, 106

Pafuri Game Reserve 98–9
Pafuri River 38
Papenfus, H.B. 69
Penguin 8
Percival, A.B. 110, 111
Piet Retief 27, 49
Pinchot, G. 29
Pirow, O. 69
Pitman, C.R.S. 110, 111
Poaching 13, 22, 28, 37, 38, 39, 40, 43, 44, 49, 93–4, 97, 99, 100
Pongola Game Reserve 19–23, 27, 32, 49, 92
Pongola Poort 22
Pongola River 22

Potchefstroom 11, 27
Prance, E. 75, 76
Preller, G. 69, 72, 80, 81, 86, 99
Preservation 5, 18, 19, 30, 44, 56, 112, 116
Pretoria 27
Pretoria Zoological Gardens 69
Pretoriuskop rest camp 77, 78, 113, 114
Prison labour 94
Prospecting 37, 40
Provincial Secretary 52, 58
Punda Maria rest camp 75

Quagga 8, 63

Railway 35, 37, 51, 61, 77, 78
Rand Daily Mail 62, 113
Reedbuck 44
Reitz, D. 60, 69, 72
Reneke, N. 38
Rhinoceros 44, 106, 107, 111
Richtersveld National Park 121
Riekert, P.J. 48
Rinderpest 18, 41, 53
Rissik, J.F.B. 49, 55
Roan antelope 44
Robinson, G.A. 120
Romanticism 106, 108, 116
Rood, W.H. 69
Roosevelt, T. 30, 110
Royal Geographical Society 36
Royal Society of South Africa 88
Rustenburg 11, 16
Rustenburg Game Reserve 32, 48, 49

Sabi Bridge 38, 95
Sabi Game Reserve
  African tenants in 43
  Africans evicted from 43, 92
  boundaries of 33, 34, 37–8, 52, 58
  change of name 59
  difficulties after 1910 51–3
  difficulties after 1918 56–7
  establishment of 24–6
  finance for 39
  game rangers 38–9, 111–13
  labour in 43, 96
  nationalization of 53–8
  poaching in 40
  publicity for 61
  relations with government 41
  re-proclamation of 32–3
  threats to 41–3

Index

warden of 33, 35. *See also* Stevenson-Hamilton, James
wildlife in 44. *See also* Hunting
Sabi River 23, 24, 26, 32, 77
Sable antelope 44
Sambaan's Land 92
San 7, 90, 118
Sand River Convention 11
Sandenbergh, J.A. 79, 85–6, 115
Satara rest camp 78
Schoeman, D.J. 26
Schoemansdal 11, 13
Science 88, 113, 114, 115–16
Scoon, R. 9
Second World War 5, 73, 104
Selati Railway 37, 51
Selby, P. 69
Selous, F.C. 29, 53, 108, 109, 110
Shaka 7
Shingwedzi rest camp 75
Sinclair, T.C. 77
Singwitsi Game Reserve 38, 43, 49, 54, 56, 57, 59, 92–5, 97–8
Skukuza, origin of name 92
Skukuza rest camp 38, 78, 87, 99, 113
Smith, A. 9, 105
Smuts, Jan 32, 48, 55, 59, 84
Smuts National Park 84
Society for the Preservation of the Fauna of the Empire 29, 36, 109
South African Constabulary 40
South African Eden 15, 70, 82, 85, 110
South African Literary and Scientific Association 105
South African Museum 9, 105
South African National Park 61
South African War 27, 29, 32, 33, 37, 61, 91
Soutpansberg 12, 21, 27, 38, 54
Sparrman, A. 105
Sport-hunting. *See* Hunting, sport
Sportsmen. *See* Hunting, sport
Springbok Flats 27
Springbuck 113
Standerton 21
State Museum 26, 33
Steenbok 44, 77
Steinaecker's Horse 33, 39
Stevenson-Hamilton, James
 appointment as warden 35–6
 army career 55–6
 character 36, 67–74
 duties in Kruger National Park 70–3

 early career 36
 in England 70
 family life 71
 friendship with Stratford Caldecott 61–2
 impact on Sabi Game Reserve 44–5
 influence on nature conservation 36, 44–5, 74
 philosophy of nature conservation 36–7, 45, 46, 111–14
 powers of 39, 40–1
 publications of 36, 109–12
 relationship with Africans 42–4, 58, 92–7, 99–100
 relationship with National Parks Board 67–74, 113
 reputation denigrated 82–5
 retirement 73, 114
 views on Godfrey Lagden 40–1
 views on Paul Kruger 60–1
 views on poachers 40
 views on rangers 39, 72–3, 111–13
 views on scientists 63–4, 113–14, 117
 views on tourists 64, 74–8
Steyn, L.B. 86
Stoffberg, T.C. 69
Streeter, F. 24, 25
Strijdom, J.G. 83–4, 99
Subsistence hunting. *See* Hunting, commercial
Swart, C.R. 83
Swazi 22, 23
Swaziland 21, 22, 30, 53

Taljaard, D.P. 21, 22
Tembe-Tsonga 22
Termites 103
Ticks 112
Tipia, Majwaba 49
Tongaland 22
'Toothless Jack' 38
Tosen, C. 82
Transcendentalism 109
Transvaal Consolidated Lands Company 59
Transvaal Game Protection Association 18, 25, 27, 31, 40, 42, 51, 52, 54, 55, 57, 69, 91
Transvaal Game Reserve 59
Transvaal Game Reserves Commission 97
Transvaal Land and Exploration Company 37
Transvaal Land Owners Assocation 31, 51, 54, 57, 59

Index

Transvaal Provincial Council 54, 55
Trapping 13, 29
Trekboers 8
Trespass 8, 13, 22, 28, 38, 49, 94–5
Trichardt, L. 10
Trophies 14, 33, 117
Tsessebe 44
Tswana 49

Umfolozi 7, 28, 57
United States 29, 30, 48, 53, 55, 67, 80, 109, 110, 115
United States National Parks Service 71
University of Pretoria 115
Urquhart, Major 40

Van der Walt, H.P. 27
Van Graan, H.S. 72, 98–9
Van Oordt, H.F. 22, 23, 27, 28, 92
Van Rensburg, J.H.J. 10
Van Riebeeck, J. 8
Van Wijk, J.L. 24, 25, 83
Vaughan-Kirby, F. 42
Venda 13
Vermin 32, 42, 64, 103, 104, 109
Versfeld, N.H. 26
Verwoerd, H. 83, 100
Veterinarians 63, 64, 114
Volksraad 11, 12, 15, 17, 18, 21, 22, 23, 24, 25, 26, 27
Voortrekkers 9, 10, 18, 24, 48, 60, 87, 104
Vorster, B.J. 81, 83

Walker, W.M. 35, 85
Waterberg 27
Waterbuck 44
White River 58, 73, 86

Wild dog 32, 103, 111, 112
Wildebeest 44
Wilderness 104, 114
Wildlife. *See also* Hunting; Kruger National Park; Nature protection
   aesthetic value of 107–8
   attitudes to 13, 14, 21
   culling of 103–10
   exploitation of 7–10
   extermination of 7, 9, 17, 21
   imperialism and 107
   legal status of 4–5, 8
   legislation for 11, 12, 13, 16, 17, 18
   preservation of 5, 28
   recreational viewing of 56
   study of 3, 37, 56
   trade 7, 10, 12, 17
Wildlife management 5, 74, 88, 103, 104, 113, 115
Wildlife Protection Society of S.A. 69, 72, 80, 83, 100, 114, 115
Williams, Mr 24
Witwatersrand Native Labour Association 95
Wolhuter, H. 39, 83, 97
Wolhuter, Mrs 75
Woodlice 116
Woolls-Sampson, A. 53

Yellowstone National Park 45, 53

Zebra 40, 91
Zoological Society (British) 36, 70
Zoutpansberg 12, 21, 27
Zululand 7, 9, 22, 23, 28, 32, 53, 121
'Zwarteskutters' 12